INDUSTRIAL ORGANIZATION IN JAPAN

RICHARD E. CAVES AND MASU UEKUSA

INDUSTRIAL ORGANIZATION IN JAPAN

THE BROOKINGS INSTITUTION
Washington, D.C.

Library of Congress Cataloging in Publication Data:
Caves, Richard E
Industrial organization in Japan.
Includes bibliographical references.
1. Big business—Japan.
2. Japan—Industries.
3. Japan—Economic conditions—1945–
4. Industrial efficiency—Japan.
I. Uekusa, Masu, joint author.
II. Title.
HD2907.C38   338.7′0952   75-44509
ISBN 0-8157-1324-X
ISBN 0-8157-1323-1 pbk.

1 2 3 4 5 6 7 8 9

THE BROOKINGS INSTITUTION is an independent organization devoted to nonpartisan research, education, and publication in economics, government, foreign policy, and the social sciences generally. Its principal purposes are to aid in the development of sound public policies and to promote public understanding of issues of national importance.

The Institution was founded on December 8, 1927, to merge the activities of the Institute for Government Research, founded in 1916, the Institute of Economics, founded in 1922, and the Robert Brookings Graduate School of Economics and Government, founded in 1924.

The Board of Trustees is responsible for the general administration of the Institution, while the immediate direction of the policies, program, and staff is vested in the President, assisted by an advisory committee of the officers and staff. The bylaws of the Institution state: "It is the function of the Trustees to make possible the conduct of scientific research, and publication, under the most favorable conditions, and to safeguard the independence of the research staff in the pursuit of their studies and in the publication of the results of such studies. It is not a part of their function to determine, control, or influence the conduct of particular investigations or the conclusions reached."

The President bears final responsibility for the decision to publish a manuscript as a Brookings book. In reaching his judgment on the competence, accuracy, and objectivity of each study, the President is advised by the director of the appropriate research program and weighs the views of a panel of expert outside readers who report to him in confidence on the quality of the work. Publication of a work signifies that it is deemed a competent treatment worthy of public consideration but does not imply endorsement of conclusions or recommendations.

The Institution maintains its position of neutrality on issues of public policy in order to safeguard the intellectual freedom of the staff. Hence interpretations or conclusions in Brookings publications should be understood to be solely those of the authors and should not be attributed to the Institution, to its trustees, officers, or other staff members, or to the organizations that support its research.

Foreword

IN FEBRUARY 1976, Brookings published *Asia's New Giant: How the Japanese Economy Works,* edited by Hugh Patrick and Henry Rosovsky, in which a group of American and Japanese economists summarized their findings about the operation of Japan's economy and that nation's economic prospects. Their research was so fruitful that they found it difficult to present their findings comprehensively in single chapters. In several instances, the authors' conclusions ran to book length and warranted separate publication. *Industrial Organization in Japan* is the first such sequel to *Asia's New Giant.*

Caves and Uekusa found Japanese industry and industrial policy a particularly attractive research challenge. Japan's large and fast-growing corporations have awed Westerners with their technical skill and rapidly rising productivity. Organized groups of Japanese entrepreneurs and the close relationship between business and government have stirred feelings of envy and suspicion among Western observers, and the fate of small businesses competing with Japan's industrial juggernauts has elicited concern. The authors here bring economic analysis and statistical research methods to bear on questions such as these, over which myth and opinion have often held sway. Their study, which makes extensive comparisons between the Japanese and American industrial systems, finds that the economic forces at work in Japanese industry are similar to those in Western industrial countries. And Japan's industrial policy appears not as a miracle of national purpose but as a rolling compromise between the shifting objectives of public policy and the economic interests of the industrial sector. While the authors find Japanese industry and industrial policy in no way alien to their Western counterparts, they do identify important effects of Japan's distinctive industrial features—the industrial groups, the practice of permanent employment, the prevalence of small enterprises, and others. In their view the structures of Japanese

vii

markets differ from those of the United States, and the differences influence the performance of Japanese industries.

The authors collaborated closely, both in Japan and the United States. Uekusa organized the data and performed most of the statistical analyses reported in the study, prepared memorandums summarizing research and information published in Japanese, and brought to the project experience and insight acquired in prior work on industrial organization and competition in Japan. Caves undertook the research that could be based on English-language sources, carried out the remaining statistical analyses, and took charge of drafting the manuscript. The authors are grateful to the Japan Economic Research Center for providing a base of operations in Tokyo. The contributors to *Asia's New Giant* read a summary of this volume and provided many useful suggestions thereon; the help of Hugh Patrick and Merton J. Peck in particular is gratefully acknowledged. Uekusa received valuable assistance from Michiko Yatsunami; Caves benefited from the efficient statistical research of Ron W. Napier. The manuscript was edited by Alice M. Carroll; the index was prepared by Florence Robinson.

The project was supported by a grant from the Andrew W. Mellon Foundation. As in all Brookings publications, the authors' views are their own, and should not be ascribed to the Institution, to its trustees, officers, or other staff members, to the Japan Economic Research Center, or to the Andrew W. Mellon Foundation.

GILBERT Y. STEINER
Acting President

May 1976
Washington, D.C.

Contents

1. **Business and Industry in Japan**   1

Environmental Influences on Industrial Organization *2*
Special Features of Business Organization *6*
Conclusions *15*

2. **The Structure of Industry**   16

Seller Concentration *16*
Mergers *28*
Product Differentiation *30*
Barriers to New Competition *34*
Rapid Macroeconomic Growth *35*
Company Finance and Capital Markets *37*
International Linkages *41*
Conclusions *45*

3. **Patterns of Competition**   47

Development of Cartels *48*
Seller Coordination *49*
Government Coordination and Guidance *53*
Effects of Collusive Practices *56*
Conclusions *58*

4. **The Role of Intermarket Groups**   59

The Prewar Zaibatsu *60*
Zaibatsu Dissolution and Reassembly *62*
Other Intermarket Groupings *68*
Profitability and Efficiency of Group Membership *72*
Interdependence among Groups *83*
Conclusions *86*

5. **Allocative Efficiency**   88

Determinants of Efficiency *88*

Differences in Performance *89*
Statistical Analysis of Performance *92*
Market Structure and Wage-Price Movements *96*
Conclusions *99*

6. Technical Efficiency   101

Small Enterprise in Manufacturing *101*
Small Enterprise in the Distributive Sector *115*
Other Sources of Inefficiency *119*
Conclusions *122*

7. Imported Technology and Industrial Progress   124

Research and Economic Growth *124*
Market Structure, Innovation, and Diffusion of Knowledge *127*
Determinants of Productivity Growth *129*
Conclusions *140*

8. Government Policy toward Industry   141

Antimonopoly Legislation *141*
Exemptions from Antimonopoly Law *146*
Industrial Policy and Administrative Control of Competition *148*
Conclusions *154*

9. Reflections and Prospects   155

Appendix: Sources of Statistical Data   159

Index   165

Tables

2-1. Shares of One Hundred Largest Japanese Nonfinancial Corporations
     in Total Corporate Paid-in Capital in Their Sectors, 1958 and 1963   17
2-2. Distribution of Industries and Value of Shipments in U.S.
     and Japanese Manufacturing Sectors, by Concentration Ratio, 1963   19
2-3. Regression Analysis of Determinants of Seller Concentration
     in Japanese Manufacturing Industries, 1963   24
2-4. Indexes of Concentration in the Japanese Manufacturing Sector
     and Selected Subsectors, 1950–70   27
2-5. Number of Recorded Japanese Mergers, by Size of Capital
     of Combined Companies, 1950–70   29
2-6. Number of Mergers of Large Japanese Firms, by Type of Merger,
     1967–70   30
2-7. Average Advertising-to-Sales Ratios of Leading Firms
     in Nineteen Japanese Industries, 1961–70   31
2-8. Effective Rates of Interest Paid on Debt Capital by Japanese
     Manufacturing Corporations of Various Sizes, Selected Years,
     1956–71   38

2-9. Average Finance Costs of 243 Large Japanese Manufacturing Firms,
     1961–70   38

4-1. Distribution of Assets of Large Japanese Corporations,
     by Group Affiliation, 1955, 1962, and 1965   64

4-2. Affiliations of Principal Trading Partners of Selected Firms
     in Three Zaibatsu Groups   66

4-3. Ownership and Immediate Control of Large Japanese Joint-Stock
     Corporations, Fiscal 1966   69

4-4. Investments in and Loans to Related Enterprises by Leading Firms
     in Selected Japanese Industries, 1962 and 1967   71

4-5. Regression Analysis of Determinants of Profit Rates and Influence
     of Group Membership in 243 Large Japanese Manufacturing
     Companies, 1961–70   76

4-6. Strength of Three Zaibatsu's Affiliates in 64 Major Concentrated
     Markets, by Share of Market Held, 1955   84

5-1. Regression Analysis of Determinants of Average Profit Rates,
     35 Manufacturing Industries, 1961–70   94

6-1. Regression Analysis of Determinants of Proportion of Employers
     and Own-Account Workers in the National Labor Force,
     34 Countries, Late 1960s   104

6-2. Utilization of Subcontractors in Japanese Manufacturing Industries,
     by Size of Principal Enterprise, 1973   112

6-3. Number of Small and Medium Enterprises and Proportion
     Engaged in Subcontracting, by Principal Japanese Manufacturing
     Industry, 1971   113

7-1. Regression Analysis of Determinants of Growth of Labor
     Productivity in Japanese Manufacturing Industries, 1958–67   136

8-1. Violations of Antimonopoly Law Found by Fair Trade Commission
     of Japan, by Type of Offense, 1947–73   145

8-2. Japanese Cartel Agreements Exempted from Antimonopoly Law
     by Fair Trade Commission or Competent Ministry,
     by Exempting Statute, 1964–73   148

INDUSTRIAL
ORGANIZATION
IN JAPAN

CHAPTER ONE

Business and Industry in Japan

KNOWLEDGE OF the analytical tools of economics and also the institutional traits of the leading Western economies (principally the United States) may dispose one to believe that Japan's economy suffers from all its differences from the West. On the other hand, one might leap to the conclusion that the Japanese economy's explosive growth over the past two decades indicates that the Japanese are doing everything right. In this study we apply the analytical tools of modern economics to industrial organization in Japan, concentrating on the effects of that country's distinctive traits. After isolating the effects of these institutional traits on the allocation and use of resources in Japan, we then compare the results with data on Western economies in order to assess their importance.

The important institutional features of the Japanese economy, both current and historical, are in part responsible for Japan's rapid and recent development as an industrial nation. They reflect the traits of Japanese culture and society that differ from Western modes and thus generate differences in economic organizations and behavior.

The speed and recent start of Japan's modernization has brought about highly uneven levels of development among the nation's economic sectors. Coexisting with steel mills as large and efficient as any in the world are industries manufacturing major consumer goods by handicraft methods that have changed only modestly since the beginning of the Meiji era (1867–1912), Japan's great period of social change. Important features of the economy, from the general trading companies to the complex and relatively inefficient distribution sector, still reflect their premodern foundations, as does the role of government in Japanese industrial organization. During the Meiji period the government played an active if selective role in promoting development, much as it today maintains close and informal

1

relations with those business sectors that claim the concern of public policy. Finally, such cultural traits as Japan's relative lack of individualism and legalism imprint themselves on business and industrial organization. The employment practices and thus the cost structures of firms reflect the Japanese tendency to see the individual as part of a group, making it natural for the worker to attach himself to a large company as a permanent employee and for the company to take a pervasive and paternalistic attitude toward his well-being. The absence of a tradition of legalism in contractual arrangements affects both the relations of businesses with their customers and competitors and the "guidance" that government agencies supply on the proper direction of business behavior.

Environmental Influences on Industrial Organization

Some strategic features of Japan's social and economic organization significantly influence industrial organization. They also serve to distinguish Japan's industrial organization from that of the United States.

The Zaibatsu

That feature of Japanese industrial organization viewed with greatest awe and alarm outside the country is surely the groupings of large enterprises that are based in different industries yet bound together by ties of fractional ownership and a variety of continuing lender-borrower and buyer-seller relations. The zaibatsu represent yet another persistent legacy of the Meiji era. They reached the height of their power and coherence during the 1930s and World War II, the largest four of them controlling about one-fourth of the paid-in capital of Japanese incorporated business at the war's end.[1] The zaibatsu were dissolved by direction of the occupying powers after the war but reappeared in somewhat looser form a decade later. Originally founded as family businesses, the groups operated until their dissolution on the principle of absolute loyalty of the company managements to the regnant families. Their successors more nearly reflect the common interests of enterprises of relatively equal power and lack a hierarchical organization. They raise fascinating questions of economic behavior that are taken up in chapter 4 below. By what process does economic gain accrue to these conglomerate groups of enterprises through

1. See Eleanor M. Hadley, *Antitrust in Japan* (Princeton University Press, 1970), especially chap. 3; and T. A. Bisson, *Zaibatsu Dissolution in Japan* (University of California Press, 1954).

their mutual associations? What does it signify for the performance of a particular industry that the principal enterprises within it are affiliated with various of such groups? What might result from mutual interdependence recognized among these groups, across the boundaries of individual product markets?

Organized groupings of firms come in several types other than the lineal descendants of the zaibatsu. The Japanese ascribe significance to the relation between large banks and the nonfinancial companies that borrow principally from them. Other groups of firms, often direct competitors, are linked by fractional shareholdings in one another. Some large companies are surrounded by clusters of subsidiaries and affiliates bound by fractional ownership, loans, personal loyalties, or long-term buyer-seller relations. Is the adhesive that forges these bonds strong enough to make them important forces influencing the market behavior of Japanese enterprises?

Small Enterprises

No feature of industrial organization is studied more in Japan than the persistence of a large population of relatively small enterprises of low productivity in the manufacturing and services sectors. The situation indeed contrasts sharply with that in the United States, where in 1967 only 3 percent of manufacturing employment was in establishments with less than ten workers. The figure for Japan was 16 percent in 1967, and it had been 23 percent in 1954. Value added per worker in these small plants was about 25 percent of that in Japan's largest manufacturing establishments, whereas in the United States the fraction was 70 percent.[2]

Small business in Japan has received ample attention from modern economists but even more from scholars of the German historical and Marxist schools. Is the sector still in a precapitalist state of development? Indeed, it does in part employ preindustrial technology to produce traditional Japanese consumer goods, and still shows elements of the putting-out system. Is the sector subject to exploitation by large business enterprises? Indeed, many small manufacturing firms are subcontractors dependent on the large businesses they supply. The sector's disappearance has been freely predicted as sustained full employment erases the dual structure of the labor market, yet since World War II all classes of enterprises but the smallest have raised their productivity fast enough to offset the erosion of their wage advantage.

2. Data from U.S. and Japanese census sources, analyzed by Ron W. Napier, "The Labor Market and Structural Change in Postwar Japanese Development" (senior honors thesis, Harvard College, 1972), chap. 1.

In chapter 6 we examine the small-business sector of Japan and the changes it is experiencing. Is it monolithic and unique to Japan, as many scholars have implied? How rapidly is it responding to changing cost conditions? Does its persistence inflict heavy costs in technical inefficiency on the Japanese economy? If so, are these costs being eliminated by market forces?

Discrimination in Factor Markets

Both capital and labor markets in Japan show imperfections that are closely tied to the economy's historical development. These affect the cost structures of firms, their market behavior, and the allocative efficiency of the economy. In the labor market a substantial wage differential favors small enterprises as against large, and it is closing only slowly as Japan loses the traits of a dual economy and as competitive pressure gnaws at the labor supply of the smaller enterprises. Its persistence is associated with the low productivity of smaller firms, the relatively abundant labor supply still flowing from agriculture, a supply of cheap female labor (including part-time) enlarged by discrimination, and discrimination in capital markets against small enterprises. It also reflects the practice common in large enterprises of hiring only new graduates and employing them through their whole working career until a relatively early retirement age (generally fifty-five). "Permanent employment" means that work is continued unless the firm is in dire straits, and the employee can look forward to relatively elaborate fringe benefits and seniority raises in pay during his working years. One of the numerous and complex effects of this system is to convert much of the firm's wages bill into a fixed cost. When 90 percent of a large firm's employees are typically on permanent status and even seniority raises are governed by strong convention, the firm's chances to reduce its input costs in an emergency are sharply limited.

An opposite discrimination appears in the capital market, where corporations with paid-in (equity) capital of less than ¥10 million must pay roughly 50 percent more to borrow funds than firms with capital of more than ¥1 billion. Although Japan's financial structure is an elaborate one with giant banking enterprises as well as many small and local ones, it retains traces of the economy's earlier history and rapid development. Banking enterprises have generally not been independent of nonfinancial firms, although the direction of dependence is complex. The lack of a mature market for debentures and other long-term debt instruments makes the loans of banks and other financial intermediaries critical in company finance.

Because of these special features of Japan's factor markets, large and small enterprises face markedly different relative prices of capital and labor. The ratio of interest rate to average wages paid can easily be four times as high for small as for large firms.[3] When firms choose technologies in light of the factor prices they face, these differentials introduce distortions into the use of factors of production. The special features of the factor markets also influence the amount by which firms' costs vary when their levels of output change. The institution of permanent employment fixes much of a company's wage bill in the short run, and the highly leveraged financial structures of Japanese corporations make most capital costs equally unavoidable. If profit recipients and managers are risk-averse, Japanese firms are likely to strive to reduce the natural variability of their streams of earnings, thus affecting the character of competition and the allocation of resources.

Rapid Economic Growth

Rapid growth itself abrades against the economy's peculiar legacies and supplies an important feature of the environment of business decision-making and market competition. The way in which individual firms respond to rapid growth depends on how they interpret the macroeconomic growth process that is taking place. What they see as their problems of adjustment depends critically on the sources of growth, and how fully they anticipate and adjust to growth affects their competitive behavior and the performance of industries. It is not the absolute rate of expansion that is important but the actual rate relative to the expected rate that businessmen have built into their plans. (This relativism is reflected in the Japanese practice, piquant to the ears of those attuned to slow growth, of referring to a temporary decline of the real growth rate as a depression.) In chapter 2 we consider the evidence that rapid growth has exerted systematic effects on the market behavior of firms, and thus on economic performance. And in chapters 4 and 5 we consider the effect of rapid growth on the applicability of standard research techniques to Japanese industry, because the techniques assume long-run equilibrium whereas rapid growth puts it out of short-run reach.

3. Miyohei Shinohara, "A Survey of the Japanese Literature on Small Industry," in Bert F. Hoselitz, ed., *The Role of Small Industry in the Process of Economic Growth* (Humanities Press, 1968), pp. 51–54. Japan's financial markets are described in Henry C. Wallich and Mable I. Wallich, "Banking and Finance," in Hugh Patrick and Henry Rosovsky, eds., *Asia's New Giant: How the Japanese Economy Works* (Brookings Institution, 1976).

Economic Policy

Public policies affecting industrial organization in Japan differ greatly in both substance and process from those of the United States. Antitrust legislation following the American model was impressed upon Japan's statute books during the occupation after World War II, but it was weakened by subsequent amendments and has been only partially enforced. Indeed, the Fair Trade Commission, which is responsible for enforcement, has played a role subordinate to other government agencies—notably the Ministry of International Trade and Industry (MITI)—which have held sharply differing views on the means and ends of industrial policy. In those industries that have attracted its attention, MITI's concern has been with ensuring the construction of large-scale plants, limiting the competitive disturbances associated with foreign investment in Japan, containing the erosion of profits through competition in periods of retarded growth and in industries where market shares of oligopolists are in dispute, and sustaining export volumes and prices consistent with government objectives. Recently MITI's role has been weakened by the relaxation of controls over imports of foreign goods and technology, and by a shift of national priorities away from maximum economic growth and toward greater concern with the environment and the quality of life. But whether the ministry's microeconomic influence has suffered any decline is difficult to tell.

Indeed, we can only speculate about the effect of industrial policy in Japan. Policy is made and executed behind the scenes, so that it is impossible to separate MITI's role from the other forces affecting economic behavior. This situation reflects the absence of a legalistic tradition in Japan, but that pattern has not rendered MITI's interventions free from criticism in Japan. These government-business relations are discussed in chapters 3 and 8.

Special Features of Business Organization

No feature of an economy's organization more closely reflects its social traditions and history than does the organization and management of its business enterprises. The motivation of business decisions and the abilities of firms to perceive opportunities and threats and to carry out plans are central to the behavior of industries and the performance of the economy. The quality and motivation of entrepreneurial talent and the effectiveness of a nation's business practices and business organization are of critical importance in determining national levels of productivity and rates of growth.[4] In Japan's case they can certainly not be ignored.

Motivation

The copious literature on entrepreneurship in Japan's economic development reveals the deep historical roots of present business motives.[5] The pursuit of profit, like the activity of selling, has never been held in high esteem in Japan. Thus the business goals of some entrepreneurs and groups seem to be substitutes for the goal of pursuing profit. For others the rationalization for business activity does not sound like profit-maximization but resembles it rather closely. Before the Meiji era the largest and most advanced sector of the economy was apparently wholesaling and distribution, carried on by lower-status but in some cases very wealthy families. Insuring the continuity and growth of the commercial house became an important rationalization for business activities; the family comprising members of the business was seen as closely related to the biological family. Insuring the honor, probity, and growth of the house became an objective that could claim the full assent of employees and yet sustain honor with the external world. In economic theory, the long-run growth-maximizing firm differs from the profit-maximizer not in its utilization of the resources at hand but only in its rate of reinvestment in the business.[6] The strong emphasis on frugality in the entrepreneurial families, the high rate of reinvestment, and their concern with maintaining the quality of family managerial talent all suggest that the maximization of growth should be considered one of their goals.[7]

Both the samurai and the lower classes were important as founders of the new industrial enterprises.[8] The samurai role is distinctive in that the

4. Richard E. Caves and associates, *Britain's Economic Prospects* (Brookings Institution, 1968), especially chaps. 6–8.

5. For example, see Johannes Hirschmeier and Tsunehiko Yui, *The Development of Japanese Business, 1600–1973* (Harvard University Press, 1975), chaps. 1 and 2; M. Y. Yoshino, *Japan's Managerial System: Tradition and Innovation* (MIT Press, 1968), chaps. 1–3; and S. Prakash Sethi, *Japanese Business and Social Conflict: A Comparative Analysis of Response Patterns with American Business* (Ballinger, 1975), chap. 5.

6. John Williamson, "Profit, Growth and Sales Maximization," *Economica,* vol. 33 (February 1966), pp. 1–16.

7. See Yasuzō Horie, "The Role of the *Ie* in the Economic Modernization of Japan," *Kyoto University Economic Review,* vol. 36 (April 1966), pp. 1–16, especially pp. 9–10.

8. Yoshino, *Japan's Managerial System,* chap. 3; and Yasuzō Horie, "Modern Entrepreneurship in Meiji Japan," in William W. Lockwood, ed., *The State and Economic Enterprise in Japan: Essays in the Political Economy of Growth* (Princeton University Press, 1965), chap. 4.

class's traditions ran heavily toward public service, rationality, and a faith in education. Just as the latter traits suited them well to serve as importers of foreign technology, their zeal for public service may have led them to incorporate the public welfare and the officially voiced interests of the state in private business goals. The close and informal relations between business and government that mark present-day Japan certainly have their antecedents in the earliest days of industrialization.

Some evidence of the present-day motives of business management can be found in a survey of the views of the presidents of sixty-four companies in Japan's electrical machinery industry on the three most important (of seven) business goals. Profit and growth rate of sales ran tandem in the lead, with market share and rate of new-product introduction coming next and equally favored. Motives weighted toward risk avoidance (composition of capital, dividend rate) ran far behind.[9] Many observers believe that their members' extraordinary interest in market share renders Japanese oligopolies effectively if not excessively competitive. Our statistical investigation in chapters 4 and 5 leads us to reject that conclusion. Still, the premise about the motive of maintaining and raising market share need not be totally false. In a fast-growing market where a firm's share in one time period depends on those in preceding periods, it maximizes long-run profit by sacrificing some short-run profit to expand its share of the market. Furthermore, there is evidence that access to finance on the capital market and to favors from the government may be improved by possession of a large market share.[10]

The early period of development of the Japanese economy has affected the organization as well as the motivation of business enterprise today. The swift acceptance of the corporate form of organization in the Meiji period has been ascribed in part to sophisticated forms of organization found in

9. Matsutarō Wadaki and others, "Decision-Making by Top-Management and Business Performance in Firms of Japan," *Keio Business Review*, no. 11 (1972), pp. 1–8. In a comparison of the presidents' attitudes and the performance of their firms, a *negative* correlation appears between a firm's actual growth and its president's stress on growth as a goal (pp. 12–27). Unfortunately, another finding, that firms with founder-presidents grow faster than those with promoted or hired presidents, tells little about the administrators' effectiveness since the sample includes both large and mature firms that have passed into managerial control and young and highly successful ones still run by their founders.

10. See, for example, Herbert Glazer, "Capital Liberalization," in Robert J. Ballon, ed., *Joint Ventures and Japan* (Tokyo: Sophia University, 1967), p. 16. The government has sometimes rewarded firms holding market shares by allocating important inputs subject to exchange control in proportion to shares of sales or capacity, or enforcing production cutbacks in proportion to capacity.

commercial houses during the Tokugawa period. The ancient Mitsui house, for example, was at least implicitly a joint-stock company held by descendants of the original founder.[11] The system of permanent employment emerged from the entrepreneurial problems and social evils of early industrialization, when the industrial labor force was fresh from the farm and quite dependent on the employer for the paternalistic services that are still provided by large Japanese enterprises.[12] One result of samurai influence is the continuing tradition of education for Japanese business executives. In 1924, 64 percent of top executives in the 181 largest operating companies held college degrees (or the equivalent)—a proportion that could not have been matched in the United States.[13] The pattern continues today; in 1966, 94 percent of the top management group of 25 large companies were college or university graduates, as were 74 percent of middle management.[14]

Entrepreneurial Skill

The sheer level of entrepreneurial ability in a society and the degree to which social values and conventions give it free play are important determinants of an economy's ability to adapt and grow. The overall growth rate of industrial output since World War II, the great shifts in the mixture of outputs, and the elevation in the quality of many products are often taken to indicate that Japanese entrepreneurs are both abundant and active. The striking purge for wartime activities of 2,210 officers from 632 zaibatsu corporations and 2,500 high-ranking officers and major stockholders of other large companies might have crippled an economy with limited entrepreneurial resources. It furthered the cause of postwar revival and growth in Japan, however, for purged zaibatsu executives were caught in two highly dysfunctional traditions. They were accustomed to filling the orders of industrial buyers, especially the government, not to adapting their products to the market's emergent needs. They were selected for their total loyalty to the zaibatsu families, not for their independent decision-making ability. And they were on average quite old, having gained their formative experience in the 1920s and 1930s. Their replacements, generally subordinates next in line, were younger men who showed a marked ability to adapt to their own (and their companies') new-found indepen-

11. Horie, "The Role of the *Ie*," pp. 1–9.

12. James C. Abegglen, *The Japanese Factory: Aspects of Its Social Organization* (Free Press, 1958).

13. Hirschmeier and Yui, *Development of Japanese Business*, pp. 164–65.

14. James C. Abegglen, ed., *Business Strategies for Japan* (Tokyo: Sophia University, 1970), chap. 2.

dence. The later reversal of the occupation measures brought few of the purged officials back into office, and their displacement is generally counted a clear net gain.[15]

Since the end of the war, many giant and successful companies have been built up from scratch. That is partly due to the ripeness of conditions, but pervasive entrepreneurial success stories (in small as well as large enterprises) suggest that favorable circumstances were not all.[16] Even the well-established tradition of top university graduates taking employment only with large companies is being broken occasionally by those who strike out on their own.

Ownership and Control

In the process of economic growth, large corporations typically slip from the control of their founders (or their heirs). Stockholdings become widely dispersed, and management in large measure controls its own fate. Evidence for the United States suggests (somewhat weakly) that dispersed ownership and the structure of management compensation both influence companies' performance in complex ways.[17] In Japan it appears that the divorce of ownership from control has proceeded rapidly, especially due to the zaibatsu dissolution and dispersion of the families' shareholdings after the war. In 1959, 33 of the largest 200 companies remained owner-controlled. Sixty more were affiliates of the zaibatsu groups' successors, with substantial proportions of their shares held by their corporate affiliates but in individually moderate blocs. If control of these companies eludes their managers, it is because of the influence of other affiliated companies and not the presence of major personal or institutional shareholders. The remaining 107 companies (95 nonfinancial, 12 financial) are controlled by their managers. Eighty-five of the nonfinancial concerns are affiliated with important financial institutions and thus may be subject to some extra-

15. Kazuo Noda, "Postwar Japanese Executives," in Ryūtarō Komiya, ed., *Postwar Economic Growth in Japan* (University of California Press, 1966), pp. 231–35; Hirschmeier and Yui, *Development of Japanese Business,* chap. 4; and Yoshino, *Japan's Managerial System,* pp. 86–87.

16. Noda, "Postwar Japanese Executives," pp. 243–44; and Hirschmeier and Yui, *Development of Japanese Business,* chap. 4.

17. See Robert T. Masson, "Executive Motivations, Earnings, and Consequent Equity Performance," *Journal of Political Economy,* vol. 79 (November–December 1971), pp. 1278–92; and John Palmer, "The Profit-Performance Effects of the Separation of Ownership from Control in Large U.S. Industrial Corporations," *Bell Journal of Economics and Management Science,* vol. 4 (Spring 1973), pp. 293–303.

managerial control.[18] In 1963 only 23 of the largest 200 nonfinancial companies in the United States were under owner control and 8 more were controlled through a legal device. Managers controlled 169.[19] Thus, Japan has not proceeded quite so far as the United States with the divorce of control from ownership.[20] Indeed, recent data show a rapid shift of shareholding toward companies and financial intermediaries. For some firms cohesive minority owner control may be restored. Individuals held 61.3 percent of the shares of listed companies in 1950, only 37.4 percent in 1971, while monetary institutions climbed from 12.6 percent to 32.6 percent.[21] Japanese financial intermediaries seem much less passive than American ones in voicing their views on the operation of companies whose shares they hold.

The managers of a Japanese company with widely dispersed shareholdings, though, do find themselves in a position of great independence. A 1950 change in the commercial code raised the position of professional managers, reducing the power of shareholders relative to boards of directors and allowing nonshareholders to become directors.[22] Individual shareholders are notably passive, and "corporate raiders" of the American and British stripe are unknown. Frequently, boards of directors consist mostly of employees subordinate to top management and thus not likely to play an independent critical role. In 1964, 44.1 percent of 397 large companies had no outside directors, and another 33 percent only one or two nonemployees.

What influence the divorce of ownership from control has on company behavior depends not only on the locus of control but also on the terms of managerial compensation. Recent U.S. investigations have shown that

18. Yūichi Hirose, *Kabushiki gaisha shihai no kōzō* [Structure of Corporate Management] (Tokyo: Nihon Hyōronshinsha, 1963), summarized by Noda, "Postwar Japanese Executives," pp. 236–37. In 50 of the 95 management-controlled nonfinancial companies, financial institutions' shareholdings exceed 20 percent of the shares outstanding; 35 of the 95 had accepted one or more officers assigned from nonzaibatsu financial institutions. Ties between nonfinancial and financial companies are discussed in chap. 4, below.

19. Robert J. Larner, "Ownership and Control in the 200 Largest Nonfinancial Corporations, 1929 and 1963," *American Economic Review*, vol. 56 (September 1966), p. 781.

20. In a 1965 study Yoshimatsu Aonuma found that only 6 percent of 1,500 executives in 375 large firms achieved their positions through ownership. By contrast, in a similar population for the year 1900, 80 percent were owner-managers. See Yoshino, *Japan's Managerial System*, pp. 88–89.

21. "Stockholdings by Corporations," *Oriental Economist*, vol. 41 (May 1973), pp. 18–22.

22. Noda, "Postwar Japanese Executives," p. 235.

the total executive compensation package (not just salary) is likely to be significantly related to the company's profit rate.[23] In that case, managerial incentives still lie with profit maximization. Japanese evidence suggests a shift away from executive compensation geared to profit: corporate managers hold company stocks in much smaller proportion than did prewar managers and receive conspicuously smaller bonuses—a component of pay at least partly dependent on profits.[24] We conclude that in large Japanese companies the scope for management to act on motives other than profit maximization is rather great, although there is not much evidence on what those other motives are.[25]

Organizational Form and Management Technique

Contemporary business organization, in its literal sense, is generally the same in Japan as in the United States, and there is an active movement toward divisional profit centers.[26] Management techniques diverge in the two societies because of the practice of permanent employment and the roles of merit and seniority in determining promotions in Japan.

Japan emerged from World War II behind in managerial techniques as well as industrial technology. About 1955, there was a great wave of interest in absorbing managerial techniques used in the West, particularly the United States. The "management science boom"—a widely recognized phenomenon—and the many organized efforts to spread the gospel of scientific management have been called a necessary ingredient for Japan's greatly accelerated growth.[27] A large majority of executives now feel that long-run planning should be a staff function that entails the systematic exploration of alternatives,[28] and the development of information relating to

23. Wilbur G. Lewellen and Blaine Huntsman, "Managerial Pay and Corporate Performance," *American Economic Review,* vol. 60 (September 1970), pp. 710–20.

24. Noda, "Postwar Japanese Executives," p. 235. Before the war high-paid zaibatsu executives tended to buy heavily into their companies and become relatively substantial owners.

25. Only 18 percent of executives asked to choose between two statements, one favoring the sacrifice of profit for social responsibility and the other sticking with qualifications to long-run profit maximization, chose the former, 77 percent the latter. See Yasuo Kotaka, "Survey of Top Executives' Views on Business Organization," *Keio Business Review,* no. 3 (1964), pp. 10–14. But we believe that maximization of growth may be the chief goal of some Japanese firms.

26. They were employed by 34 percent of a group of large firms surveyed in 1963. See Ryōichi Iwauchi, "Adaptation to Technological Change," *Developing Economies,* vol. 7 (December 1969), pp. 446–47.

27. Noda, "Postwar Japanese Executives," pp. 237–40; compare p. 249.

28. As against a consensus process devolving from the chief executive. See Kotaka, "Survey," pp. 14–17. Also, see Japan, Economic Planning Agency, *Economic Survey of Japan, 1968–1969* (Tokyo: Japan Times, Ltd.), table 116.

cost control is given high priority.[29] The 1960s saw a catch-up in the use
of computers by Japanese business.[30]

Japanese industry continues its tradition of seeking employees with high
levels of general education and providing large amounts of on-the-job training. Japanese business depends little on academic business instruction, but
does provide a great deal of training within the company. A 1961–63 survey found that 69.6 percent of all new recruits were put through general
business education programs under long-term training plans. While a major
aim of these programs is to inculcate loyalty to the company rather than to
provide intensive education, 29.3 percent of the recruits got specialized
training programs for particular jobs. On-the-job training is one of a range
of devices employed to cope with rapid technological change and with the
introduction of more and more processes involving complicated control.
Others include the rearrangement of supervisory functions and a greater
emphasis on skill in promotion to foreman-type jobs.[31]

Certain Japanese business practices that accord with traits of the national culture obviously work against organizational effectiveness. Many of
these surround the practice of permanent employment, which continues unchanged despite predictions of its demise.[32] Some mobility among top executives is now evident, however. A 1965 study of 1,410 professional managers
found that 46 percent had spent their entire careers with a single company; of
the others, 19 percent had moved from financial institutions, 9 percent from
government.[33] There is also evidence of emphasis on merit rather than on
seniority in promotions, and seniority does not control the staffing of a company's top jobs. A survey of large enterprises published in 1967 found that
the merit system was adopted in 40.3 percent "but with some elements of
the seniority system . . . maintained." But 47.9 percent of firms based promotions on seniority tempered by some elements of merit, and 10.4 percent
relied totally on seniority.[34] Persons whom we interviewed on Japanese
management practice stressed that permanent employment often means
putting up with unsatisfactory performance in significant positions, and
Abegglen in his study of the Japanese factory blamed it for much of the

29. In Kotaka, "Survey," pp. 22–26, 84 percent favored a statement lauding its
value, only 13 percent an opposed statement suggesting that cost control is overrated.

30. Iwauchi, "Adaptation to Technological Change," pp. 447–48.

31. Ibid., pp. 428–34 and 442.

32. See the evidence on employee turnover rates in Abegglen, *Business Strategies*,
pp. 48–51, and a survey cited by Iwauchi, "Adaptation to Technological Change," p.
450.

33. Cited in Yoshino, *Japan's Managerial System*, p. 89.

34. Iwauchi, "Adaptation to Technological Change," p. 449; and Abegglen, *Business
Strategies*, p. 48.

evident overmanning.[35] It also supports a broad preoccupation with harmonious interpersonal relations and developing group solidarity, perhaps at some expense in the development of technical competence. It furthers informal cliques built on personal loyalty that cut across business organization charts and can apparently create rivalries and complicate the business decision process.[36] On the other hand, permanent employment, apart from its consistency with Japanese desires for secure and ordered personal affiliations, has some direct benefits in reducing recruitment costs and resistance to technological change and job reassignment. It also makes it easier for the firm to capture the rents from on-the-job training. If these advantages can be retained while the system's dysfunctional emphasis on seniority is reduced, then the system seems an efficient one in Japan's society.

Another feature of business organization rooted in Japan's culture is an emphasis on the group rather than the individual as the acting unit. Some observers have placed great emphasis on the need of business management to consult widely within the company and develop a consensus before any decision is taken. Partly because of lifetime employment, harmony must be maintained among the ranks. A prime manifestation of this feature is the *ringisho* system: relatively low-level employees draft proposals for action; their documents then circulate among numerous offices, collecting approvals, and finally work their way to top management. Staff support for the planning function can be quite weak because the substantive proposal comes from nonspecialized personnel, and there is no way for alternatives to be systematically explored. The system can be slow and precludes fixing definite responsibility for actions taken.[37]

In view of the dynamism and bold maneuvers widely noted in Japanese business, we are skeptical that executive decisions are really preceded by great amounts of communing and soul-searching—at least when there is pressure of time. The evidence from surveys seems to suggest that consideration of the views and interests of subordinate employees is important for successful management in Japan, but that top executives must act with a firm and responsible hand.[38]

35. Abegglen, *The Japanese Factory,* especially chap. 2.

36. Yoshino, *Japan's Managerial System,* chap. 7, especially pp. 206–10.

37. See Ichinō Hattori, "Management Practices," and Susumu Takamiya, "Business Organization," in Robert J. Ballon, ed., *Doing Business in Japan* (Tokyo: Sophia University, 1967). Some companies are experimenting with modifying or abolishing the *ringisho* system in order to fix the responsibility for decisions and their execution. Also see Wadaki and others, "Decision-Making," pp. 9–12.

38. Kotaka, "Survey," pp. 3–10, posed a statement emphasizing the desirability of democratized decisionmaking against one favoring firm but considerate executive leadership. The former got agreement from only 15 percent, the latter from 75 percent of the executives surveyed.

Conclusions

In this study of the structure and performance of Japanese industry we apply Western analytical tools to develop and test hypotheses about Japan's distinctive institutional features. Among the general and pervasive features are the prevalent role of government and the relative lack of individualism and legalism in the culture. Important factors in industrial organization are the heterogeneous groupings of large enterprises (including the former zaibatsu), the survival of a large number of relatively small and unproductive plants, the prevalence of price discrimination in factor markets (small enterprises favored in the purchase of labor, large enterprises in the purchase of capital), the rapid and uneven pace of economic growth, and the lack of a strong antimonopoly policy and the encouragement of collusive behavior.

The motivation and organization of business enterprises are fundamental influences on their economic performance. Although the profit motive per se lacks strong cultural roots in Japan, loyalty to the enterprise and concern for its survival and growth work to emphasize long-run profits tempered by some preference for growth. The separation of ownership from control, which has proceeded rapidly since World War II, joins with the weak role of boards of directors and other liberating forces to give the managements of large enterprises ample room to indulge a preference for growth or other sources of managerial utility. The evident high quality of entrepreneurial talent in Japan and rapidly rising productivity of the labor force are both associated with high levels of general education, the intensive use of in-company training, and the rapid development of modern management techniques. But some features of business organization have questionable or adverse effects on Japan's productivity. Permanent employment in large enterprises increases internal flexibility but supports seniority against competence as a basis for promotion. And the culturally rooted system of collective responsibility may slow decisionmaking and discourage the systematic and sophisticated investigation of alternatives.

CHAPTER TWO

The Structure of Industry

IN JAPAN as in other countries, most of the evidence on the major elements of industrial market structure deals with the manufacturing sector. In this discussion, therefore, only casual references are made to other parts of the economy.

Seller Concentration

The common impression of Japanese industry seems to be that it is monopolistic in the extreme. Such an impression leans heavily on the role of cartels and other collusive arrangements—a matter distinct from seller concentration. It also pays undue respect to the organized groups of large enterprises, for the members of any such group are typically oligopolistic firms in different industries and not direct competitors. Important though these phenomena may be for the performance of Japan's economy, their influence can only be measured in terms of their effect on competitive conditions in individual markets for goods, services, and factors of production. The concentration of sellers in the typical industry, a prosaic element of market structure, becomes an important filter for the influence of these more dramatic economic institutions. Therefore, we compare concentration in Japanese manufacturing with that in the United States.

Overall Concentration

In fiscal 1963 the one hundred largest nonfinancial corporations controlled 53.2 percent of all paid-in corporate capital in Japan—39.4 percent directly, another 13.8 percent through affiliates. As table 2-1 shows, their

16

Table 2-1. *Shares of One Hundred Largest Japanese Nonfinancial Corporations in Total Corporate Paid-in Capital in Their Sectors, 1958 and 1963*

	Largest corporations, fiscal 1958			Largest corporations, fiscal 1963		
Sector	Number	Paid-in capital, in millions of yen	Percentage of sector's total corporate capital	Number	Paid-in capital, in millions of yen	Percentage of sector's total corporate capital
Agriculture, forestry, and fishery	4	16,800	55.9	3	29,500	74.3
Mining	4	15,550	23.0	1	7,022	4.4
Construction	0	0	n.a.	1	6,800	3.9
Manufacturing	59	398,091	38.0	65	1,396,967	43.5
Textiles	10	50,107	n.a.	8	109,181	n.a.
Chemicals	15	82,655	n.a.	13	173,648	n.a.
Metals, machinery	31	255,634	n.a.	40	1,080,439	n.a.
Other	3	9,695	n.a.	4	33,699	n.a.
Distribution, hotels, restaurants	4	14,800	4.6	9	103,412	16.0
Real estate	1	5,160	15.2	1	16,500	14.5
Transportation, communication, warehousing	15	102,880	39.3	8	119,536	26.7
Electricity and gas	11	160,485	n.a.	12	482,990	93.7
Services, et cetera	2	6,280	9.0	0	0	n.a.
Total	100	720,046	35.4	100	2,162,727	39.4

Source: Japan, Fair Trade Commission, *Annual Report, 1967*, p. 23.
n.a. = not available.

share of directly controlled paid-in capital[1] was greater than it had been in 1958; much of the increase was concentrated in manufacturing. Concentration of operating profit or value added is not nearly so great; in fiscal 1964 the largest hundred accounted for 39.0 percent of paid-in capital but only 28.7 percent of operating profit and 21.3 percent of value added.[2]

Later data on overall concentration are distinctly limited in value because they do not take account of the affiliates of the largest corporations. The concentration of sales in the hundred largest manufacturing enterprises (not including their affiliates) was approximately constant between 1959 and 1973, having fallen irregularly in the early 1950s. The concentration of employees rose slightly after 1959 while the concentration of total assets fell rather sharply (from 38.8 percent in 1959 to 31.8 percent in 1973).[3] Hence

1. This measure of the size of corporate capital, commonly used in Japan, includes only preferred and common shares (legal capital actually issued), not accumulated profit surplus or debt capital. Thus it differs greatly from a measure based on total assets, especially in view of the high debt-equity ratios common for Japanese corporations. Readily available data supply no information on whether paid-in capital is more or less concentrated than total assets; we discern no source of net bias that should on a priori grounds be controlling.

2. Japan, Fair Trade Commission, *Annual Report, 1967*, pp. 22–24. The greater concentration of paid-in capital is difficult to interpret because the measure excludes retained earnings, and it is not obvious how the proportional importance of retained earnings varies with size of firm.

3. Tomio Iguchi, "Seizogyō ni okeru shūchū to mobirity" [Concentration and Mobility in Manufacturing Industries], *Rokkodai ronshū*, vol. 22 (October 1975), p. 13;

it is not clear that concentration in the largest manufacturing enterprises has changed over the last decade, although the picture might change significantly if their affiliates were included or if all nonfinancial companies were considered.

Data from official sources on overall concentration in the United States pertain only to the manufacturing sector, but some investigators have calculated measures of concentration of total assets in all nonfinancial corporations that are roughly comparable to the data for Japan. Using balance-sheet asset figures (thus reflecting the degree of consolidation reported by companies themselves) and excluding depreciation reserves whenever possible, Kaplan found the hundred largest nonfinancial corporations in 1960 controlled 30.8 percent of total corporate assets as reported in U.S. taxation statistics. Thus, concentration in Japan would seem to be substantially higher than in the United States unless the concentration of paid-in capital greatly exceeds the concentration of total assets in Japan.[4] Also, unincorporated enterprise may control a significantly larger share of economic activity in Japan than in the United States, which would lessen the difference in the concentration of control over total industrial assets and of corporate assets.

It is impossible to compare overall concentration in manufacturing exactly because Japanese figures do not take account of affiliates. The largest hundred manufacturing enterprises in Japan controlled 29.2 percent of manufacturers' sales in 1967. In the United States, concentration of *net output* in the hundred largest manufacturing companies was 33 percent in 1967 (30 percent in 1958); in the United Kingdom it was 42 percent in 1968 (33 percent in 1958).[5] Japanese figures would increase by a large but unknown amount if they included affiliates' sales.

---

also see Yoshishige Higuchi, "Sangyō shūchū to shijō keitai" [Industrial Concentration and Forms of Market], in Miyohei Shinohara and Masao Baba, eds., *Sangyō soshiki* [Industrial Organization] (Tokyo: Nihon Keizai Shinbunsha, 1974), p. 81.

4. The U.S. figures, from A. D. H. Kaplan, *Big Enterprise in a Competitive System,* rev. ed. (Brookings Institution, 1964), pp. 120 and 124, are for 1960. The only estimates of the concentration of control by the hundred largest nonfinancial corporations over total assets in Japan are for 1970; 40.0 percent were controlled if affiliate relations are neglected, 49.9 percent if they are included (see Japan, Fair Trade Commission, *Nihon no kigyō shūchū* [Corporate Mergers in Japan] [Ministry of Finance, 1971], p. 41). Concentration surely rose in the United States in the decade after Kaplan constructed his chart, but not by enough to reach this upper limit.

5. Both the U.S. and the U.K. figures are on a census establishment basis, treating each company as consisting only of all owned or controlled manufacturing establishments. The denominator in each case is total (not just corporate) value added in manufacturing. These data are assembled and analyzed in an unpublished study by S. J. Prais (National Institute of Economic and Social Research, London).

Concentration in Manufacturing Industries

Ultimately more important than overall concentration is the concentration of sellers in particular markets. Table 2-2 compares the distribution of Japanese and American manufacturing industries by concentration ratios in 1963—the only year for which Japanese data are comprehensive. Both measures are based on the proportion of industry shipments accounted for by the largest four firms. The two countries' industrial classification systems are quite similar, though Japanese manufacturing at this level is divided into 512 sectors and U.S. manufacturing into 417. If the classification scheme is assumed to be an approximation of the number and distribution of "true" economic industries (groups of competing sellers of homogeneous products), the slightly lower American concentration ratios could signal the same level of effective concentration in the underlying "true" markets.

According to the data of table 2-2, the weighted average concentration ratio is 40.9 percent for U.S. industries, 35.4 percent for Japanese; unweighted figures are 38.3 percent and 37.5 percent, respectively. If anything, concentration in Japan appears lower. In the cumulative distribution of unweighted concentration ratios Japanese industries appear to be more dispersed than American: 40 percent have concentration ratios over 80 percent or under 20 percent, while only 29 percent of U.S. industries lie in the tails of the distribution. This may reflect the survival of the dual structure of the Jap-

Table 2-2. *Distribution of Industries and Value of Shipments in U.S. and Japanese Manufacturing Sectors, by Concentration Ratio, 1963*[a]

	Industries				Value of shipments			
	United States		Japan		United States		Japan	
Concentra-tion ratio	Num-ber	Cumulative percent of total	Num-ber	Cumulative percent of total	Billions of dollars	Cumulative percent of total	Billions of dollars[b]	Cumulative percent of total
80–100	27	6.5	46	9.0	50.9	12.2	3.7	5.6
70–79	18	10.8	21	13.1	14.3	15.6	3.5	10.8
60–69	29	17.8	29	18.8	23.8	21.3	1.8	13.4
50–59	43	28.1	61	30.7	49.3	33.2	10.6	28.9
40–49	49	39.8	56	41.6	31.9	40.9	8.5	41.3
30–39	80	59.0	63	53.9	72.8	58.4	7.6	52.5
20–29	81	78.4	79	69.3	90.5	80.2	9.7	66.7
0–19	90	100.0	157	100.0	82.4	100.0	22.7	100.0
Total	417	100.0	512	100.0	415.7	100.0	68.2	100.0

Sources: *Concentration Ratios in Manufacturing Industry, 1963*, Report Prepared by the Bureau of the Census for the Subcommittee on Antitrust and Monopoly of the U.S. Senate Committee on the Judiciary, 90 Cong. 1 sess. (1967), pt. 2, p. 259; and Japan, Ministry of International Trade and Industry, *Seisan shūchūdo chōsa hōkoku, 1963* [Report of Survey of Concentration Ratios of Production, 1963] (1966). Figures are rounded.

a. Concentration ratio based on proportion of industry shipments accounted for by four largest firms in the country.

b. One dollar equals 360 yen.

anese manufacturing sector, comprising both a traditional sector of extremely small-scale enterprises and a modern sector in which public policy and private interest have concurred on the choice of very large scales for both plants and firms. The pattern does not, however, appear in the shipments-weighted figures.

More detailed information is available on finely defined product classes (the equivalent of five-digit or seven-digit industries in the U.S. standard industrial classification) in the concentrated tail of the distribution of Japanese industries. Of 157 industries surveyed in 1966, 28 can be ranked "partial monopolies": the largest firm controls at least 50 percent of production, the largest five more than 90 percent. Another 53 are "highly concentrated oligopolies": the largest firm's share is at least 30 percent, and the largest five account for 70 percent or more.[6] Most markets of this type, according to the Fair Trade Commission of Japan, have concentration patterns that are quite stable over time.

Higuchi's comparison of concentration in ninety-three corresponding manufacturing industries of Japan and the United States[7] suggests that their rank correlation is quite high. And research by Pryor[8] on the industrial structures of Western countries confirms this close similarity of concentration patterns.

To check this similarity of concentration ratios and also to explore the determinants of concentration in Japanese industries, we developed a statistical analysis. Concentration is an exogenous determinant of industries' performance only in the short run; in the long run, concentration itself appears to be determined by technological factors and by the past patterns of behavior of sellers in an industry. We made a casual exploration of these determining factors for Japan and undertook to identify the significant determinants of concentration in a single country when the common technical factors that influence concentration in a given industry in *all* countries are controlled.

The analysis is based on a sample of ninety-nine manufacturing industries that are comparably defined in the American and Japanese censuses

6. Japan, Fair Trade Commission, *Nihon no sangyō shūchū—1963–1966* [Industrial Concentration in Japan—1963–1966] (Tokyo: Tōyō Keizai Shinpōsha, 1969), pp. 24–25 and 76.

7. Yoshishige Higuchi, "Shūchūdo no kokusai hikaku—Nihon to Amerika" [International Comparison of the Degree of Concentration—the United States and Japan], *Kōsei torihiki,* June 1968.

8. Frederic L. Pryor, "An International Comparison of Concentration Ratios," *Review of Economics and Statistics,* vol. 54 (May 1972), pp. 130–40.

of manufactures[9] and for which data on the concentration of shipments in the largest four, eight, and twenty companies are available. The dependent variables in the analysis are:

$JC4$ = share of industry total shipments accounted for by the four largest companies, Japan, 1963

$JC58$ = marginal concentration ratio: share of industry shipments accounted for by the largest eight companies minus share accounted for by the largest four companies, Japan, 1963

$JMGC$ = proportional marginal concentration ratio: equal to $JC58/JC4$ when $JC4 \leqq 50$ percent, equal to $JC58/(100 - JC4)$ when $JC4 > 50$ percent.

The variable $JMGC$ takes account of the facts that $JC58$ cannot be larger than $JC4$ and that it cannot exceed the difference between $JC4$ and 100 percent. $JMGC$ thus expresses $JC58$ as a percentage of the maximum value that it can take given $JC4$.

The independent variables include, first of all, measures of concentration in the United States. Our hypothesis is that concentration in each industry is due to a number of underlying traits of production technology, transportation costs of inputs and outputs, and the nature and social context of the output's consumption or final use. Since these traits are specific to the good itself and not to the culture, topography, factor prices, and so forth, of a particular country, the concentration ratio in a large and fully developed industrial country can be included as a means of controlling for the sector-specific determinants of concentration. $USC4$, $USC58$, and $USMGC$ are analogous to the three Japanese concentration measures. $USC8$ represents the concentration ratio for the largest eight companies and $USC820$ the difference between $USC8$ and the U.S. 20-firm concentration ratio.

In addition to this control for industry-specific traits, certain factors that depend on conditions in the Japanese economy are included among the independent variables.[10] Scale economies in manufacturing plants provide one possible basis for concentration of enterprises. The larger is the plant of minimum efficient scale, given the size of the market, the fewer will be the plants that can economically serve the market, and the higher will be seller concentration. Average plant size, while it is a determinant of the concen-

9. This data base, prepared mainly for an analysis of productivity changes presented in chap. 7, is described in the appendix to this volume.

10. Variables similar to those nominated in the text have been used in S. I. Ornstein and others, "Determinants of Market Structure," *Southern Economic Journal*, vol. 39 (April 1973), pp. 612–25, and papers cited therein.

tration of companies, may not be independent; it is also connected to company concentration through the size of the market and the extent of firms' multiplant development. In fact, all the variance of any one of these factors can be explained by the other three, so that a statistical relation between concentration and average plant size does not establish causation. Concentration can be high because efficient-scale plants are large, or plants can be large because leading firms can command large market shares and build large plants to serve them. Lagging the independent variable helps some:

$AVSIZE$ = value added in all plants in the industry employing fifty or more workers divided by the number of these plants, 1958

$LGSIZE$ = value added in the largest plants accounting for 50 percent of the industry's value added divided by the number of these plants, 1958.

Most industries can be expected to contain plants of varying sizes, some of them producing below, and others at or beyond, a minimum-efficient scale. Various statistical studies of industrial organization in the United States have used differences in the average size of the larger plants as a proxy for interindustry variations in minimum-efficient scale, and $LGSIZE$ is constructed in that spirit. But the proportion of plants that attain minimum-efficient scale may vary greatly from industry to industry. Then average plant size (after excluding very small plants) may be a superior indicator. It can also be defended because of its sensitivity to the number of relatively small plants in an industry. If these are quite numerous, the disadvantages of inefficiently small plant scales are probably small. Thus, a low value of $AVSIZE$ tends to indicate both a small value of minimum-efficient scale and relatively small diseconomies to the inefficiently small plant.[11]

The causal effect of plant size on concentration of course depends not on absolute plant size but plant size relative to the market. Many studies roll these two variables together, expressing plant size as a fraction of market size. We prefer to enter the two variables separately, and therefore define:

JVA = total value added in the Japanese industry, 1967.

JVA will depend on many structural traits of the Japanese economy, including consumers' preferences for various goods and Japan's comparative advantage in international trade. If there were no foreign trade, if the Japanese consumed industries' products in the same proportions as do Ameri-

11. See William S. Comanor and Thomas A. Wilson, "Advertising Market Structure and Performance," *Review of Economics and Statistics,* vol. 49 (November 1967), pp. 423–40, especially table 8; and Peter Pashigian, "The Effect of Market Size on Concentration," *International Economic Review,* vol. 10 (October 1969), pp. 291–314.

cans, and if factor prices were the same, *JVA* would be perfectly correlated with its U.S. counterpart, the influence of which is embedded in the U.S. concentration measures. Hence, a statistically significant result for both *JVA* and the U.S. concentration variable indicates some independence of Japanese market size.

Another positive influence on concentration is an industry's capital intensity. Capital intensity in production is thought to be associated with scale economies because the technological bases for scale economies often depend on the physical properties of pieces of equipment. Also, capital intensity when combined with large minimum-efficient scales of production raises absolute-capital-cost barriers to entry. Hence we include the variable:

JCAP = capital employed per regular worker in the Japanese industry, 1958.

What matters is the capital intensity observed at Japanese factor prices. The less closely this is correlated with capital intensity in the U.S. industries, the more likely are *JCAP* and *USC4* to exert independent influences on concentration in Japan.

Table 2-3 presents linear regressions incorporating these variables. The fits are notably good and most of the coefficients are significant at the 0.01 level. Each of our hypotheses about *JC4* is confirmed. Equations (2) and (3) show the effect of using different combinations of variables measuring concentration in the United States. Equation (1) shows the regression of *JC4* on *USC4* alone. The relation is close, with the constant term significantly positive and the slope coefficient significantly less than one (a pattern that holds after other variables are added). The observations in this regression are weighted by value added in the Japanese industry, as a heteroscedasticity correction and in order to give greater weight to larger industries in testing the hypotheses. Therefore equation (1) accords with the finding on value of shipments in table 2-2 that Japanese concentration ratios are somewhat less dispersed than American ratios after being weighted by value added. Comparing *F* ratios, we find that *USC8* provides a slightly better explanation of *JC4* than either *USC4* and *USC58* (which sum to *USC8*) or *USC4* alone. Whatever the forces that compel the great similarity of an industry's concentration from country to country, they seem to persist through a substantial part of the cumulative distribution of firms by size. The determinants of *JC4* do fade, however, beyond the eight-firm U.S. concentration ratio; in equation (4), *USC820* is not significant.

Measures of marginal concentration in Japan are also closely related to their U.S. counterparts. The relation is less interesting for *JC58* than for

Table 2-3. *Regression Analysis of Determinants of Seller Concentration in Japanese Manufacturing Industries, 1963*[a]

Equation number	Dependent variable	Independent variable										Regression statistic	
		USC4	USC58	USMGC	USC8	USC820	JVA	JCAP	AVSIZE	LGSIZE	Constant	$\bar{R}^2$	F
(1)	JC4	0.573[b] (8.09)	...	...	...	...	...	...	...	...	13.2[b] (4.20)	0.397	65.4
(2)	JC4	0.472[b] (8.02)	0.430 (1.44)	...	...	...	-3.69[b] (-4.53)	3.33[b] (3.11)	...	0.0075[b] (5.63)	9.05[c] (2.32)	0.712	49.5
(3)	JC4	...	...	...	0.470[b] (8.44)	...	-3.62[b] (-5.44)	3.27[b] (3.37)	...	0.0075[b] (5.93)	8.68[b] (3.21)	0.715	62.5
(4)	JC4	...	...	...	0.472[b] (8.19)	0.026 (0.143)	-3.60[b] (-5.25)	3.23[b] (3.15)	...	0.0074[b] (5.82)	8.22[d] (1.95)	0.712	49.5
(5)	JC58	0.088[b] (4.20)	0.389[b] (4.15)	...	...	...	...	1.10[b] (2.79)	...	0.0018[b] (4.54)	0.84 (0.70)	0.638	44.2
(6)	JC58	...	0.908[b] (6.23)	...	...	-0.300[b] (-3.21)	1.24[b] (5.15)	1.06[c] (2.16)	0.0017 (0.79)	...	1.34 (0.92)	0.582	28.9
(7)	JMGC	...	...	0.418[b] (3.88)	...	...	2.44[c] (2.43)	-0.55 (-0.39)	...	-0.0006 (-0.34)	19.76[b] (3.66)	0.120	4.3

a. See text for definition of variables. Values of $\bar{R}^2$ are adjusted for degrees of freedom; t values appear in parentheses.
b. Significant in a two-tailed test at 0.01.
c. Significant in a two-tailed test at 0.05.
d. Significant in a two-tailed test at 0.10.

JMGC, because the former could be due to the correlation between the marginal and four-firm concentration ratios. The relative marginal concentration ratio is constructed in a way that insures a low correlation with other concentration measures, so the significant relation of *JMGC* to *USMGC* strongly supports our conclusion that an industry's cumulative concentration curve varies little from country to country. In equation (6), however, *USC820*'s relation to *JC58* is negative and significant. Again, the constancy of the concentration curve vanishes after the eighth firm (or so); we have no explanation for the significant negative coefficient.

In equations (2)–(4), concentration has a strong negative relation to market size, but a significant positive sign appears in equations (6) and (7) explaining marginal concentration. We can only conjecture what causes this reversal. In many studies the correlations in cross-section between market size and the size of plants or firms are positive. If this relation were strong enough, it would extinguish the negative relation between *JC4* and market size shown in equations (2)–(4). If this were true of the smaller firms in an industry but not the leaders, the relative marginal concentration ratio *(JMGC)* in particular could then become positively related to market size. This exploratory study cannot provide a more confident explanation for this change in relations.

The two measures of plant size are both significantly related to *JC4* and *JC58,* except for occasional lapses in *AVSIZE*'s relation to *JC58*. Substituting *AVSIZE* for *LGSIZE* in equations for *JC4* generally raises the variable's *t* ratio and the equation's *F* ratio somewhat. With the dubious causality and identity relation connecting plant size and concentration we push the conclusions no further.

Finally, capital intensity bears the predicted positive relation to concentration, at least for *JC4* and *JC58*. It is unrelated to *JMGC,* however, suggesting that its effect prevails only at the top end of the concentration curve (that is, for the top few firms). This may be due to the great differences in relative factor prices facing Japanese firms of different sizes, and to the relation between capital intensity and firm size often observed in other countries.

We examined the residuals from the equations in table 2-3, especially equations (2)–(4), for clues about the variables omitted from the model. Actual concentration tends to exceed its estimated levels in industries producing differentiated consumer goods that are relatively new in Japan, and in high-technology industries. The latter effect is probably due to public policy, the former to the dynamics of product differentiation. Concentration falls short of its estimated value in some industries that are heavy exporters or in which small-scale enterprises have been long established either as subcontractors or independent sellers.

In all countries the data on concentration tend to be much more complete for the manufacturing sector than others, and Japan is no exception. Casual empiricism suggests that concentration patterns in other sectors differ little from those in the United States. Agriculture, the services, and distributive trades are unconcentrated. The important public utilities and transportation sector is highly concentrated in Japan and partly under public ownership, partly private but regulated.

Like previous investigators, we find no great difference in concentration between Japan and the United States. Bain found that industrial concentration is "about the same or slightly greater in Japan than it is in the United States," while Rotwein held that "even with the incomparabilities removed it is unlikely, conservatively speaking, that the results would reveal a substantially higher level of concentration in Japan than in the United States."[12]

In the United States the average level of seller concentration in industrial markets has been quite stable over the long term, occasionally marked by an upward or downward trend. Is Japan's pattern similar, despite the rapid growth and the shocks of World War II and its aftermath? Examining 35 industries in 1937 and 1950, Rotwein reports a decline in the unweighted average share of the top three Japanese firms from 67 percent to 59 percent; 23 industries showed declines, 11 increases. For 1950–55 a 64-industry sample shows another modest decline in the average from 64 percent to 61 percent (decreases in 40 industries, increases in 20).[13] Annual indexes for selected industries surveyed by the Fair Trade Commission, as shown in table 2-4, confirm the impression of a decline from 1950 at least into the 1960s; the food and kindred products sector is an exception, however. The overall indexes of concentration in manufacturing since 1960, with broader coverage than the sectoral ones based on 1950, do indicate an upturn after 1965. Because the commission's series contains a downward bias for statistical reasons, the recent upturn strongly suggests a reverse of the earlier trend.[14] Considering that the Herfindahl index gives a heavy weight

12. Joe S. Bain, *International Differences in Industrial Structure* (Yale University Press, 1966), p. 83; and Eugene Rotwein, "Economic Concentration and Monopoly in Japan," *Journal of Political Economy*, vol. 72 (June 1964), p. 276.

13. Rotwein, "Economic Concentration," pp. 264–65. The samples both appear to be weighted toward the (initially) more concentrated industries. Hence it is possible that increases in the initially less-concentrated industries could modify or reverse the conclusions. Also see Eleanor M. Hadley, *Antitrust in Japan* (Princeton University Press, 1970), pp. 330–42.

14. The index covers an unchanged sample of industries that were highly concentrated in 1960. Their concentration was bounded from above and could not rise much. A downward trend in the index could be consistent with unchanged (or increasing) con-

Table 2-4. *Indexes of Concentration in the Japanese Manufacturing Sector and Selected Subsectors, 1950–70*[a]

Industry and concentration level	1950	1955	1960	1965	1970
Food and kindred products					
3 firms	100.0	104.7	119.4	127.1	...
10 firms	100.0	106.7	119.7	126.2	...
Textile mills, pulp and paper products					
3 firms	100.0	69.9	63.5	66.6	...
10 firms	100.0	69.0	62.9	63.0	...
Chemicals, petroleum, and ceramic products					
3 firms	100.0	94.1	84.4	82.5	...
10 firms	100.0	98.3	90.6	89.0	...
Metals					
3 firms	100.0	96.4	92.6	86.9	...
10 firms	100.0	99.5	98.7	98.9	...
Machinery					
3 firms	100.0	89.0	77.5	106.4	...
10 firms	100.0	91.9	83.1	99.7	...
Overall[b]					
3 firms	...	...	100.0	97.8	104.0
10 firms	...	...	100.0	100.4	102.8
Herfindahl	...	...	100.0	96.8	110.1

Sources: Japan, Fair Trade Commission, *Nihon no sangyō shūchū—1963–1966* [Industrial Concentration in Japan—1963–1966] (Tokyo: Toyō Keizai Shinpōsha, 1969), pp. 58–59, and *Shuyō sangyō ni okeru seisan shūchūdo: 1955–1970* [Concentration Ratios of Production in the Main Industries: 1955–1970] (Tokyo: Fair Trade Institute, 1973), p. 2.

a. The concentration index for 3 firms is based on three-firm concentration ratios; for 10 firms on ten-firm concentration ratios; and for "Herfindahl" on Herfindahl concentration ratios (the Herfindahl measure is defined as $\sum_i s_i^2$ where s_i is the fraction of industry shipments accounted for by the ith firm).

b. Coverage for the overall indexes differs from that for the subsectors.

to inequality among the leading firms, the three overall indexes together suggest some fluctuation in concentration since 1960 among the top few firms but less change among larger oligopoly groups. The commission points to horizontal mergers among large firms as an important component in the increase after 1965. We conclude that the trend of declining concentration gave way in 1965 to an upward trend, and there is no reason why that trend should not persist.

Not only do these overall indicators show no strongly sustained long-term trend in concentration; in addition, the position of individual industries has tended to stay rather constant. Nishikawa found a (Kendall) rank

centration if industries omitted from the index were becoming increasingly concentrated at a rate that offsets (or more than offsets) the decline for the included industries. Kōzō Yamamura, *Economic Policy in Postwar Japan: Growth versus Economic Democracy* (University of California Press, 1967), chap. 6, puts the upturn earlier than 1965, around 1960.

correlation of 0.53 among five-firm concentration ratios for twenty-eight commodities between 1937 and 1962.[15]

Little statistical evidence is available on the determinants of changes in industrial concentration. The economic reforms of the occupation can get little credit for the apparent decline of concentration from the prewar period, because the more effective measures were aimed at zaibatsu holding companies and intercorporate shareholding rather than monopoly per se. A more likely explanation for any postwar decline in concentration is rapid growth itself. At least in cross-industry comparisons, growth often appears to favor the entry of new firms to an industry and the reduction of concentration. Nishikawa examined data for 50 commodities over the years 1956–62. The change in concentration was negatively correlated with growth both before and after 1959, though significantly in the 1959–62 period only; the change in concentration and the change in the number of firms showed a significant negative relation for both periods.[16]

Mergers

In most industrial countries there have been a large number of corporate mergers in the past two decades and a rising trend throughout the 1960s. In the United States mergers were diverted into the conglomerate channel during the 1950s, when horizontal and vertical mergers were branded illegal where there is even a modest possibility that they might reduce competition. Conglomerate mergers surely contributed to the increasing share of assets held by America's largest hundred corporations, but their direct role in elevating seller concentration in individual product markets has been modest, and any indirect influence (because vertical integration and large firm size raise concentration) remains conjectural.

In Japan, as in the European countries, public policy imposed no strong check on horizontal and vertical combinations. Most of the combinations since 1950 have been among relatively small companies, as table 2-5 shows.[17] In the 1960s, however, mergers among very large enterprises be-

15. Shunsaku Nishikawa, "Concentration under Rapid Economic Growth: Japanese Manufacturing, 1956 to 1962," discussion paper no. 7 (Economic Research Institute, Economic Planning Agency, Tokyo, 1969), pp. 3–4.

16. Ibid., pp. 7–9. Compare Willard F. Mueller and Larry G. Hamm, "Trends in Industrial Market Concentration, 1947 to 1970," *Review of Economics and Statistics*, vol. 56 (November 1974), pp. 511–20.

17. The series shows some tendency to move inversely with the business cycle. See Jirō Ono, "The Characteristics of Recent Corporate Mergers in Japan," *Kōbe Economic and Business Review*, vol. 17 (1970), pp. 53–67.

Table 2-5. *Number of Recorded Japanese Mergers, by Size of Capital of Combined Companies, 1950–70*

	Number of mergers, by size of capital (billions of yen)				
Year	Under 0.1	0.1–1	1–10	Over 10	Total
1950	413	7	0	0	420
1951	317	14	0	0	331
1952	359	23	3	0	385
1953	315	24	5	0	344
1954	293	28	4	0	325
1955	311	19	8	0	338
1956	359	15	7	0	381
1957	367	22	9	0	398
1958	348	25	8	0	381
1959	372	37	8	0	417
1960	381	49	9	1	440
1961	519	54	16	2	591
1962	585	101	26	3	715
1963	821	131	33	12	997
1964	730	104	21	9	864
1965	771	109	11	3	894
1966	763	78	25	5	871
1967	852	103	33	7	995
1968	876	116	21	7	1,020
1969	965	162	34	2	1,163
1970	925	179	37	6	1,147

Source: Japan, Fair Trade Commission, *Nihon no kigyō shūchū* [Corporate Mergers in Japan] (Ministry of Finance, 1971), p. 171.

came increasingly common. About half of the large mergers in the 1967–70 period were horizontal; table 2-6 tends to confirm the suggestion that these mergers have been a major force in the reversal of the declining trend of seller concentration in Japanese manufacturing industries. The distribution of assets acquired in all mergers that took place in 1970 leaves the same impression: 50.3 percent were absorbed in horizontal combinations, 9.2 percent in vertical mergers, and 38.0 percent in conglomerate acquisitions (13.7 percent were market-extension mergers); 2.5 percent were unclassified.

The Fair Trade Commission offers an explanation for the upswing of mergers in the 1960s that echoes one often heard in Western Europe. A liberalization of international trade in 1962 allegedly prompted Japanese corporations to merge in order to enlarge their size and extinguish competition among themselves, the better to defend themselves against foreigners. Mergers in 1967–69 are attributed to a similar reaction of larger firms

Table 2-6. *Number of Mergers of Large Japanese Firms, by Type of Merger, 1967–70*[a]

Type of merger	1967	1968	1969	1970
Horizontal	21	17	24	31
Vertical	6	5	4	4
Backward	2	3	2	3
Forward	4	2	2	1
Conglomerate	12	12	27	24
Market extension	2	7	14	11
Product extension	8	4	8	4
Other	2	1	5	9
Total	39	34	55	59

Source: Fair Trade Commission, *Nihon no kigyō shūchū*, p. 66.
a. Combined assets of companies in merger are greater than one billion yen.

faced with the liberalization of controls over foreign investment in Japan, but also to efforts to improve the productive technique and capital facilities of smaller firms by rationalization and modernization.[18] The influence of public policy is surely also significant. Many measures have been designed to encourage rationalization in smaller companies through merger, among other means, although it is difficult to link the policies to the timing of the merger wave. Among large companies, public policy has been important at least in its permissiveness and some combinations received active public encouragement.

Product Differentiation

The ability of producers to differentiate their products through advertising and related techniques has proved a potent influence on market competition in the United States and the United Kingdom. It not only insulates sellers from their rivals' actions but also tends to raise barriers to the entry of new sellers.[19] In the abstract, one might expect that a country with social patterns and values much different from Western norms might exhibit a different level of product differentiation, both overall and in indi-

18. Fair Trade Commission, *Nihon no kigyō shūchū*, p. 49. Data on the distribution of acquired assets, cited above, are given in ibid., pp. 68–71. Also see Ono, "Characteristics of Recent Mergers," pp. 61–67.

19. Comanor and Wilson, "Advertising Market Structure and Performance"; and Javad Khalilzadeh-Shirazi, "Market Structure and Price-Cost Margins in United Kingdom Manufacturing Industries," *Review of Economics and Statistics,* vol. 56 (February 1974), pp. 67–76.

vidual industries. Yet the most casual traveler in Japan quickly writes off that possibility, finding the methods of sales promotion quite similar to those in Western countries. Whether on cosmetics, pharmaceuticals, or convenience foods, sales-promotion techniques seem to be exploited with relentless thoroughness. The average advertising-to-sales ratios for leading firms in nineteen Japanese industries shown in table 2-7 are not matched to comparable U.S. data, but their rankings clearly would be similar.

One difference in Japanese and American product differentiation lies in the recent development and unsettled state of Japan's pattern. True, sales promotion is not a new phenomenon in Japan: advertising first emerged early in this century among sellers introducing Western-style goods, with breath fresheners, toilet articles, tea, and seasonings the chief advertisers noted in a 1910 survey. But large-scale manufacturing enterprises have grown up in the differentiated consumer-goods industries only since World War II. Thus the structural consequences of mass advertising are still working themselves out. Consider the percentage distribution of total expenditure

Table 2-7. *Average Advertising-to-Sales Ratios of Leading Firms in Nineteen Japanese Industries, 1961–70*

Industry	Number of firms	Advertising as a percentage of sales
Cosmetics	2	13.0
Drugs	10	9.4
Detergents	5	7.0
Dairy products	3	5.8
Cameras	4	5.8
Photographic films	2	5.5
Sodium glutamate	1	4.7
Electrical apparatus	8	3.4
Sewing machines	4	2.7
Motorcycles	2	2.5
Pianos and organs	2	2.3
Tires and tubes	5	1.5
Beer	3	1.2
Automobiles	8	1.2
Watches	2	1.2
Synthetic fibers	8	1.2
Sheet glass	2	1.0
Woolen and worsted fabrics	5	0.9
Paints	5	0.9

Source: Masu Uekusa and Tsuruhiko Nanbu, "Gōsei sen'i" [Synthetic Fiber], in Hisao Kumagai, ed., *Nihon no sangyō soshiki* II [Industrial Organization in Japan, II] (Tokyo: Chūō Kōronsha, 1973), p. 161.

between the channels used for sales promotion in Japan and the United States:[20]

	Japan	United States
Newspapers	35.4	29.2
Magazines, trade publications	5.6	12.5
Television	32.8	16.5
Radio	4.4	6.0
Direct mail	4.0	15.2
Outdoor billboards, signs	15.0	1.2
Miscellaneous	2.8	19.4
Total	100.0	100.0

The one safe conclusion seems to be the relative predominance in Japan of general and nationwide media—television and newspapers (largely national in Japan). The firm trying to break into the circle of successfully differentiated producers thus may face a problem of scale economies in nationwide sales promotion at least as great as his U.S. counterpart. A difference from the United States not evident in the data is the extensive use of rebates and premiums in Japan. Their significance differs somewhat from other sales-promotion strategies, for they represent disguised forms of price reduction and thus inject a measure of price flexibility. Moreover, they can be managed so as to increase with the size of a buyer's total purchases, providing an effective strategy for the already dominant firm.

Another important feature of product differentiation in Japan lies in the extensive control exercised by many manufacturers over their channels of distribution. Among large-scale manufacturers of consumer goods, control is aimed partly at getting around the complexities and inefficiencies of Japan's fragmented distribution system, partly at securing and insulating market power.[21] In some industries the cooperation of the distribution channels is important in establishing the identity of individual brands. Control over distribution then provides important advantages to the manufacturer: he can insure that on-the-spot efforts by the retailer to display, promote, price, and service the product are to his maximal advantage, and he can force

20. M. Y. Yoshino, *The Japanese Marketing System: Adaptations and Innovations* (MIT Press, 1971), p. 105; and F. M. Scherer, *Industrial Market Structure and Economic Performance* (Rand McNally, 1970), p. 326. In each case diverse original sources were used. Japanese figures pertain to 1968, U.S. to 1965. The expenditure categories may not be comparably defined; the figure for outdoor advertising in the United States, for instance, is clearly understated.

21. Various changes in the distribution sector reveal the influence of increasing product differentiation. See chap. 6, below, and Kisou Tasugi, "Modernization of the Functions of the Assemblers in Each Local Producing Area in Japan," *Kyoto University Economic Review*, vol. 41 (April 1971), pp. 1–28.

potential entrants to incur heavy fixed costs to set up exclusive distribution channels of their own.

Before World War II, distribution in Japan was dominated by wholesalers and large-scale trading companies whose market information guided the production of the small manufacturers who supplied them. Since then, vertically integrated control by the manufacturers has become quite common in oligopolistic and fast-growing consumer-good sectors.[22] The extent and variety of this control appears to exceed what is found in the United States. In a few industries (sewing machines, Western-style beds) it takes the form of fully owned entry into wholesale and retail distribution, in others exclusive or nonexclusive franchises (gasoline, automobiles, some confectionery). Still other industries have organized their distribution outlets into affiliated groups of wholesalers and retailers. For instance, Shiseido, the leading maker of cosmetics, holds controlling interests in its seventy-three wholesalers who, in turn, sell to affiliated or controlled retail outlets. Electrical manufacturers have gained control by pooling their wholesalers in each region into a company with equity participation by the manufacturer, and independent wholesalers have become nearly extinct. Exclusive dealing is not the general practice in electrical appliances, but 70–80 percent of an outlet's sales are generally of its affiliated brand. In the pharmaceutical industry, resale price maintenance has helped in the establishment of a system of nonexclusive affiliates.

Many of these developments can be rationalized in terms of producers' efforts to combat the manifest inefficiencies of Japan's distribution sector (see chapter 6). Intentionally or unintentionally, however, their effect is to reduce competition among rival sellers and raise the barriers to entry among new ones. Yoshino points out that organizing the traditionally independent distributors entails heavy fixed costs in managerial effort, which impose greater burdens on smaller manufacturing firms. Unfortunately, data on concentration in Japan do not allow a clean comparison of trends in differentiated consumer-goods industries (an area of rapid concentration in the United States) with trends in other industries. The Fair Trade Commission's data on detailed commodity groups contains about four times as many producer goods as consumer goods, and neither group appears representative. We classified 135 industries roughly into these two categories and tabulated the percentage-point changes in three-firm concentration ratios between 1959 and 1970. The median change was +0.6 point for the producer-goods sector and +1.9 points

22. Much of this discussion is drawn from Yoshino, *The Japanese Marketing System*, chap. 3; and Distribution Economics Institute of Japan, *Outline of Japanese Distribution Structures* (Tokyo: Distribution Economics Institute of Japan, 1971).

for consumer goods,[23] a difference that can hardly settle the issue one way or the other. The differential trend toward higher concentration in the U.S. consumer-good industries is much stronger, or at least more clearly demonstrated.[24]

Barriers to New Competition

Barriers to entry of new firms, a vital trait of market structure, depend partly on technological factors, and to that extent should vary little from country to country. A country's institutions can, however, raise or lower the fences that protect the market power of established sellers. Certain structural features of Japan's economy seem to lower these barriers.

In the United States, product differentiation due to advertising and other sales-promotion activities appears to be the most potent inhibitor of new entry. While product differentiation in Japan is following the Western pattern, recent developments suggest that many going Japanese firms are less well entrenched than their American counterparts. In general, the disturbed and fast-changing condition of the economy since World War II has favored entry of new firms by increasing the uncertainty and vulnerability of established firms.[25] Compared to industrial countries other than the United States, Japan's economy is a large one, so that smallness of markets is not a serious barrier to entry. Absolute costs also pose relatively low barriers in Japan. Because most raw materials are imported and bought at arm's length on the international market, going firms do not tie up known domestic sources of inputs. Similarly, Japan depends on imported technology that is often available from numerous foreign suppliers, so that control of technology is not a major force excluding entrants. On the other hand, the practice of permanent employment may make it difficult for new firms to secure scarce and specialized labor skills.

The sheer size of the capital needed to enter an industry and the lender's risk in supplying a new firm often raise barriers to entry. Japan's economy is greatly favored, however, by the ready entry of going firms from other industries and by methods of financing that can spread the risks of large-scale entry. The internal flexibility of the output mixes of large firms and their willingness

23. Japan, Fair Trade Commission, *Shuyō sangyō ni okeru seisan shūchūdo: 1955–1970* [Concentration Ratios of Production in the Main Industries: 1955–1970] (Tokyo: Fair Trade Institute, 1973).

24. Mueller and Hamm, "Trends."

25. See M. Y. Yoshino, *Japan's Managerial System: Tradition and Innovation* (MIT Press, 1968), chap. 6, especially p. 166.

to shift into new lines of activity also further entry.[26] The general trading companies have become quite active as general promoters of new business ventures, both within Japan and abroad.[27] The zaibatsu successors and principal bank groupings have often spawned new firms to enter promising industries, with many members contributing to the initial capital of the new firm.[28]

This structural analysis of the sources of entry barriers is confirmed by a survey of the difficulties faced by large public corporations in entering new industries.[29] Many of the 182 respondents cited more than one source of difficulty:

	Number	Percent of respondents
Control of distributive outlets	96	53
Brand image	92	51
Lack of specialized skills (technical or marketing)	80	44
Capital requirements	58	32
Patents and special technology	45	25
Low profitability or slow growth of demand	42	23
Scarcity of land or water	29	16

The responses give prominent place to product differentiation contrived through the control of distributive outlets, and the relatively small proportion of respondents mentioning capital requirements confirms the effectiveness of Japan's institutions for sharing risks and raising large sums to finance new businesses.

Rapid Macroeconomic Growth

Japanese industry's periods of extraordinarily rapid growth of output have evidently been important to business decisionmaking and market competition. When the growth rate of demand significantly influences the way sellers interact with one another, it becomes one of the major determinants of market structure. How this rapid growth affects microeconomic behavior depends on how the macroeconomic growth process affects businessmen's plans and decisions. Tentatively, we suggest that for extended periods in the latter

26. George Rosen, "Japanese Industry Since the War," *Quarterly Journal of Economics,* vol. 67 (August 1953), pp. 445–63, especially pp. 450–51.

27. See *Oriental Economist,* vol. 40 (June 1972), pp. 22–27.

28. For an example involving 49 contributors, see *Oriental Economist,* vol. 40 (August 1972), pp. 14–15.

29. Japan, Economic Planning Agency, *Seihin shijō eno shinki shinshutsu ni kansuru chōsa* [Survey on New Entry into Product Markets] (forthcoming).

1950s and latter 1960s, many industries found the possibilities for profitable expansions of output limited only by short-run supply and planning constraints. The favorable exchange rate of the yen placed selling prices for many internationally traded goods high enough to make profitable seemingly unlimited expansions of output.[30] At the same time there were a large labor supply available that could be shifted from agriculture and other low-productivity sectors, and a high rate of saving to supply capital. The effect of the undervalued yen on industries' decisions to expand output depends on the expansion being profitable at international prices, and not necessarily on actual sale of the output in international markets. This is to say, an increasing proportion of manufactured output being exported would strongly support the interpretation but is not necessary to it. Between 1960 and 1968, fourteen of seventeen broadly defined manufacturing industries did increase their (direct and indirect) dependence on exports; but the evidence suggests that this shift came primarily toward the end of the period and should thus not be branded "export led" growth.[31]

The microeconomic effect of such a combination of factors is to extinguish producers' concern about their interdependence, so far as each anticipates selling all he can produce at the going world price—whether on foreign or domestic markets. Market strategies to improve a firm's position at the expense of its rivals take on a low priority, and fear of retaliation is reduced. Sellers' concentration in the market then should have little influence on the rate of profit they earn: taking the profit rate as an indicator of resource misallocation due to monopoly makes sense only if we are observing industries in long-run equilibrium. Indeed, variations in the reported rates of profit are likely in such circumstances to result mostly from varying short-run windfalls. Where producers can adapt their actual plant capacities only slowly to the levels they would desire in a rapidly growing market, profits will be inflated by short-run windfalls whatever their long-run equilibrium level; where expansion comes quickly, windfalls will not accrue.

30. Powerful evidence is contained in a study of productivity in matched Japanese and American manufacturing industries in 1958–59 and 1963. The variance of U.S.-to-Japan productivity ratios among industries was great, of course, but the average clearly reflected the money-cost advantage enjoyed by many Japanese industries. In 1958–59, productivity differential was 2.7, but the average wage differential about 6; in 1963 the figures were 2.4 and 5. See Kenzō Yukizawa, "A Comparison of Labour Productivity in Japanese and American Manufacturing Industry," *Kyoto University Economic Review*, vol. 38 (April 1968), pp. 49–50.

31. See Japan, Economic Planning Agency, *Economic Survey of Japan, 1969–1970* (Tokyo: Japan Times, Ltd.), p. 78; and Tuvia Blumenthal, "Exports and Economic Growth: The Case of Postwar Japan," *Quarterly Journal of Economics*, vol. 86 (November 1972), pp. 617–31.

But fast growth can also affect the rivalry among sellers directly. Suppose that the share a seller can command in a market today depends on the share he held yesterday, because demand for his product depends on such inter-temporal factors as experience and goodwill and the cumulative effects of advertising. The more rapidly the market is growing, the more will it pay the seller to "invest" in market share for tomorrow by selling more today than short-run profit maximization would indicate. And if his productivity increases with the cumulative volume he produces, he gains a further incentive to compete aggressively.[32] With Japan's abundant entrepreneurial capacity, conditions of rapid growth thus are likely to promote the entry of new firms and the diversification of established ones into the more rapidly growing sectors.

The same incentives to raise market share in the short run affect the stability of the shares held by growing firms in an oligopoly market. Also, rapid growth probably means larger disturbances and potential changes in relative advantage for these firms. One Japanese study found that for industries whose output grew more than five times between 1958 and 1967 the variability in their shares of the market was almost 50 percent higher than for those whose output grew less than three times.[33] For this reason also, one might expect that rapid growth would limit firms' ability to maintain collusive arrangements.

Company Finance and Capital Markets

Certain features of factor markets in Japan have an unusual effect on the allocation of resources. These special features of the capital market in combination with the particular financial structures of Japanese firms strongly affect market structure.

The capital market's discrimination in favor of large firms is apparent in table 2-8, which suggests that the largest class of firms pays a third less for its debt capital than those with less than ¥100 million in paid-in capital. The differential shows no signs of closing over the fifteen-year period covered by the table. Unfortunately, the table's figures pertain principally to relatively small firms. The lower boundary of the open-ended largest category corresponds to firms with paid-in equity capital of only $2.8 million (using the ex-

32. James C. Abegglen and William V. Rapp, "Japanese Managerial Behavior and 'Excessive Competition,'" *Developing Economies*, vol. 8 (December 1970), pp. 432–43.
33. The "variability coefficient" was simply a sum of absolute values of changes in individual firms' shares. The study by Mitsubishi Economic Research Institute is reported in Economic Planning Agency, *Economic Survey of Japan, 1968–1969*, p. 112.

Table 2-8. *Effective Rates of Interest Paid on Debt Capital by Japanese Manufacturing Corporations of Various Sizes, Selected Years, 1956–71*

Paid-in capital of firm, in millions of yen	Effective interest rate[a]			
	1956	1961	1966[b]	1971[b]
Under 2	15.36	14.90	14.79	14.47
2–4	14.52	14.90	14.79	14.02
5–9	14.28	14.90	16.55	15.08
10–49	14.19	14.02	16.41	14.64
50–99	13.35	13.57	15.22	14.62
100–999	12.24	12.06	13.87	12.84
1,000 and over	12.24	8.65	9.90	9.26

Source: Japan, Ministry of Finance, *Hōjin kigyō tōkei nenpō* [Annual Statistics on Corporations] (annual).

a. Interest paid plus discount divided by short-run and long-run term loans plus debentures; insurance deposits against discount and compulsory deposits as a condition for loans are excluded, so the figures should measure the effective net cost of capital.

b. Short-run term debentures are included from 1965 on.

Table 2-9. *Average Finance Costs of 243 Large Japanese Manufacturing Firms, 1961–70*[a]

Size of assets, in billions of yen	Number of firms	Average annual finance cost, in percent[b]
Less than 10	38	5.64
10–19	59	5.16
20–29	36	5.18
30–39	30	5.64
40–49	15	4.96
50–99	28	5.24
100 or more	37	4.82

a. See the statistical appendix to this volume for a description of this sample of 243 firms.

b. Borrowed capital is defined as total assets minus equity.

change rate of 360 yen to the dollar). Table 2-9 indicates that the average finance costs of 243 large manufacturing firms, most of them with capital assets of more than ￥10 billion, are roughly consistent with the notion of some favoritism toward the larger corporations.[34] Average capital costs for companies with total assets exceeding ￥40 billion is evidently less than that for smaller companies. Nonetheless, the pattern is not particularly sharp. It appears that capital-market discrimination in Japan favors large companies relative to small ones.

34. The absolute magnitudes in table 2-9 are not comparable to those in table 2-8. No adjustment is made in table 2-9 for compensating balances, and the denominator includes current liabilities on which interest is seldom paid.

Another distinctive feature of company finance in Japan is the exceptionally high leverage of companies' capital structures. The ratio of owners' equity to total capital in Japanese corporations is not only low but has been declining, as the following percentages show:[35]

	Manufacturing firms	All industries
1950	31.4	26.9
1955	34.0	29.0
1960	27.6	22.6
1965	23.1	19.0
1970	19.9	16.1

The decline, which may be partly a reflection of accounting practices, has been greater for large firms than for small ones, almost erasing the once significant differences among firms of various sizes. The end of the trend to increasing leverage has been predicted as Japanese growth slows somewhat and the self-financing capabilities of business firms increase,[36] but the data do not yet show a turnaround.

The effect of this high financial leverage on the economy's performance depends on whether Japanese holders of debt instruments view their risk-bearing function the same as debt lenders in Western countries. The large lenders are chiefly banks, because debentures represent only a few percent of new corporate funds (4 percent in 1966).[37] They have adapted to the risk imposed by high corporate leverage partly by spreading the risks and partly by exercising control that in the United States would imply equity participation. The banks are very large relative to the corporations they finance. The largest hold deposits about four times the sales of the leading manufacturing company, whereas in the United States the relation would be closer to parity. Also, banks' risks on their business loans are hedged in several important ways. A given corporation borrows from many different banks, the leading bank usually accounting for no more than 30 percent of a company's borrowings. In Western countries, the risks of a given large firm's default are probably not spread so widely among lenders. Furthermore, loans to large (although not small) companies seem in effect to be guaranteed by the Bank of Japan, which will assist in a rescue if a large company gets in trouble.[38]

35. Japan, Ministry of Finance, *Hōjin kigyō tōkei nenpō* [Annual Statistics on Corporations] (annual).

36. See discussion in Economic Planning Agency, *Economic Survey of Japan, 1968–1969*, pp. 116–21.

37. James C. Abegglen, ed., *Business Strategies for Japan* (Tokyo: Sophia University, 1970), p. 58.

38. See Hadley, *Antitrust in Japan*, pp. 234–35; Abegglen, *Business Strategies*, p. 62; and Abegglen and Rapp, "Japanese Managerial Behavior," p. 430.

Finally, it appears that banks somehow manage to share in the riches when their principal borrowers do particularly well. One study found the city banks' profits fairly closely related to the growth rate of their client enterprises. It is possible, of course, that this relationship is due solely to the shares of corporate stocks the banks hold.[39]

The high leverage and low liquidity characteristic of Japanese industry are possible because of the relative absence of long strikes. If these were a normal feature of labor-management relations, corporations carrying low liquidity could not face the threat of wage settlements that would put them at a unit-cost disadvantage.[40] Another factor favoring corporations is the help available (documented below in chapter 4) to faltering members of Japan's conglomerate groups from their nonfinancial brethren. These and the financial factors mitigate the effects of high leverage, but do not neutralize them.

The fact that interest rates favor large firms causes artificial (private but not social) economies for large-scale enterprise and encourages firms to grow larger and markets more concentrated than necessary. (Labor costs, of course, cut the other way; it is not possible to tell how the two factors balance out, especially since industries vary in their opportunities to substitute capital for labor.) High leverage, by Western standards, should also affect the conduct of firms and the performance of industries. In general, it should tend to increase their preference for safe conduct, including collusive arrangements that remove the uncertainties associated with competitive moves to improve one firm's position at the expense of its rivals. Some types of collusive arrangements, however, can actually destabilize profits. Nonetheless, studies of industries in the United States suggest that high leverage (along with other heavy fixed costs) raises firms' *desires* to collude, whether or not structural conditions are such as to make collusion effective.[41] Quite apart from its competitive significance, high leverage should discourage innovative risk-taking.

These predicted effects of the high leverage in corporate financial structures are the more important because other traits of the Japanese economy contribute to the fixity of large firms' costs and thus amplify the effects.[42]

39. Economic Planning Agency, *Economic Survey of Japan, 1968–1969*, pp. 121–22. The sample of enterprises used in the study was probably biased toward those in which financial institutions' equity holdings are relatively high. Usually a bank's loans to a firm are much larger than its holding of the firm's equity.

40. Abegglen and Rapp, "Japanese Managerial Behavior," p. 430.

41. Roger Sherman and Robert Tollison, "Technology, Profit Risk, and Assessments of Market Performance," *Quarterly Journal of Economics*, vol. 86 (August 1972), pp. 448–62.

42. For evidence from the behavior of Japanese companies, see the case study of the steel industry in Eugene J. Kaplan, *Japan—The Government-Business Relationship: A*

Chief of these, of course, is the practice of permanent employment. Most of a large firm's workers can be discharged only in the most dire circumstances.[43] Furthermore, there seem to be no alternative sources of flexibility, for money wages and even semiannual bonuses seem largely independent of the firm's short-run position. Firms in certain industries that rely on subcontracting benefit from their subcontractors' less rigid costs that allow these smaller firms some flexibility in responding to shifts in supply and demand. The practice of subcontracting can also cut a large firm's total costs by giving it access to labor at wages lower than it would have to pay itself. But subcontracting can further complicate the cost structure of a large firm with high fixed costs of capital and labor. Consider the effect of a decline in demand (or over-extension of capacity) on a firm that subcontracts part of its production processes but uses its own labor for work of the same type. The firm can avert the impact of the demand decline by stopping orders to its subcontractors and keeping its own (permanent) labor force busy. However, work done by its high-wage workers is apt to be more costly per unit than that done by the subcontractor. Thus the short-run average costs of production tend to exceed or at least equal costs at the firm's normal operating rate (the cost curve is downward sloping or at least less upward-sloping than otherwise). This tendency reinforces the adverse effects of cost fixity, which has exactly the same tendency.[44] Our predictions about the aversion of Japanese industry to the private risks of rivalrous conduct are thus strengthened.

International Linkages

Studies of industrial organization often neglect the international linkages associated with international trade, foreign direct investment, international technology agreements, and the like. By and large, these linkages have a

---

Guide for the American Businessman, U.S. Department of Commerce, Bureau of International Commerce (1972), especially p. 143.

43. "Regular workers" account for 95 percent of the labor force of firms employing 1,000 or more, 60 percent in firms employing 4 to 9 workers. The proportion of workers enjoying some sort of permanent employment is estimated to be about one-third of the total Japanese labor force. See Solomon B. Levine, "Labor Markets and Collective Bargaining in Japan," in William W. Lockwood, ed., The State and Economic Enterprise in Japan: Essays in the Political Economy of Growth (Princeton University Press, 1965), chap. 14.

44. Masu Uekusa and Tsuruhiko Nanbu, "Gōsei sen'i" [Synthetic Fiber], in Hisao Kumagai, ed., Nihon no sangyō soshiki II [Industrial Organization in Japan, II] (Tokyo: Chūō Kōronsha, 1973), chap. 4, pp. 200–01.

favorable effect on competitive behavior and performance in a market. But they offer no guarantee of improvement, and their impact varies from market to market.[45]

Among Japanese industries that are heavy exporters, there is an evident trend away from light industry and competitive sectors populated by small firms, and toward the heavy and chemical industries dominated by large firms. The proportion of output exported by small businesses dropped from 10 percent in 1960 to 7 percent in 1971, and their share of exports fell by a considerable amount. The share of output exported by large companies rose from 7 percent to 12 percent.[46] Large companies make most expenditures on research, and exports are now positively associated with industries' research intensity, a trend not evident a decade ago.[47] The small-business sector increasingly is exposed to competition from imports produced in the lower-wage Asian countries undergoing rapid industrialization.[48]

In certain circumstances the effects of import competition and export opportunities symmetrically restrain industries from exploiting their monopoly power in the domestic market. This symmetry tends to break down, however, when the export industries are concentrated enough (and protected by high enough tariffs) to charge different prices in the home and export markets. Thus the shift of Japan's concentrated industries into export status is probably adverse to effective competition in the domestic market, although the liberalization of trade controls on imports reduces exporters' ability to dump as well as increasing the pressure on import-competing industries. But, of course, the cartelizing of Japanese industries in order to implement "voluntary quotas" on exports to other industrial countries cuts in the opposite direction.

Foreign direct investment can also be a significant element of market structure.[49] In an industry with significant barriers to entry, the foreign enterprise

45. Richard E. Caves, *International Trade, International Investment, and Imperfect Markets,* Special Papers in International Economics, no. 10 (International Finance Section, Princeton University, 1974).

46. Economic Planning Agency, *Economic Survey of Japan, 1971–1972,* p. 76. This source puts the small-business share of exports in 1971 at 40 percent, but that is evidently an overestimate. On the long-run trend see William V. Rapp, "Firm Size and Japan's Export Structure: A Micro-view of Japan's Changing Export Competitiveness since Meiji," in Hugh Patrick, ed., *Japanese Industrialization and Its Social Consequences* (University of California Press, forthcoming).

47. Economic Planning Agency, *Economic Survey of Japan, 1967–1968,* p. 93.

48. Ibid., pp. 120–22.

49. This discussion is limited to the effects of investment in Japan by enterprises abroad. While the opportunity to invest abroad can also affect a firm's posture in the home market, Japan is just emerging as a foreign investor.

is an important potential entrant, and the foreign subsidiary (especially in its younger days) may provide a significant competitive force. Foreign investment can also provide a channel for the international transmission of technology for which there are no perfect substitutes.

Patterns of foreign investment in Japan are quite different from those in Western industrial countries, chiefly if not solely because of government restrictions. In 1967, most manufacturing enterprises with foreign participation were in the producer-goods sector—the chemicals, electrical engineering, and nonelectrical engineering sectors accounted for 58 percent of all foreign-affiliated enterprises included in a government survey.[50] Overall, foreign-affiliated firms are not very numerous. In 1969, firms in which there was some investment of foreign equity employed only 0.5 percent of Japan's labor force, and only 1.2 percent of its workforce in manufacturing. And in 1971, firms actually under foreign control (foreign majority ownership of equity) made only 11 percent of all sales by foreign-related firms.[51] These data imply that the joint venture is the characteristic form of foreign-affiliated enterprise. The share of foreign equity is exactly 50 percent in 23 percent of the foreign-affiliated firms, 30–50 percent in 57 percent of them, over 50 percent in only one-third. The foreign-affiliated enterprises are mostly new ventures (72 percent started since 1960), and their foreign parents are mostly American (70 percent). The Japanese partner in a joint venture is most often in the same industry (57 percent); in an important minority of cases it is diversifying from another industry, or is a general trading company. The joint ventures often have a complex ancestry, averaging 1.6 investors per company on the Japanese side, 1.1 on the foreign side. The influx of foreign-affiliated firms is closely correlated with agreements on the transfer of technology, and the motives of the Japanese partners have been heavily weighted toward securing foreign technology. The foreign partner has typically sought to secure access to the Japanese domestic market or to low Japanese costs of production.

Many features of company management and performance in the foreign-affiliated enterprises testify to the peculiar character of joint ventures, the servants of at least two masters.[52] As young companies, their immediate objectives run toward the establishment of market position rather than financial

50. Japan, Ministry of International Trade and Industry, *Foreign-Affiliated Enterprises in Japan,* Japan Industry Series, no. 26 (Tokyo: Trade Bulletin Corp., 1969), p. 15. The balance of this paragraph draws heavily on this report.

51. Dan Fenno Henderson, *Foreign Enterprise in Japan: Laws and Policies* (University of North Carolina Press, 1973), chap. 1.

52. This paragraph is based on MITI, *Foreign-Affiliated Enterprises in Japan,* pt. 3, Japan Industry Series, no. 33 (Tokyo: Trade Bulletin Corp., 1969).

results. The joint ventures operate in a quite constricted range of products, however, and seem distinctly short on long-term plans and objectives. The managements of those without a single dominant parent are constrained by the need to seek parental approval of their actions, and troubles often arise from the parents' divergent objectives.[53] From the evidence, the joint-venture enterprise appears to carry significantly less clout as an entity in the market than does the subsidiary with a single parent. As the Japanese government has intended, joint ventures serve as a means of admitting foreign capital and securing foreign technology without turning loose a major new competitive threat on Japanese product markets.[54] The competitive significance of direct investment in Japan is thus less than the number of foreign-affiliated enterprises would suggest.

A final significant international link is the agreement to import foreign technology to Japan, a major feature of productivity growth since World War II. Under these agreements Japanese firms are able to enter new product markets, or at least to improve the quality and/or lower the cost of old products. Thus access to foreign technology is a significant competitive element, as is evident in the fact that one standard source of absolute-cost barriers to entry is control over technology.

Statistical evidence shows that technology imports have become more numerous but probably individually less important over the postwar years. At first the province only of dominant firms, they have become accessible to more companies and also have ceased to supply such quantum leaps in Japan's stock of technology. The degree to which technology imports are concentrated in large companies has dropped sharply, as has the average amount of investment associated with each introduction.[55] The drop is probably due more to a shift in the composition of industries than it is to changes in the pattern of the typical industry's technology imports. One reason for this decreasing concentration of control over imported technology seems to lie on the supply side: more and more, firms elsewhere in the world have been successfully imitating or inventing around monopolized technologies, so that multiple sources are more often available. As Japan's technology level ap-

53. See Herbert Glazer, "Capital Liberalization," and Yōtarō Kobayashi, "Human Aspects of Management," in Robert J. Ballon, ed., *Joint Ventures and Japan* (Tokyo: Sophia University, 1967).

54. Henderson, *Foreign Enterprise in Japan,* chaps. 6–7, describes the administrative control apparatus and assesses the degree to which foreign investment has been effectively liberalized. Under foreign pressure Japan has relaxed her controls on foreign investment somewhat, but the de jure liberalization exceeds the de facto one.

55. Economic Planning Agency, *Economic Survey of Japan, 1966–1967,* pp. 66–67.

proaches that of the leading Western industrial country, the role of international movements of technology will surely change, but it has been important in the postwar years.

Conclusions

The concentration of corporate enterprise in Japan is greater than in the United States—much greater, once affiliates are taken into account. However, no such difference appears in concentration in individual manufacturing industries—levels in the two countries are about the same. Concentration in Japanese manufacturing industries is closely related to concentration in their U.S. counterparts, but size of national market, capital intensity, and size of establishments each have a statistical influence on concentration in the Japanese economy. Concentration in Japanese manufacturing had apparently been declining from 1937 to the early 1960s, and has been increasing since then. The resurgence is due in part to widespread horizontal mergers, recently one-half or more of all mergers involving large amounts of assets.

Product differentiation in Japan resembles that in the United States, and levels of expenditure for sales promotion vary similarly among industries in the two countries. Differentiation in Japan seems to depend more on nationwide sales promotion, and control of distribution channels is also important for effecting it. Broadly speaking, the structure of Japan's economy seems to make barriers to new competition somewhat lower than in the United States. Product differentiation is not as great. Lending institutions and group relations among nonfinancial firms reduce capital-cost barriers to entry and favor entry by established firms. But public policy, as chapter 8 indicates, largely works to deter entry.

Rapid macroeconomic growth has been an important environmental influence on industrial competion, reducing the force of oligopolistic interdependence, promoting the entry of new firms, and destabilizing collusive arrangements.

Capital markets are notable for their discrimination in favor of large firms, and the capital structures of Japanese companies for their exceptionally high debt-equity ratios. The burden of this leverage is eased because the leading debt holders (the large banks) accept an implicit risk-bearing role and because the hovering presence of the Bank of Japan and other potential rescuers provides insurance for a troubled company. Nonetheless, we expect high leverage to increase firms' preference for safe and collusive conduct, especially because the fixity of capital costs is matched by the fixity of the wage bill for the permanent employees making up much of the work force of large companies.

Sharp shifts since World War II in Japan's international competitive position have taken the large-enterprise sector from import-competing to export status, probably reducing thereby the discipline of international trade on market distortions. Sharp restrictions on foreign direct investment in Japan curb another competitive force, for the evidence shows the international joint ventures operating in Japan to be less potent rivals than independent companies—domestic or foreign—would be.

These elements make up the structural environment of Japanese industry. Some appear more favorable to competitive markets than their U.S. counterparts (entry barriers, probably product differentiation). Others are surely less favorable (cost fixity, superconcentration). And the levels of seller concentration seem to be on an equal footing.

CHAPTER THREE

Patterns of Competition

THE PRICE charged and the character of the product sold by an industry result from interaction among the competing sellers—that is, their market conduct. When these sellers are few, or when they are numerous but collude
formally, their interaction is sure to differ from the theoretically pure competition. One school of American students of industrial organization tends to
write off the importance of market conduct, holding that its essential features
are determined by the market structure within which the rival firms are embedded. Some dissenters, however, believe that although the essential features of conduct may be determined by structure in the short run, in the long
run they can modify structure and thus assume an independent causal role.
Other dissenters hold that various patterns of conduct can have quite diverse
effects on the performance of the economy, and that it is only because of the
half-heartedness of research efforts that it appears impossible to predict the
consequences of particular kinds of seller conduct.

Consideration of market conduct is a justifiable feature of any study of an
economy outside of Western cultural and legal traditions. Patterns of business
behavior reflect the conventions of social behavior and the constraints and
opportunities created by public policy. A given market structure cannot con-
fidently be expected to cast up the same conduct patterns in Japan as in the
United States. Hence, in this chapter the historical origins and characteristics
of market conduct in Japanese industry are examined in terms of their relation
to Japanese industrial policy. One expects, of course, that collusive practices
will prove more widespread in Japanese than in U.S. industries having comparable market structures, if only because of the more lenient attitude of
Japanese public policy. But how effective are these collusive arrangements
and how much do they displace the economy's performance?

Development of Cartels

Patterns of market conduct are highly diverse, but their significance turns on a single critical question: To what extent do rival sellers recognize their mutual interdependence and aim at maximizing their joint profits? Alternatively, to what extent do they neglect this interdependence, assuming that their own acts will not lead other sellers to adjust their behavior? It is easy to invoke the conformist and group-centered character of Japanese society to support a prediction of easy resort to collusive practices, and fuller adherence to formal and informal collusive agreements once they go into force. Why should the loyalty that Japanese employees give to their business organization not be paralleled by a respect of rival business organizations for their common interest and harmony? But the question of collusive versus independent action is one of how to do best for one's own enterprise, not whether to do so. And loyalty to one team or organization presupposes an obstacle to be conquered, an enemy or outsider to be bettered. Although in this discussion the collusive aspects of market conduct in Japan are stressed, one cannot take for granted that collusion will always find easy agreement, or ready adherence.

The roots of collusive and parallel behavior in Japanese business run back to the pre-Meiji associations, resembling medieval guilds, that anticipated the modern trade association in their arrangements for members' common welfare: quality standards, joint programs for insurance, training facilities, and welfare programs, as well as price-fixing arrangements. These were particularly important in such sectors as textiles, paper, sugar, milling, and coal mining. As industrialization proceeded in the Meiji period, the paper-makers' (1880) and spinners' (1882) associations took on the aspects of modern cartel operations.[1] The large enterprises that spearheaded the development of new industries during the Meiji period initially had few if any domestic rivals, and so the formation of collusive arrangements among them came to be a pressing matter only later. According to Eleanor Hadley's tabulation, only three modern formal cartels antedate 1920. The development of cartels during the 1920s and their rapid spread during the 1930s were probably due to a combination of economic and political events: the price collapse of the early postwar depression, the financial crisis of 1927, and later the Great Depression on the economic side, along with the start of a round of military engagements and preparation for the larger one to come. Legislation in 1925

1. Johannes Hirschmeier and Tsunehiko Yui, *The Development of Japanese Business, 1600–1973* (Harvard University Press, 1975), chaps. 1 and 3.

authorized cartels and provided for compulsory adherence by members, and a 1931 enactment authorized the government to compel membership of all firms in an industry when more than two-thirds requested it. Wartime controls instituted in 1938 dictated compulsory cartels under government supervision, and by the end of the war 1,538 of these "control organizations" were in operation. Although the wartime controls in effect expropriated many smaller enterprises, two decades of a cartelized economy had their effect. As Hadley puts it, "Japan's business leaders had come to like the cartel way of doing business; certainly it was enthusiastically subscribed to by a number of the ministries."[2]

Cartels in Japan have an extremely complex legal history.[3] An Antimonopoly Law modeled on U.S. lines was imposed in 1947, but partially dismantled after the occupation ended. A series of general and special legislative acts followed, timed to periods of excess capacity or rivalry over shares in some market, either creating general escape-hatches for industries wishing to form temporary cartels (for example, to combat depressions, or to rationalize production facilities) or exempting particular industries from the remaining prohibitions of cartels. Over the past decade the legally authorized cartels have numbered about one thousand. Despite their plenitude, the cartel acts far from authorized the cartelization of each and every industry. On the other hand, these acts are not the sole means of coordination among sellers in Japanese industry.

Seller Coordination

Many Japanese industries use the same devices of tacit coordination that are known in the United States. Price leadership by the dominant firm is common in highly concentrated sectors, and has included such products as beer,[4] film, flat glass, aluminum ingot, synthetic fibers, metal cans, newsprint, wire and cable, and many steel products. The leadership patterns have not been consistently stable, and in some industries subject to fast technological change have been particularly weak. Resale price maintenance, now losing its legal status, has served as an important device for blocking the erosion of

2. Eleanor M. Hadley, *Antitrust in Japan* (Princeton University Press, 1970), pp. 357–72 (quotation p. 372).

3. See ibid., chaps. 6 and 9; Kōzō Yamamura, *Economic Policy in Postwar Japan: Growth versus Economic Democracy* (University of California Press, 1967), chaps. 3–5; and Hiroshi Iyori, "Cartel and Concentration Trend in Japan," *Internationales Asienforum*, vol. 4, no. 3 (1973), pp. 416–32. See also chap. 8, below.

4. The price of beer was government controlled until 1964.

price structures from the retail end in goods such as soap and detergents, drugs, cameras, cosmetics, books, and phonograph records. Trade associations provide a device for coordinating sellers in those producer-good industries that are only moderately concentrated and sell homogeneous products —the same ones appearing in the classic U.S. court cases dealing with trade associations. Trade associations are widely prevalent in Japan, with 20,553 registered with the Fair Trade Commission as of March 31, 1974 (18,125 voluntary associations, 2,428 associations based on various kinds of laws). Common practices among them include open-price reporting (especially chemicals and steel), the publication of common price lists, and the maintenance of statistics on inventories and production.[5]

The behavior of industrial prices alone, reflected in parallel announcement of price changes by rival sellers, indicates a great deal of collusive price-fixing in Japanese industry. For instance, when the oil crisis struck Japan in 1973, many Japanese industries announced coordinated increases of the prices of their products on the pretext of sharply rising oil prices.[6]

The significance of collusive arrangements is best seen in fluid situations, where the sellers are responding to some disturbance or breakdown in consensus. For instance, in December 1970 the Ministry of Welfare banned the pharmaceutical manufacturers' long-standing practice of giving away large amounts of free medicines to hospitals and physicians who purchased their products. Evidently, because prices were maintained markedly in excess of marginal costs of production, manufacturers could profitably make large side-payments to purchasers of their goods. The ban prompted fierce price-cutting, and the growth of sales declined significantly in value terms. In order to stabilize the situation the producers resorted to special sorts of price-maintenance contracts with wholesalers, overall rationalization programs, and heavy sales-promotion measures.[7] Thus, price collusion in an incomplete cartel can lead to varied forms of nonprice competition, which might have quite different consequences for the efficient use of resources.

In the early 1960s there was sharp rivalry for markets among firms in the electrical appliance industry. Inventory was forced onto the distributive channels, which prompted price cutting there and pushed the weaker distributors toward bankruptcy. A dominant firm, Matsushita, took the lead in a retrenchment designed both to restrict short-run competition and to tighten the com-

---

5. The data presented in chap. 8, below, on the prevalence of these practices in cases decided by the Fair Trade Commission may or may not indicate their actual prevalence in the economy.

6. *Oriental Economist,* vol. 42 (August 1974), p. 34.

7. Ibid., vol. 41 (August 1973), p. 36.

pany's links with the distributive channels. The company granted exclusive
territories to two hundred of its sales subsidiaries, supporting them with
credit and service organizations. In the process it achieved tight control over
resale prices and the structure of trade discounts. Sony went further, shipping
on consignment in order to maintain absolute control over prices.[8] Aggregated rebate schemes have also been used to control an industry's distributive sector. They provide a strong weapon for the firm with a broad product
line to block its narrow-line competitor's access to distribution channels.[9] In
general, in consumer-goods industries where rivalry is emerging in or shifting
to product competition, firms have moved to consolidate control over their
distribution channels.[10] Thus, under a variety of conditions the interaction of
oligopolists can lead them to choose strategies to manage their distribution
channels and incidentally erect barriers to new competitors.

Other devices in use, although falling short of full cartel arrangements, provide the basis for even more forceful restrictions on competition. One is the
joint selling agency, a variant of which is the joint agency that handles finance
for the Japanese computer manufacturers. This sector, consolidated in 1971
from six firms into three, has been under pressure from the government
to take further parallel action to increase its strength relative to foreign
computer manufacturers.[11] Another device to increase cooperation among
oligopolists is the acquisition by an industry's leading firms of fractional
shareholdings in their competitors. This action could tip the balance when a
firm faces a choice between an action expected to increase joint profits for the
industry and one designed to raise its own net revenues at the expense of its
rivals. The shareholding makes the reward to its stockholders a weighted
average of its own commercial profits and those of its competitors.[12] Reciprocal subcontracting arrangements sometimes form a similar basis for
understanding among competing firms.

A critical question about all collusive devices, formal or informal, is the
degree to which firms adhere to them. The more successful firms are in raising
the profitability of marginal sales, the greater is the private temptation to

8. M. Y. Yoshino, *The Japanese Marketing System: Adaptations and Innovations*
(MIT Press, 1971), pp. 113–17. At pp. 117–19 a contemporary episode in the pharmaceutical industry is discussed.

9. Distribution Economics Institute of Japan, *Outline of Japanese Distribution
Structures* (Tokyo: Distribution Economics Institute of Japan, 1971), pp. 45–47.

10. See ibid., pp. 54 and 59–60, for examples.

11. *Oriental Economist,* vol. 41 (June 1973), pp. 14–17 and 43–44.

12. The case of the Japanese metal can industry is documented in a decision of the
Japan Fair Trade Commission concerning Tōyō Seikan Kaisha, Ltd. (FTCJ decision of
Sept. 18, 1972, 1972[R] no. 11).

cheat and perhaps undermine the agreement. In Japan, members seem to have adhered to the terms of legally sanctioned cartels with moderate regularity, but little is known about clandestine and invisible arrangements. Many collusive arrangements have been shaken or even demolished by large firms unwilling to moderate their market-share goals. Foreign-affiliated firms have proved difficult to integrate into the patterns of parallel action sustained by trade associations, and the associations have objected to acquisitions of Japanese companies by foreign firms and to innovations undertaken by joint ventures.[13] There is a tendency also for the terms of collusive arrangements to expand and grow more complex, as rivalry suppressed in one activity springs up in another. For instance, in the 1950s the fertilizer cartel's terms grew into an elaborate scheme for calculating each member's output and fixing his prices for home and export sales. The iron and steel industry had to make monthly output allotments of each product to each firm and to designate the use of wholesalers who would observe set resale prices. Even so, the nonadherence of small producers caused trouble.[14] One cannot say whether the leakage in these arrangements was greater or less than would have occurred in similar circumstances in the United States.

Do patterns of market conduct support at all the Japanese tendency routinely to term competition "excessive"? Generally, no. But certain forces have promoted active and sustained rivalry among oligopolists in some industries.

First, as our analysis of enterprise organization and goals in chapter 1 suggests, large Japanese companies enjoy some scope to indulge their desire to maximize the size or the growth of the enterprise. This objective certainly supports rivalrous behavior, for competitive strategies can easily involve an expansion of sales at the expense of short-run profits.

Second, the entry of new firms may involve intense oligopolistic rivalry. Professor Miyazaki has argued that rivalry among the large banks to develop parallel and complete families of affiliated industrial firms has led to the compulsive promotion of new entrants by banks building up a set of industrial clients.[15] It is often asserted in Japan that this behavior gives rise to cutthroat competition and the construction of excess capacity in many industries. These relationships, called the "one set" hypothesis, may indeed have explained

13. Dan Fenno Henderson, *Foreign Enterprise in Japan: Laws and Policies* (University of North Carolina Press, 1973), p. 146; also *Oriental Economist,* vol. 41 (August 1973), p. 36, and vol. 41 (June 1973), pp. 14–17.

14. Yamamura, *Economic Policy in Postwar Japan*, pp. 66–67.

15. Yoshikazu Miyazaki, *Sengo Nihon no keizai kikō* [Economic Organization of Postwar Japan] (Tokyo: Shinhyōronsha, 1966).

some behavior during the period of rapid industrial development in the late 1950s, but we believe it could only apply now in new and fast-growing industries.

Third, a fast-growing market may dampen oligopolists' recognition of the short-run effects of their strategies on one another. For differentiated products, a seller's market share today usually affects his share tomorrow, because use of his product today builds habits in ultimate buyers, consolidates distribution channels, and so forth. The more rapidly a market is growing, the greater is the present value of the profit expected from an increment of market share tomorrow, and the greater the short-run sacrifice the firm will make to retain or increase today's market share. This may have helped to weaken interdependence among firms in some differentiated industries during Japan's periods of most rapid growth. It may also explain the alleged strategy of maximizing production and selling the output for whatever it will bring.

Finally, in times when markets are soft and some firms have excess capacity, the high fixity of costs for large enterprises means that a wide gap emerges between price and marginal cost, creating a corresponding temptation to cheat on oligopolistic consensus in order to utilize capacity fully. This force would tend to work in slack times, whereas the effect of the interdependence of demand in different time periods should appear when demand is growing rapidly.

Market conduct in Japan's concentrated industries reflects forces in sharp contrast. On one hand, collusive practices are widely evident, and they have incurred little hostility and gained much support from the government. On the other hand, we have found evidence that collusion is not fully effective and that structural factors discourage Japanese oligopolists from clinging effectively to the goal of maximizing joint industry profits. Such a combination of forces could produce a low level of stability in some industries' patterns of market conduct, with bouts of active rivalry followed by repentance and a return to cooperation. Only the tests of market performance reported in chapters 4 and 5 can show whether conduct has been unruly enough to upset the normal determining force of market structure on performance.

Government Coordination and Guidance

An important if fluid role in coordinating the actions of rival sellers has been played by agencies of the Japanese government, particularly the Ministry of International Trade and Industry. In a number of industries MITI has taken an active hand to promote coordination directly through "administrative guidance." The practice is without explicit statutory authority or legalistic procedure—it would be unthinkable in the United States, and is at least somewhat controversial in Japan's less legalistic political system. It has rested partly on specific enforcement powers held by MITI, first over the allocation of foreign exchange, later over the approval of licenses for imports of technology. But it demands no formal authority and reflects above all a recognized common interest between MITI and the leading firms in certain oligopolistic industries, the latter recognizing that guidance may occasionally impair their profits but in the long run will promote joint net revenues in the industry.[16]

The ministry's guidance is aimed particularly at the construction of new capacity and the entry of new firms into an industry, for MITI is concerned about the creation of efficient-scale plants as well as fearful of excess capacity and ensuing price competition. Rather than working to establish minimum prices, MITI seeks to control investment. When an oligopoly sells in a growing market, the maintenance of an excess of price over long-run marginal cost ultimately turns on the rate at which rival firms allow the industry's capacity to expand and the method by which they dole out the increments of capacity among themselves. The maintenance of prices yielding excess profit is a short-run matter managed in the context of production capacity already determined by these investment decisions. Price collusion that overlooks mutual dependence in expanding capacity can lead to such socially deficient performance as chronic excess capacity, but it is unlikely to generate much monopoly profit. Agreements on capacity may allow each seller occasionally to construct a new plant of efficient scale, but they may as easily lock the rivals into simultaneous, continual investment in inefficiently small units. The Ministry of International Trade and Industry has been concerned both with preventing excess capacity and insuring efficient-scale plants.

Fast-growing producer-good sectors have principally attracted MITI's attention. For example, petrochemical manufacturers, both established firms and newcomers, were quite aggressively rivalrous in their plant and equipment investments in the 1960s. In December 1964 a Petrochemical Coordinating Council was organized with the cooperation of MITI to control the rate of expansion and enlarge the scale of new plants. The resultant tripling in the basic scale of new ethylene plants between 1965 and 1967 was subsequently

16. For general discussions see Yamamura, *Economic Policy in Postwar Japan*, chap. 5; Hadley, *Antitrust in Japan*, pp. 380–86; and Thomas F. M. Adams and Noritake Kobayashi, *The World of Japanese Business* (Tokyo and Palo Alto, Calif.: Kōdansha International, 1969), p. 177.

held to overestimate the attainable economies of scale, but it may have been aimed also at reducing the number of independent production facilities.[17] In the steel industry MITI has actively promoted cartel arrangements to divide new capacity among five leading firms.[18] It has also intervened to stem rivalry over market shares. Sumitomo, seeking to break into the circle of leading steel makers and equipped with a World Bank loan, constructed a large integrated mill in 1959 that greatly increased its capacity. When a 1964 recession led the steel makers to negotiate output quotas among themselves, Sumitomo initially refused to go along with the low quota dealt to it. The company's president was summoned to the ministry, however, and wisdom prevailed.[19]

The ministry has also supported cartel activities in older industries where profits suffer from excess capacity or slow growth. These conditions after the Korean War encouraged the revival of the cartel in cotton spinning. It achieved some success despite easy entry into the industry because MITI allocated foreign exchange for raw-cotton imports only to cooperating firms. Even so, the largest ten firms' share declined from 89 percent in 1950 to 50 percent in 1957 as extra output was attracted by fattened margins. After the import-control curb on uncooperative behavior was lost with the relaxation of exchange control, MITI shifted to using legislation that authorized the moth-balling of facilities deemed surplus by a government-sponsored cartel. Though government agencies may offer guidance or formal support of collusive activities, they are evidently not able to guarantee that the practices will be effective.[20]

Clearly, MITI engages in a bargaining process with large firms while plying its guidance, and the acceptance of restrictions at one time is often premised on favors dispensed at another. Toyō Rayon had in June 1951 taken a great and successful gamble in licensing nylon technology from Du Pont. Its highly profitable domestic monopoly persisted for some time, but eventually the government granted four other producers permission to license nylon technology from other Western firms. Nylon prices then collapsed, and with

17. *Oriental Economist,* vol. 40 (January 1972), pp. 17–23.
18. "Administrative Guidance Questioned," *Oriental Economist,* vol. 42 (September 1974), p. 8.
19. See the case studies in Eugene J. Kaplan, *Japan—The Government-Business Relationship: A Guide for the American Businessman,* U.S. Department of Commerce, Bureau of International Commerce (1972).
20. William W. Lockwood, "Japan's 'New Capitalism,' " in William W. Lockwood, ed., *The State and Economic Enterprise in Japan: Essays in the Political Economy of Growth* (Princeton University Press, 1965), pp. 500–01.

them Toyo's profits. When the firm next applied for permission to license technology for entry into the field of silicones, it received "the fastest approval in post-war history" despite the presence of two other domestic producers.[21]

The ministry has been especially solicitous about curbing the threat of competition from imports or foreign subsidiaries, often working behind the scenes. Foreign companies investing or selling in Japan are expected, as an unwritten rule, to respect traditional Japanese channels of distribution. This raised an issue when the American cosmetics firm, Avon Products, applied for permission to open a sales branch, because of Avon's well-known system of direct distribution. However, Avon could not be refused outright because two Japanese cosmetics firms were already making some use of Avon's methods. Hence a promise was secured from Avon to "proceed slowly, to refrain from disrupting the market or engaging in excessive competition and to abide by other unwritten conditions."[22]

The policies of the Ministry of International Trade and Industry have surely had complex and devious effects. At times they have probably supplied an artificial incentive to enter certain industries. When it seems that MITI will shortly slam the door on further entry, creating bright prospects for future profits in an industry, wise firms are likely to seize the chance to enter while it lasts. Also, MITI's fears about cutthroat competition have been strongly self-validating. The ministry considers allowing a few firms to enter an industry. A large crowd of would-be entrants, anticipating substantial profits if they are chosen, collects at the door. Observing the queue, MITI officials become convinced that, but for their resolute efforts, all the applicants would actually enter and the market would collapse into cutthroat competition.

Effects of Collusive Practices

The extent and character of collusive arrangements employed in an industry can affect its performance in two principal ways. First, they can alter its allocative efficiency by changing the actual level of output relative to the competitive ideal. Second, they can affect technical efficiency, increasing or decreasing the real cost of producing at whatever level of output actually prevails.

Evidence on the influence of collusive arrangements is conjectural. It is never easy to separate their influence from that of the market structure that

21. James C. Abegglen, ed., *Business Strategies for Japan* (Tokyo: Sophia University, 1970), pp. 124–25.
22. Adams and Kobayashi, *The World of Japanese Business*, pp. 178–79.

makes them possible or, alternatively, dooms them to failure. Some data suggest that prices may be higher in the cartelized small-business industries than in other small-business industries. A study of reductions in monthly outputs of industries under official depression cartels shows that some contraction of output did occur, but usually less than the officially designated amount.[23] Beyond that, we can conclude only that illegal cartels are probably somewhat more cohesive (not to mention more prevalent) in Japan than in the United States, and probably more effective in restricting output.

The effects of cartels and other collusive practices on technical efficiency are equally hard to identify, and indeed have almost never been documented in statistical investigations.[24] It does seem clear that in response to efforts to reduce rivalry for market shares, manufacturers have sought control over their distribution channels. As a consequence, resources are diverted to sales promotion; this increased emphasis on differentiation of the product encourages inefficient-scale enterprises in the manufacturing sector in the long run. The abundant evidence in Japan of tacit or formal price collusion and the luxuriant growth of these forms of nonprice competition suggest that these efficiency costs might be significant.

The efforts of MITI to regulate the scales of plants within industries may or may not be helpful. Oligopolistic behavior could induce firms to make additions to their production capacity too often and on too small a scale, but a greater degree of collusion in some cases could lead to a higher level of technical efficiency.[25] In our statistical investigation of the relative productivity performance of matched Japanese and U.S. manufacturing industries in chapter 7, one of the variables tested is the change in the share of Japanese output accounted for by very large plants. If this variable proved significant, it would suggest that plant scale economies had been a significant source of overall gains in technical efficiency. A positive result, however, would not demonstrate that MITI had sought to effect the ideal tradeoff of technical against

23. Eugene Rotwein, "Economic Concentration and Monopoly in Japan," *Journal of Political Economy,* vol. 72 (June 1964), pp. 274–75.

24. See Jack Downie, *The Competitive Process* (London: Duckworth, 1958).

25. The optimal timing of plant construction and the optimal scale of new plants must be determined simultaneously, of course. Imperfect collusion might lead to inefficiently small plant scales if excess capacity that can be used when needed is an important tool for maintaining market share in the long run. Each firm would desire then to keep up its share of installed capacity, and would be able to build at inefficiently small scale with impunity if its rivals were doing the same. Following similar reasoning, Scherer accepts the proposition that in some cases collusion may be a preferable if second-best route toward increasing technical efficiency at some cost in allocative efficiency. See F. M. Scherer and others, *The Economics of Multi-Plant Operation* (Harvard University Press, 1975).

allocative efficiency. And a negative or insignificant relation would suggest
that MITI's policies were definitely of questionable social efficiency.

Conclusions

The very strong role that cartels gained in Japan during the interwar period
has been diluted. Nowadays the conduct of sellers in Japanese industries is
controlled partly by cartels (legal and illegal) and partly through such lesser
devices as price leadership and trade-association reporting practices that are
familiar in the United States. Collusive arrangements appear to be much
more prevalent in Japan than in the United States. However, members' adherence to them is far from perfect, leaving doubts about whether they usually
effect very large restrictions of output. They certainly lead to various forms
of technical inefficiency, including protection of inefficient firms and promotion of nonprice competition. There are structural reasons why Japanese
oligopolists in some industries have tended at times to neglect their mutual
interdependence.

Collusion in many industries is promoted by sponsoring government agencies, especially the Ministry of International Trade and Industry. This ministry has been concerned with promoting orderly arrangements for expanding
capacity, insuring the construction of large-scale plants, and precluding excessive competition and the entry of undesired numbers of new sellers.

CHAPTER FOUR

The Role of Intermarket Groups

DOES A MARKET'S performance depend only on the shares of sales and capacity that rival sellers hold? Or does it matter as well that some of the sellers may be extraordinarily large firms, or that they may face each other as rivals in a number of markets? The competitive significance of a firm's extra-market assets and activities is a controversial question in industrial organization—and nowhere more so than in Japan, where zaibatsu and other affiliations link industrial, commercial, and financial firms in a thick and complex skein of relations matched in no other industrial country.

Japan is a group-oriented society, and its economy exhibits a startling variety of groupings of firms that extend beyond well-defined commodity markets. These groups in turn are cemented by a variety of commercial linkages: between buyer and seller of goods, lender and borrower, shareholder and issuer of equity. They raise many questions about the structure and behavior of the Japanese economy.

What behavioral significance does economic theory ascribe to chains of ownership or influence linking firms that sell in different product markets? Marxists readily accept the proposition that large capitalists devour small ones, and apparently feel no need to explain how this happens via specific market forces. Neoclassicists, on the other hand, have given rather little attention to formulating and testing the mechanisms by which a firm's extra-market assets and affiliations may affect its intramarket behavior, and thus the performance of the markets it occupies. Hence, the questions raised here transcend the puzzles raised by Japan's economic institutions.

The Prewar Zaibatsu

The zaibatsu organizations are collections of manufacturing, trading, and financial corporations, each group generally including oligopolistic firms from a number of industries but few rivals in individual product markets. The present-day groups are much altered from those of the prewar period.[1] At the end of World War II the big four—Mitsui, Mitsubishi, Sumitomo, and Yasuda—controlled about one-quarter of the paid-in capital of incorporated business in Japan. Six other groups possessed similar characteristics but were generally smaller and less complete in their galaxy of financial institutions.

Ultimate control of the zaibatsu firms reposed in wealthy families. Through holding companies and other pyramidal devices, they controlled much larger amounts of corporate assets than even their vast personal wealth allowed. Direction of each zaibatsu centered in a "top holding company" under family control, with that company controlling the principal operating companies of the group, which in turn controlled many others through subsidiaries and fractional shareholdings. The manufacturing firms of the organizations were mostly in the producer-goods sectors, including mining and primary industrial materials. During the 1930s and 1940s they were important suppliers to the Japanese military machine. The organizations included large banks and other financial intermediaries, such as insurance companies. They also included giant general trading firms, that distinctive Japanese commercial institution that deals as buyer and seller with a wide variety of raw materials and semifinished and some finished goods.[2]

Holding-company relationships were only one linkage that knitted the zaibatsu together. Family ownership also reached directly into the operating companies. The banks and financial intermediaries were principal suppliers of capital to the operating companies. The trading companies bought and sold goods for the manufacturing firms, and the manufacturers traded extensively among themselves. Decisionmaking was coordinated not just through the formal equity and financial links of the groups, but also more personally

1. For background see Eleanor M. Hadley, *Antitrust in Japan* (Princeton University Press, 1970), chaps. 1–10; T. A. Bisson, *Zaibatsu Dissolution in Japan* (University of California Press, 1954); and Tsutomu Nakamura, "Business Concentration in Japan," *Academia*, no. 68 (September 1968), pp. 37–82. It is questionable whether the term *zaibatsu* should be applied to the present-day groups; we apply it purely for expository convenience to the three direct successors—Mitsui, Mitsubishi, and Sumitomo.

2. The most important activities of the trading companies today are in international commerce; see Lawrence B. Krause and Sueo Sekiguchi, "Japan and the World Economy," in Hugh Patrick and Henry Rosovsky, eds., *Asia's New Giant: How the Japanese Economy Works* (Brookings Institution, 1976).

through the families' control of key personnel in the operating companies and the absolute loyalty that the operating executives owed to the families.

The members of a given zaibatsu were seldom the individual or joint monopolists of product markets, but rather oligopolists with shares of various markets that might run from modest to dominant. Their relations with one another were generally vertical, but carried on within the complex network of input-output relations typical among major sellers of producer goods. Thus, conglomerate relations and business reciprocity come much closer to describing zaibatsu market linkages than does single-market monopoly. To perceive the formal implications of these business relations, consider a general-equilibrium situation in which n traders barter m commodities among themselves.[3] Markets are not assumed free from monopoly power, and so equilibrium price ratios are in general not equal to marginal opportunity costs of production. Suppose that a subgroup of traders band together to explore the possibility of changing their trading arrangements so as to maximize their joint profits. They can do so by trading among themselves at "competitive" shadow prices computed to align price ratios to the relevant opportunity-cost ratios among members of the group. And they would trade jointly with the outside world at prices that would make profit-maximizing use of their joint monopoly-monopsony power.

Such arrangements would leave several tell-tale marks in the group's commercial relations. First, the prices charged on transactions among members would in general not be the same as those in their transactions with the outside world. Second, the group's transactions with the outside world would have to pass through a single set of hands, if the joint monopoly-monopsony power were efficiently exploited. Third, because the optimal pricing arrangements would tend to lower the commercial profits of some members while raising those of others (and the group as a whole), either profits must be transferred in lump sums among the members or they must flow into a central treasury.

Such forces do seem, from descriptive evidence available, to have been at work within the old zaibatsu. Internal transfer prices among members were not always the same as the prices attached to transactions with outsiders. The general trading companies manipulated transactions with the outside world

---

3. This interpretation is based on a model advanced to explain the nature of profit-maximizing "reciprocity" or trading relations among a subgroup of diversified transactors. The model, which has its roots in the theory of customs unions, is set forth in Richard E. Caves, "The Economics of Reciprocity: Theory and Evidence on Bilateral Trading Arrangements," in Willy Sellekaerts, ed., *International Trade and Finance: Essays in Honour of Jan Tinbergen* (London: Macmillan, 1974), pp. 17–54.

to maximize the monopoly power of the group. And the common ownership links stretching up to the top holding companies meant that shareholders would be indifferent about the distribution of commercial profits among the member companies (although the interests of outside minority shareholders at various stages of the pyramid could have provided some check on the jointly optimal arrangements). Although we have not formally tested this model, we are impressed with the casual evidence that is consistent with it.[4]

Zaibatsu Dissolution and Reassembly

The zaibatsu were a major target of the economic reforms imposed on Japan during the period of occupation. Although the leading zaibatsu were reassembled in the decade after the 1952 peace treaty, both their form and substance were substantially changed.

The occupation, begun with the aim of democratizing the nation's society and economy and removing its war-making potential, later shifted toward the reconstruction of Japan as an economic ally of the United States against the Soviet bloc countries. In the course of this shift, an ambitious program of projected antitrust legislation and deconcentration measures was undermined and then largely dropped. Of the 257 industrial firms and 68 in distribution and the service trades that had been designated for reorganization because they embodied excessive economic power, only 18 were ultimately subject to antitrust action.

The zaibatsu organizations, however, were transformed by the deconcentration measures. Chief among these was dissolution of the top holding companies of the four major and six lesser organizations—along with all other holding companies. The owning families were deprived of their shares in the holding companies and some proportion of their direct equity holdings in the operating companies. Their compensation took the form of fixed-yen securities that were nonnegotiable for ten years and were thus effectively expropriated by the ensuing inflation. In an enormous rearrangement of asset ownership, the families' holdings were dispersed in relatively small personal stockholdings. Cross-ties of ownership were forbidden among the operating companies under a former holding company, although other intercorporate shareholdings were left unaffected. Banks were precluded by the Antimonopoly Law from holding more than 5 (later 10) percent of the stock of

4. It seems consistent with the evidence and interpretations put forth by Hadley, *Antitrust in Japan,* especially chaps. 2, 3, and 8; and Eugene Rotwein, "Economic Concentration and Monopoly in Japan," *Journal of Political Economy,* vol. 72 (June 1964), pp. 262–77.

a given operating company. The two largest general trading companies, Mitsui and Mitsubishi, were dissolved on the theory that they served as linchpins in the discriminatory policies that erected barriers to entry into competition with the zaibatsu operating companies. The banks and financial intermediaries escaped serious restraint, despite the fact that they had clearly discriminated in favor of member firms in extending credit. A purge of top executives from the zaibatsu and other companies removed key officers who were thought to have played a major part in the war effort; they were replaced by subordinates promoted from within the companies. Finally, further use of the old zaibatsu trademarks was forbidden.[5]

After the occupation terminated, three leading zaibatsu—Mitsui, Mitsubishi, and Sumitomo—began to reassemble themselves. Once more they have become a major and conspicuous force in the Japanese economy, though they have not regained the coordinated musculature that the groups displayed in the 1930s and 1940s. The prohibition on the zaibatsu trademarks was quickly rescinded. The two major trading companies were put back together, as were some of the key manufacturing firms that had been dissolved (notably Mitsubishi Heavy Industries). The top holding companies and the controlling family equities were gone forever, and the purged top executives did not return. Nonetheless, loyalties among the group operating firms survived, and coordination mechanisms were restored in the form of "presidents' clubs," which include in Sumitomo's case all eleven of the old first-line companies or their successors and nearly complete rosters (with a few additions and deletions) in the cases of Mitsui and Mitsubishi. The smaller and less complete of the prewar groups did not reappear in their previous form. However, three major groups have emerged centered on giant banks—especially Fuji (successor to the Yasuda zaibatsu), Dai-ichi, and Sanwa.

Changes over a ten-year period in the distribution of assets of the larger corporations, grouped according to their affiliations, are shown in table 4-1. The public sector bulks large in the total because of its predominance in the capital-intensive transportation and public utilities sectors, but its growth is slowing and its share declining. Independent private corporations outside the affiliate system have been expanding most rapidly, although each private-sector group has picked up part of the state enterprises' drop in share.

How extensive are the linkages among today's groups? Do they enjoy the degree of internal coordination that apparently marked the former zaibatsu? Within the Mitsubishi zaibatsu in 1966, 20 percent of the issued equity capital of the median firm was held by other members of the group. The percentage had been over twice as high at the end of World War II. Furthermore,

5. Hadley, *Antitrust in Japan,* especially chaps. 2, 4, 5, 8, and 10.

Table 4-1. *Distribution of Assets of Large Japanese Corporations, by Group Affiliation, 1955, 1962, and 1965*[a]

Affiliate group	Percentage of total assets		
	1955	*1962*	*1965*
Public corporations whose capital is wholly or partly government owned	62.2	50.1	38.3
Affiliates of long-term credit banks whose capital is partly government owned	2.1	3.3	4.3
Affiliates of zaibatsu and large private banks	23.3[b]	28.4[b]	29.2[b]
Mitsui	6.1	3.8[c]	5.0
Mitsubishi	5.0	6.4	7.2
Sumitomo	3.2	5.9	5.4
Fuji Bank (Yasuda)	2.9	3.6	3.8
Dai-ichi Bank	3.1	3.5	3.2
Sanwa Bank	1.4	2.2	2.6
Giant industrial corporations with vertical and conglomerate structures of subsidiaries and affiliates	5.6	9.5[c]	8.8
Foreign-owned enterprises	1.0	1.4	1.4
Companies outside the affiliate system	5.8	7.3	18.0
Total	100.0	100.0	100.0

Sources: Yoshikazu Miyazaki, *Sengo Nihon no keizai kikō* [Economic Organization of Postwar Japan] (Tokyo: Shinhyōronsha, 1966), p. 208, and "Shōwa 40 nendo kigyō shūdan hyō ni tsuite" [On Corporate Group Tabulations in 1965], in Shigeto Tsuru, ed., *Atarashii seiji keizaigaku o motomete* III [For a New Political Economics III] (Tokyo: Keisō Shobō, 1970), p. 381, table 2.
a. The population is corporations with tangible assets of more than ¥5 billion.
b. Total includes smaller bank groups not shown in breakdown.
c. If Tōshiba Electric is transferred, Mitsui's figure increases by 1.6, and giant industrial corporations' figure decreases by 1.6.

group holdings now are split into smaller pieces than before and can repose in as many as forty-eight different companies. Often they are relatively dispersed compared to those of outsiders, who frequently hold large blocks of shares. Because insiders' holdings seldom exceed half the total of the largest ten shareholdings overall, Mitsubishi dominance of the actions of one firm depends on the group members acting in concert. The patterns of shareholding in the Mitsui and Sumitomo organizations suggest even greater dispersion and weakening of insiders' control.[6]

6. These figures are from Hadley's careful survey of intragroup connections in ibid., pp. 213–19. The percentage of equity shares reciprocally owned among members of each leading industrial group has been increasing. For the three zaibatsu organizations and the three leading bank groups, not separately identified, the percentages in 1963 and 1967, respectively, were: 9.85 and 11.75; 14.26 and 16.99; 12.91 and 15.03; 6.96 and 8.96; 10.18 and 12.62; 8.27 and 10.04. Japan, Economic Planning Agency, *Economic Survey of Japan, 1968–1969* (Tokyo: Japan Times, Ltd.), p. 124. Also see "Stockholdings by Corporations," *Oriental Economist*, vol. 41 (May 1973), pp. 18–22.

Another form of linkage among zaibatsu firms lies in loans from group banks. Long-term bank loans to Japanese industrial firms are heavily leveraged on equity, and as either cause or consequence seem to convey more control to the lender than would be expected in most Western industrial countries. Hadley found that bank borrowings by the principal zaibatsu industrial firms were several times as large as the value of their equity: on average 3.09 for Mitsubishi firms, 4.47 for Mitsui, 2.58 for Sumitomo. Thus, it is conceivable that debt as well as equity obligations of the firms could provide the avenues for effective control and integration of the groups. Not nearly all the loans to a group's industrial firms, however, are from member banks—the weighted average is apparently about half for Mitsubishi and Sumitomo firms, less for Mitsui. Companies sampled by Hadley show indebtedness to between five and twenty banks outside the group. She notes that "Japanese analysts characteristically ascribe great significance to the bank from which the largest loan comes." However, there is often not a marked difference between the largest and next largest indebtedness. Conceivably the financial institutions of a given zaibatsu might act in concert so that a borrowing firm's behavior would be governed by the group of banks it was indebted to rather than by individual lenders. However, mutual shareholdings among financial institutions within a group are small, making effective liaison possible but not particularly likely. Hadley also examines share ownership and the assignment of personnel to group nonfinancial companies as possible channels of control. Overall, these rather thin linkages do not suggest to her "in the *usual* situation that banks are the inheritors of the former top-holding company role," although banks may be important as agents and promoters of projects.[7]

Effective coordination might come directly through the presidents' clubs or interlocking directorates. The clubs, however, are informal groups of ostensibly equal individuals, with neither special staff to coordinate their actions nor enforcement mechanisms. They are probably important as channels for collaboration on new ventures and forums for resolving disputes among members, but they do not seem capable of providing the close coordination that was once attained by the top holding companies. Committees of lower-level management exist and may be significant for coordination, but not much is known about them.[8]

Finally, the extent of current transactions among the zaibatsu members may supply some index of their internal coordination. The trading companies provide a possible vehicle (as suggested in the theoretical analysis on page

7. Hadley, *Antitrust in Japan*, pp. 219–46 (quotations pp. 226 and 244).
8. Ibid., pp. 249–54.

Table 4-2. *Affiliations of Principal Trading Partners of Selected Firms in Three Zaibatsu Groups*

Zaibatsu group and type of transaction	Number of principal transaction partners, by affiliation of trading firm[a]			
	Mitsui	Mitsubishi	Sumitomo	None
Mitsui (35 firms)				
Purchases	76	12	16	196
Sales	65	16	16	191
Mitsubishi (31 firms)				
Purchases	18	60	9	149
Sales	9	39	10	145
Sumitomo (25 firms)				
Purchases	25	19	43	130
Sales	16	12	31	138

Source: Eugene Rotwein, "Economic Concentration and Monopoly in Japan," *Journal of Political Economy*, vol. 72 (June 1964), p. 267.

a. Attribution of group membership of trading partners is quite generous. A less liberal attribution would raise the share of outside partners, but would probably not remove the emphasis from transactions within zaibatsu groups.

61, above). They are active in securing economies through joint advertising using group trademarks, and they have close ties with personnel in other member firms of the groups. However, the core manufacturing companies sometimes use the trading companies, but sometimes buy and sell on their own.[9] Direct buyer-seller relations among group firms, necessary for joint maximization of profits, could also indicate the extent of internal coordination. Firms of the three groups whose transactions are summarized in table 4-2 appear to do more business with other members of their own groups than a random distribution of buyers and sellers inside and outside the groups would yield. Since there is no way, however, to control for the distribution of potential suppliers inside and outside the groups, the conclusion is tentative.

This evidence does not suggest the extensive group coordination that has been attributed to the older zaibatsu. The "business reciprocity" revealed by table 4-2 would be rational in the absence of any group coordination whatsoever, as an extension of the theory of bilateral trading arrangements reveals. Suppose that producer goods are generally subject to some monopolization, so that posted prices exceed marginal costs. When firm A chooses between B and C as its supplier, paying the list price for its purchases, it confers a rent on the chosen supplier. If A owns a fractional equity share in B, part of that rent returns to A in incremental dividend payments as "trading stamps" when it buys from B. Hence, given intragroup minority shareholdings, reciprocity

9. Ibid., pp. 247–49.

in current transactions is a rational procedure for group members individually and jointly, and a partial substitute for the predicated price discrimination that would be needed to attain the maximum joint profits for a zaibatsu's members.

Among other conglomerate groupings identified in Japanese industry, those clustering around certain principal banks are most similar to the present-day zaibatsu. Indeed, they are often referred to jointly as keiretsu. The most widely recognized groups are the firms to which three large banks are the principal lenders—Fuji, Dai-ichi Kangyō, and Sanwa. The Fuji group is a literal successor of the Yasuda zaibatsu, and the others contain subgroups of firms that were affiliated in prewar groups. Hadley's study convinces her that the level and stability of ownership and transactions relations within these groups are relatively weak, and their potential significance thus quite modest. "Controls are not sufficient to compel unity of behavior. . . . Corporate decisions may be influenced by member companies, but hardly compelled."[10]

Reports on the present-day activities of the zaibatsu and principal bank groups strongly confirm these interpretations.[11] Although intragroup ties have recently been strengthened by expansion of interlocking directorates and stockholdings, as well as financial links, the only proposals for common action normally considered are those unlikely to raise disputes within the group. One company president declares: "Unlike what was the practice of the prewar Zaibatsu 'main company,' there can be no resolution calling for specific behavior on the part of a member-company."[12] The bank groups show little cohesion except among subgroups of firms, and the cross-ties of ownership are relatively weak. Among the zaibatsu, Mitsui is described as lacking a driving force and strong leadership. Direct competition between members of a zaibatsu, never unknown, keeps breaking out and causing disputes. For instance, Sumitomo Light Metal and Sumitomo Chemical are cited as disagreeing on the unification of all Sumitomo activities in the aluminum industry, and the same group includes not one but two trading firms, Sumitomo Shōji and C. Itoh and Company.

On the other hand, recent reports document the continuing importance of business reciprocity among the group members, lubricated by fractional shareholdings. They also underline the importance of the groups as pools of entrepreneurial talent and capital available to float joint ventures in promis-

10. Ibid., pp. 257–69 (quotation pp. 268–69).
11. See, for example, the *Oriental Economist* series titled "Industrial Groups under Reorganization," August through November 1972.
12. *Oriental Economist*, vol. 40 (November 1972), p. 21.

ing new fields. The trading companies are pivotal for this purpose, but the resources and risk-sharing potential of the groups as a whole are important. Finally, the groups continue to mount rescue operations for members that have fallen into difficulty.[13]

Other Intermarket Groupings

Beyond the zaibatsu successors and principal bank groups, some commentators claim to find a ring of lesser but still significant groupings of nominally independent enterprises. One is the sets of firms for which each of the larger banks (eleven large banks, nine city banks, and two long-term credit banks) is the principal lender. They believe that a firm's borrowings from its principal bank usually represents about 30 percent of its external debt, and that it possesses an unspecified but close and continuing relation to this bank. Hadley's statistical analysis, covering a sample of firms that are dominant in their chief product lines, does not reveal much strength in these relations. Typically they borrow from a number of banks. In 1966, fourteen out of twenty firms borrowed less than 30 percent of their debt from the principal bank. Between 1959 and 1964, five of these twenty changed their principal bank affiliation. Finally, the firms often had borrowings from governmental or foreign financial sources large enough to call into question the primacy of the relation to their principal bank. Ownership ties might further cement these relations, and indeed in eighteen of twenty cases the principal bank (and its affiliates) owned some of the company's stock. The ownership fractions, however, were small. Likewise, in seventeen of twenty cases the company owned a fraction (very small) of the bank; but in all seventeen cases the company also owned shares of at least one other bank. Personnel ties, through transfers from the bank to its customers, are another very weak connection, and the principal bank is only one of several banks typically represented among a firm's directors and officers.[14]

Intercorporate shareholdings within the zaibatsu and bank groups are among the potentially significant intermarket linkages. They are prevalent

13. For instance, when Shōwa Denkō, a chemical company belonging to the Fuji Bank group, ran into difficulty, its unprofitable cement division was taken over by Nihon Cement, and 100 surplus employees were temporarily shifted to Nissan Motor (both Fuji companies). There was talk of lending executives from Fuji Bank or Marubeni Corp., the Fuji general trading company. See *Oriental Economist*, vol. 40 (September 1972), p. 20; and "Sumitomo: How the 'Keiretsu' Pulls Together to Keep Japan Strong," *Business Week*, March 31, 1975, pp. 43–48.

14. Hadley, *Antitrust in Japan*, pp. 269–85.

Table 4-3. *Ownership and Immediate Control of Large Japanese Joint-Stock Corporations, Fiscal 1966*[a]

Status	Number of companies controlled by outside owner, by concentration of shareholding					Number of companies controlled by management	Total number of companies	Percentage of all companies
	Over 90 percent	50–90 percent	30–50 percent	10–30 percent	Under 10 percent			
Outside shareholder control								
Family	1	4	6	18	12	...	41	8.8
Corporate affiliate	0	3	6	22	9	...	40	8.6
Single company	12	15	19	36	24	...	106	22.8
Domestic, nonfinancial	9	13	17	28	4	...	71	15.2
Banking	0	0	0	4	20	...	24	5.2
Insurance	0	0	0	4	0	...	4	0.9
Foreign	3	2	2	0	0	...	7	1.5
Multicompany group	12	26	17	68	31	...	154	33.1
Domestic, nonfinancial	4	12	3	5	1	...	25	5.4
Domestic, including financial	0	7	7	57	29	...	100	21.5
Foreign	0	2	0	0	0	...	2	0.4
Foreign and domestic	8	5	7	6	1	...	27	5.8
Central and local government	1	4	1	2	0	...	8	1.7
Management control	...	...	...	...	...	117	117	25.1
Total	26	52	49	146	76	117	466	100.0
Percentage of all companies	5.6	11.2	10.5	31.3	16.3	25.1	100.0	...

Source: Yoshikazu Miyazaki, *Kasen* [Oligopoly] (Tokyo: Iwanami Shoten, 1972), p. 42.
a. The population is corporations with tangible assets of more than ¥5 billion.

among large Japanese corporations generally, in forms ranging all the way from coherent controlling interests down to small fractional shareholdings scattered among a group of companies. In 1966, as table 4-3 reveals, one-fourth of all companies reported ownership or significant minority participation by single financial or nonfinancial companies, and for one-third, control or minority participation rested in coherent groups of companies (for example, affiliated financial institutions or nonfinancial companies having recognized ties with one another). When intercorporate shareholdings are traced through to the "ultimate" controlling group, 38 percent of the companies as opposed to 25 percent shown in table 4-3 are free of shareholder control because their ultimate control is in firms that are themselves under management control.[15]

Intercorporate shareholding in Japan is significant in several ways. If it were more common among large than among small firms—an issue on which no data appear to exist—the control over corporate assets would be more

15. Yoshikazu Miyazaki, *Kasen* [Oligopoly] (Tokyo: Iwanami Shoten, 1972), p. 42. Miyazaki's conclusions about the extent of management control differ substantially from those of Hirose (see p. 10, above): 25.1 percent versus 53.5 percent of their respective samples of companies. The difference results because Miyazaki counts very small shares of equity as yielding minority control. Hirose's figures hold interest because of their closer comparability to U.S. data. Miyazaki's show the extent of intercorporate shareholding.

concentrated than table 2-1 indicates. Also, some intercorporate shareholdings create links between leading firms that compete with one another in the same product markets, which implies that conventional concentration ratios understate seller concentration. Finally, intercorporate shareholding encourages business reciprocity and gives firms an incentive to buy other than from the cheapest source.

More direct ties of ownership extend to the cluster of subsidiaries that surrounds the typical large nonfinancial corporation. In 1965 the top 100 nonfinancial corporations had 4,270 firms dependent on them—that is, an ownership interest of 30 percent or more in the subsidiary, or 10–30 percent ownership plus other control linkages such as loans or common directors. They had ownership interest of 50 percent or more in 58.8 percent of the dependent firms and of 30 percent or more in 82.4 percent, interlocking officerships in 75 percent, and loans to 36 percent. Subsidiaries in which the top 100 nonfinancial corporations hold an ownership interest of 50 percent or more increased from 1,576 in 1960 to 2,818 in 1970, while those in which they hold 10 percent or more rose from 3,475 to 7,612.[16] The capital investments in related enterprises by the leading firms in five of seven industries reviewed in table 4-4 increased over the period 1962–67. More recent evidence suggests that all forms of intercorporate shareholding have gone on increasing apace: whereas in 1960, 53.2 percent of the shares of companies listed on Japanese stock exchanges were owned by corporations, 62.4 percent were so owned in 1971; the increase was concentrated in monetary institutions and business and industrial firms. The continued concentration of stock in corporate hands is ascribed both to the tightening of relations within trading groups and the cementing of control by firms over their subsidiaries or supplying affiliates.[17]

The product-market relation between parent and subsidiary can be anything—vertical, horizontal, conglomerate—and there is not much aggregate information on the importance of the various types. For many large firms engaged in assembly-type manufacturing operations, subsidiaries function chiefly as suppliers of parts and components. Their separate existence is explained in part by peculiarities of Japan's factor markets. Being much smaller than their parents, the subsidiaries apparently pay wages appropriate to firms

16. Information from a 1965 study by Japan, Fair Trade Commission; summarized in Hadley, *Antitrust in Japan,* pp. 291–92. Also, Fair Trade Commission, *Nihon no kigyō shūchū* [Corporate Merger in Japan] (Tokyo: Ministry of Finance, 1971), p. 43.

17. "Stockholdings by Corporations," *Oriental Economist,* vol. 41 (May 1973), p. 18. Recent increases in the holding of subsidiaries' shares are blamed on the threat of acquisition by foreign corporations under newly liberalized regulations.

Table 4-4. *Investments in and Loans to Related Enterprises by Leading Firms in Selected Japanese Industries, 1962 and 1967*

| Industry[a] and year | Percentage of capital invested in[b] | | | | |
| | Subsidiaries | | | Competing enterprises | Subsidiaries and competing enterprises |
	Stocks	Loans	Total		
Motor vehicle (3 firms)					
1962	4.66	1.97	6.63	2.21	8.84
1967	5.10	3.63	8.73	2.13	10.86
Shipbuilding (4 firms)					
1962	1.12	0.67	1.79	3.15	4.94
1967	1.12	0.81	1.93	3.17	5.10
Heavy electric (3 firms)					
1962	3.04	1.90	4.94	1.97	6.91
1967	4.06	2.13	6.19	3.04	9.23
Electrical appliance (3 firms)					
1962	5.75	1.67	7.42	1.32	8.74
1967	7.11	2.32	9.43	1.82	11.25
Synthetic fiber (3 firms)					
1962	1.85	1.91	3.76	2.75	6.51
1967	3.23	2.54	5.77	5.12	10.89
Cotton spinning (3 firms)					
1962	5.64	3.51	9.15	4.28	13.43
1967	4.36	2.86	7.22	5.18	12.40
Iron and steel (6 firms)					
1962	2.64	1.30	3.94	3.61	7.55
1967	1.79	1.26	3.05	4.14	7.19

Source: Japan, Economic Planning Agency, *Economic Survey of Japan, 1968–1969* (Tokyo: Japan Times, Ltd.), p. 123.

a. Number of leading firms included in the survey is shown in parentheses.

b. Invested capital expressed as a percentage of total liabilities plus net worth.

of their own size rather than that of their parents. They also appear to be less locked into the permanent employment system, and provide inter alia a place to locate the parent's retired but still useful employees. Thus, looked at from the viewpoint of the parent firm, the subsidiary provides both access to lower labor costs and flexibility in dealing with fluctuations in the level of production. The prevalence of subsidiaries is thus related to the general phenomenon of subcontracting (which is discussed in chapter 6, below).

Unlike the bank groupings, and probably unlike the present-day zaibatsu, the networks of subsidiaries do entail important relations of dependence among firms. Whatever the market relation between parent and subsidiary, it is safe to assume that the enterprises are operated for the joint pursuit of profit or other objectives.

Profitability and Efficiency of Group Membership

The zaibatsu and other diversified groupings of firms may have important effects on allocative efficiency and the technical performance of the Japanese economy. Empirical research on these groups, however, seems to have been confined to examining their structural linkages to determine whether they possess the coherence needed for unified action. Their linkages now appear rather weak to bear the load of coordinated decisionmaking required for joint action. But evidence from inspection of their anatomy is hardly sufficient. Group coordination is a matter of degree and ought to be assessed on the basis of ex post results.

Commercial arrangements of the old zaibatsu, according to our model of preferential trading, can yield increased joint profits for a group's members. An appropriate test for present-day groups thus is whether firms counted as group members earn higher profits than independent firms (allowing, of course, for structural differences in their respective markets). This test is carried out using data on a sample of 243 large manufacturing firms, each assigned to the manufacturing industry encompassing its principal activity.[18] All were in operation continuously over the years 1961–70 and could be classified as to affiliation with one of the zaibatsu or bank groups. Data were gathered on a number of variables in order to test hypotheses other than the one immediately at hand.

If group affiliation raises the profits of member firms, our hypothesis holds that they should on the average earn higher profits than independent large companies (after the firms' individual market power and other firm-specific variables determining profit rates are controlled for). We employ two measures of profit:

PE = average annual rate of profit after taxes on owners' equity for the years 1961–70

PA = average annual rate of profit after taxes but before interest on total assets for the years 1961–70.[19]

---

18. The design draws on several statistical studies using U.S. data, especially Marshall Hall and Leonard Weiss, "Firm Size and Profitability," *Review of Economics and Statistics,* vol. 49 (August 1967), pp. 319–31; and Bradley T. Gale, "Market Share and Rate of Return," *Review of Economics and Statistics,* vol. 54 (November 1972), pp. 412–23. Details on the sample and sources of data are presented in the appendix to this volume.

19. The denominator, total assets, undesirably includes current liabilities as well as debt and equity. Current liabilities include trade credit on which interest is not normally paid. Hence a measurement error is involved that we have to assume to be random.

If debt capital were acquired on a perfectly competitive capital market and *PE* served as an accurate measure of the firm's internal rate of return, *PE* would be the theoretically appropriate measure of monopoly profit. Averaging over ten years should reduce the dangers of bias in reported net profit on equity due to the vagaries of depreciation schedules and other accounting practices.[20] Nonetheless, *PA* provides a desirable alternative measure of profits for at least two reasons. Firms' owners may vary in their attitudes toward risk, some preferring high leverage and variance of profits, others safety and lower leverage. If the price of high leverage includes a premium on the market cost of debt capital, the interfirm variance of monopoly rents can be identified more precisely if profits and interest are lumped together. Secondly, the role of banks in the group organizations raises the possibility that interest payments may differ for group firms and comparable unaffiliated firms. The difference could run either direction: banks may discriminate in favor of their affiliates or, as dominant figures in the groups, siphon out some monopoly rents earned by their nonfinancial brethren in the form of inflated interest payments. We therefore include interest payments in the *PA* measure of profitability, and also undertake an independent study of the determinants of firms' average costs of finance:

FI = average annual finance charges paid by the firm divided by total assets minus equity capital averaged over 1961–70.

The independent variables explaining profitability include several elements of market power well established in U.S. industries:

CR = concentration ratio—percentage of shipments accounted for by the four largest firms in the company's principal industry, 1963

AD = average ratio of advertising outlays to total sales by the company, 1961–70

TA = total assets of the firm, average of semiannual end-of-period figures, 1961–70

GR = average rate of growth of sales by the firm, 1961–70, computed as the average of annual percentage growth rates

VS = coefficient of variation of semiannual sales by the firm, 1961–70

20. Japanese accounting practice appears to allow ample room for shifting profits between years, so there is a strong case for averaging over a long period. See T. W. M. Teraoka, "Accounting Practices," in Robert J. Ballon, ed., *Doing Business in Japan* (Tokyo: Sophia University, 1967); Yōtarō Kobayashi, "Human Aspects of Management," in Robert J. Ballon, ed., *Joint Ventures and Japan* (Tokyo: Sophia University, 1967); and Gerhard G. Mueller and Hiroshi Yoshida, *Accounting Practices in Japan* (Graduate School of Business Administration, University of Washington, 1968). Of course, the problem remains that long-period average accounting rates of return can still be biased indicators of economic or discounted-cash-flow rates.

DI = diversification, measured inversely by the primary-product specialization ratio for establishments classified to the firm's principal industry in 1970.

In most studies, concentration has proved to be a significant determinant of profitability, and thus should indicate the market power shared among dominant firms. (It would also be most desirable to include the firm's own share of the market, in the light of Gale's results,[21] but the data are not available.) When concentration fails to prove statistically significant, variables measuring product differentiation and barriers to entry—themselves likely determinants of concentration—are usually included in the study. We include only AD to depict these forces (a more comprehensive measure of sales-promotion outlays than advertising was tried as a numerator for AD; its considerably inferior performance may confirm the significance of nationwide advertising as a barrier to entry). Another dimension of the firm's market power is measured by DI. A diversified firm can threaten to dip into its "deep pocket" to discipline rivals.[22] And it can conceal excess profits from a particular product line in a consolidated income statement. Notice that the variable DI pertains to the firm's base industry, not just to the firm itself. Whether this is desirable or undesirable depends on whether diversification is thought to increase the firm's specific market power, or only to increase the market power of the oligopoly group when carried out by all firms. The latter view is favorable to our measurement which is, in any case, the only one feasible.

Usually GR is included in analyses of this type to capture the windfall component of profit due to sales having expanded faster or slower than the firm's management expected. Its importance for the purpose, however, is proportional to the shortness of the period for which profits are measured. Long-run growth and profitability can be connected via causal hypotheses that predict opposite signs, so GR is likely to pick up too many influences to allow a clear interpretation. If a firm has discovered some innovation or acquired a special rent-yielding asset during or before the 1961–70 period, its sales will grow faster and its profit rate should rise. Therefore GR reflects the effect of endogenous as well as exogenous shifts in the demand facing a firm. It should capture the influence of some unique assets possessed by a firm and thus the variation of profits due to certain rent components—but not rents due to shared monopoly power.

21. Gale, "Market Share and Rate of Return."
22. Stephen A. Rhoades, "The Effect of Diversification on Industry Profit Performance in 241 Manufacturing Industries: 1963," *Review of Economics and Statistics*, vol. 55 (May 1973), pp. 146–55, and "A Further Evaluation of the Effect of Diversification on Industry Profit Performance," ibid., vol. 56 (November 1974), pp. 557–59.

Another variable included to purge profits of a component not due to monopoly rent is VS, the coefficient of variation of sales over time. If suppliers of equity capital are risk-averse, they should demand a higher rate of return from a firm facing more variable market conditions. Gale argued that variations in leverage among firms chosen from different industries would reflect their reactions to the varying market risks they face and thus could be used as a proxy for those risks. But leverage and profit variance are simultaneously determined, and so we prefer a measure of sales variability, which should be largely exogenous.[23]

The assets variable TA can be justified, following Hall and Weiss, as an embodiment of the suggestion that a large firm can do anything that a small firm can, but not vice versa. More plausibly, it can register the ability of large borrowers to command lower interest rates due to lower lender's risk, bargaining power, or simple discrimination against small firms. On the other hand, diseconomies of managing large enterprises could, beyond some point, generate a negative relation between size and profitability. For that reason the term TA^2 is included in some regressions reported below.

After controlling for these forces, a dummy variable signifying membership in a group should capture its residual effect. The dummies for the zaibatsu are $D1$ for Mitsui, $D2$ for Mitsubishi, and $D3$ for Sumitomo; for the Fuji and five other big-city bank groups, DC; for the three zaibatsu groups taken together, DZ; and for the zaibatsu and city bank groups together, DZC. Firms vary in their degrees of adherence to their groups because the links of ownership, indebtedness, and purchase-sale transactions can vary greatly in their strength and regularity. Since this diversity is missed by the dummy variables, we include:

SH = proportion of a firm's equity shares held by its zaibatsu or principal bank group affiliates.

Table 4-5 shows the principal results of regressing PE and PA on these independent variables. To correct for heteroscedasticity, all variables are weighted by the square root of mean annual total assets for each firm.[24] In equation (1), profits on equity are closely related to growth, GR, but to no other continuous variable. This supports the overinclusive role that we sug-

23. Not totally, though, because the choice of market-conduct strategies can influence the intertemporal variability of sales. See R. E. Caves and B. S. Yamey, "Risk and Corporate Rates of Return: Comment," *Quarterly Journal of Economics*, vol. 85 (August 1971), pp. 513–17.

24. The effect of this weighting procedure is as usual to increase the percentage of variance explained—twofold in the case of PA—but not greatly to alter the significance of the independent variables.

Table 4-5. *Regression Analysis of Determinants of Profit Rates and Influence of Group Membership in 243 Large Japanese Manufacturing Companies, 1961–70*[a]

Independent variable	Dependent variable and equation number				
	PE (1)	PA (2)	PA (3)	PA (4)	PA (5)
CR	−0.0048	0.03[b]	0.03[b]	...	−0.0022
	(−0.18)	(3.59)	(3.81)		(−0.11)
AD	0.13	0.56[b]	0.57[b]	...	0.57[b]
	(0.45)	(5.73)	(5.95)		(4.55)
TA	0.0030	0.0059[b]	0.0057[b]	...	0.0083[b]
	(0.51)	(3.02)	(2.95)		(3.30)
TA^2	$-0.27*10^{-8}$	$-0.60*10^{-8}$ [b]	$-0.58*10^{-8}$ [b]	...	$-0.72*10^{-8}$ [b]
	(−0.55)	(−3.63)	(−3.51)		(−3.80)
GR	1.58[b]	0.10[c]	0.11[c]	...	0.10[c]
	(11.35)	(2.31)	(2.37)		(2.16)
VS	0.02	0.06[b]	0.06[b]	...	0.06[b]
	(0.61)	(4.56)	(4.74)		(4.72)
DI	0.02	0.01[c]	0.01[c]	...	−0.01
	(1.34)	(2.49)	(2.28)		(−0.95)
CR*DI	...	...	...	0.0011[b]	0.0006[c]
				(14.26)	(2.02)
TA*AD	...	...	...	$0.74*10^{-5}$ [b]	$0.69*10^{-6}$
				(9.09)	(0.75)
SH	−0.06	−0.03[c]	−0.03[c]	...	...
	(−1.34)	(−2.46)	(−2.14)		
D1	−1.23	−1.25[c]	...	...	−0.34
	(−0.68)	(−2.11)			(−0.69)
D2	0.52	−0.53	...	...	0.19
	(0.28)	(−0.87)			(0.43)
D3	−0.24	−0.48	...	...	0.24
	(−0.12)	(−0.76)			(0.52)
DC	−2.39	−0.98[d]	...	...	...
	(−1.56)	(−1.93)			
DZC	...	...	−0.93[d]	...	−1.09[c]
			(−1.93)		(−2.14)
Constant	−56.53	374.34[b]	368.29[b]	801.32[b]	494.77[b]
	(−0.21)	(4.23)	(4.20)	(10.62)	(4.41)
R^2	0.663[b]	0.822[b]	0.822[b]	0.635[b]	0.820[b]
F	35.11	81.69	107.59	139.17	74.57

Sources: See appendix.
    a. See text for definition of variables. Values of R^2 are corrected for degrees of freedom; t values appear in parentheses.
    b. Significant in a two-tailed test at 0.01.
    c. Significant in a two-tailed test at 0.05.
    d. Significant in a two-tailed test at 0.10.

gested for this variable.[25] In equation (2), gross profits on total assets are related to GR but also significantly to all other explanatory variables, and the proportion of variance explained is notably high. All signs match our theoretical expectations save DI. Contrary to some multivariate studies of U.S. manufacturing industries, concentration and advertising are both highly significant determinants of profits on total assets. Size, TA, influences profits positively but only up to a point, because the sign of TA^2 is negative and its

25. When we replaced GR with the growth of shipments in the firm's principal industry, 1961–70, the significant relation disappeared. We conclude that high values of PE and GR both reflect some valuable asset of the firm not otherwise identified in our analysis. Other coefficients are not substantially affected.

coefficient is significant. The "advantages of scale," according to equation (2), are exhausted once a firm commands assets of ¥491.2 billion, exceeded by only three of the firms in the sample.[26] The dummies for group affiliation show a rather odd pattern: for the individual zaibatsu they are generally insignificant, but for the three banks, *DC,* and the zaibatsu and banks, *DZC,* they are always negative and significant at 0.10 or better for *PA.* And the coefficient of *SH,* representing firms' participation in the groups, is negative and significant. There is thus no evidence that group membership raises a firm's rate of profit.

To determine whether the independent variables might interact in their effects on profitability, two likely interactions are tested in equations (4) and (5). Diversification should favorably affect the profits a firm can earn in a given industry only if concentration is reasonably high, because its effect depends on the prevalence of some concentration in the base industry. Hence the interaction term CR/DI should take a positive coefficient. However, diversification (measured inversely by specialization) appears in equations (2) and (3) to have a significant *negative* influence on profits. Heeding that sign, we entered $CR*DI$ into equations (4) and (5) and obtained significant results (although *CR* and *DI* are no longer significant separately in equation [5]). This result contravenes theoretical expectations. A possible explanation is that specialization is causally related to profitability, with firms confining their growth to their base industries when these remain profitable and diversifying only when they become unprofitable or slow-growing. This causal relation might dominate the results, because the dependent variable measures profits for the dominant and well-established firms in various industries rather than the whole population of firms classified to an industry.[27]

Equations (4) and (5) of table 4-5 also include an interaction between advertising and asset size, $TA*AD.$ High rates of advertising outlay should gen-

26. Similar conclusions are reached by Alex Jacquemin and Wistano Saëz, "Compared Performance of the Largest European and Japanese Industrial Firms," working paper 7414 (Institut des Sciences Économiques, Université Catholique de Louvain, 1974; processed).

27. This ad hoc explanation may be more satisfying for Japan, where many firms have been taxed administratively to seize the growth opportunities open to them, than for the United States. Evidence does show that U.S. firms tend to diversify out of slow-growing oligopolistic industries; see David Gilbert, "Mergers, Diversification and the Theory of the Firm" (doctoral dissertation, Harvard University, 1971), chap. 2. Also see Katsuhiko Ikeda, "Industrial Structure and Firms' Diversification in Japan," *Kwansei Gakuin University Annual Studies,* vol. 22 (1973), pp. 75–87. These considerations may help to explain Rhoades's puzzling conclusion that the profits of large U.S. companies are positively related to diversification among finely defined (4-digit) industries but negatively to various measures of diversification across more broadly defined sectors (Rhoades, "A Further Evaluation").

erate profits that can raise entry barriers more readily when firms are large and the advertising they undertake involves absolutely large outlays. This interaction and $CR*DI$ are the only variables in equation (4), in contrast with equation (5) where they appear with the other variables. They are much less significant in equation (5) than in equation (4), and they throw the signs of other variables into some disarray. Notice that the numerous variables added in equation (5) make a relatively modest contribution to the explained variance of equation (4); the two interaction terms evidently capture—directly or via collinearity—a large proportion of the forces influencing PA.

So far it does not appear that group membership inflates a firm's profits. However, the channels via which rents can be collected and distributed within the groups are complex. The banks, often counted as the organizational nuclei of the present-day groups, hold small amounts of equity in the firms of their groups but lend them large amounts of money. Thus the interest payments passing to the banks may be a conduit for group-derived rents. Before examining that possibility, we need to consider some intervening complexities of corporate finance—the interrelation of risk and leverage. The rate of interest paid on corporate debt is apt to be determined simultaneously with the leverage ratio and the level and variance of the rate of profit on equity, and it seems unsafe to approach one without considering the determinants of the others.[28] We already know that the level of gross profits is systematically related to the variance of sales, so it becomes probable that external risk also affects the firm's financial structure and the mean levels and variances of payments to each class of lenders or investors.

Consider first the ratio of equity to total assets, E/A. It should be positively related to VS, our measure of the market risk facing the firm, and negatively to the growth rate, GR, because of the difficulty that fast-growing firms often face raising equity capital at a rate proportional to their growth. It should be negatively related to the firm's diversification and thus positively related to DI, representing specialization of establishments in its primary industry (and in this case an unhappy proxy for firm-specific data). Diversity of output spreads a firm's risk in ways not completely captured by VS. The relation of leverage to market-power variables is less clear. On the one hand, monopoly power may contribute to the stability of a firm's environment and allow it to choose a lower ratio of equity to assets. On the other hand, the fruits of market power may be enjoyed by management partly in the form of freedom from fixed debt-service obligations (even at the expense of some reduction in the market's valuation of the firm). The former line of reasoning

28. Gloria J. Hurdle, "Leverage, Risk, Market Structure and Profitability," *Review of Economics and Statistics,* vol. 56 (November 1974), pp. 478–85.

predicts a negative relation of CR and AD to E/A, the latter a positive one. Group membership should reduce the risk faced by firms, because affiliates can be called on for rescue operations in adverse times. Thus E/A should be negatively related to group-affiliation dummies. Loans by affiliated banks may also carry some connotation of equity capital, and the more of a firm's borrowing flows from affiliated banks the thinner should be its equity slice. Therefore we include the variable:

BL = long-term loans from the firm's affiliated banks as a percentage of all long-term bank loans, 1970.

The significance of the determinants of E/A depends fairly heavily on the employment of the square root of average total assets as a weight. When this weight is employed,

$$E/A = 559.73^b + 0.13^a\ VS + 0.03^b\ DI + 0.07\ BL + 0.24^c\ GR$$
$$\quad\ (2.46)\quad (3.71)\qquad (2.03)\qquad (1.48)\qquad (1.65)$$

$$+\ 0.17^a\ CR + 1.68^a\ AD - 1.02\ DZC.$$
$$\quad\ (6.61)\qquad (5.45)\qquad (-0.70)$$

$$\bar{R}^2 = 0.771^a;\ F = 98.89.$$

Significance levels (two-tailed test): a = 0.01; b = 0.05; c = 0.10.

The predicted relations to VS and DI are confirmed. GR is significant but perversely signed, casting doubt on any constraint on growth due to profits and retained earnings.[29] CR and AD are both significant and take signs that support the hypothesis that the firm has chosen to enjoy the fruits of its market power partly in lower leverage.[30] Group membership seems generally unrelated to E/A; dummies like DZC are always correctly signed but insignificant, and the variable BL is perversely signed though insignificant.

Now we can turn to the variability of rates of return on equity. The coefficient of variation of profits on equity, VE, should be positively related to

29. Consistent with this result, Mikitani found the proportion of gross investment internally financed to bear a strong inverse relation to the rate of growth of total assets but a weak or nonexistent relation to the rate of profit. See Ryōichi Mikitani, "Corporate Investments and Sources of Funds: Experience of Japanese Large Corporations, 1956–1963," in Jirō Yao, ed., *Monetary Factors in Japanese Economic Growth* (Research Institute for Economics and Business Administration, Kōbe University, 1970), chap. 4.

30. The Mitsubishi Economic Research Institute in a study of 56 large companies found that the mean profit rate on equity increased as financial leverage declined, and the coefficient of variation of profits fell. This is quite consistent with the conjunction of low leverage, low risk, and high profits in firms enjoying monopoly power. See Japan, Economic Planning Agency, *Economic Survey of Japan, 1967–1968* (Tokyo: Japan Times, Ltd.), p. 167.

VS[31] and negatively related to E/A, on the reasoning set forth above. It should be positively related to growth, GR, because rapid growth generally entails greater disturbances and more frequent surprises for the firm. It should be negatively related to diversification (positively to DI, which unfortunately pertains to the industry rather than the firm) because one motive for diversification is to reduce risk. It should be negatively related to total assets, TA, because the larger firm is likely to be more diversified in many senses not captured by DI, for example in geographic scope or width of product line. Finally, the relation to market-power variables CR and AD is unclear for reasons set forth in connection with E/A. Weighting the regression equation that relates VE to these variables worsens the problem of multicollinearity; the equation is unweighted:

$$VE = 561.7^a - 3.32^b\ VS - 7.43^a\ E/A + 2.30\ GR - 0.39\ DI$$
$$(5.25)\ (-1.97)\quad (-3.44)\qquad (0.39)\quad (-0.52)$$

$$- 0.00023\ TA - 1.31\ CR - 2.51\ AD - 0.007\ DI$$
$$(-1.39)\qquad (-1.31)\quad (-0.29)\quad (-1.04)$$

$$- 0.005\ D2 - 0.004\ D3 + 0.002\ DC.$$
$$(-0.66)\quad (-0.55)\qquad (0.33)$$

$$\bar{R}^2 = 0.253^a.$$

Significance levels (two-tailed test): a $= 0.01$; b $= 0.05$; c $= 0.10$.

The results are disappointing. The relation to E/A is correctly signed and significant, but that to VS is significant and perverse for no apparent reason (the zero-order correlation between them is -0.08). The sign of CR suggests that market power assists in stabilizing net earnings, but the relation is insignificant. The sign of TA is as expected, but that coefficient is also insignificant. Group dummies are not significant, always negative in sign for the zaibatsu successors and positive for the less coherent bank groups—a pattern consistent with the differing coordination levels within the two sets.

In considering the determinants of average interest payments on borrowed capital, FI, risk must be allowed for. The asking price for borrowed capital should be higher the thinner is the equity slice—that is, the larger fraction is debt capital of total capital. FI should be positively related to the basic riskiness of the firm's market, VS, negatively to its total size, TA, and to extent

31. We did not explore the determinants of the interfirm variability of sales except for its relation to group membership. Membership should lower variability if group members can cooperate to stabilize the flows of transactions among themselves—a possible benefit from membership. The correlations of VS with the zaibatsu variable DZ and the zaibatsu and banks variable DZC are negative and significant at 10 percent or better.

of its base industry's diversification (positively to *DI*). Risk should also be reduced when a firm's investment in fixed capital is disentangled rapidly—for example, the capital is short-lived. This longevity is reflected in the size of depreciation flows relative to fixed assets, which we approximate by the following variable, which should be negatively related to *FI*:

DP = average annual depreciation expenses as a percentage of total assets, 1961–70.

Finance cost should be increased by a company's choice of high financial leverage, which we measure here as:

DB = debt as a percentage of total assets.

Finance cost should be negatively related to concentration, *CR*, because monopoly profits protect the firm's ability to meet its debt obligations, and negatively to growth, *GR*, because of its promise of higher short- and medium-run profits to cover payment obligations. High *CR* and *GR* should depress lenders' supply prices for funds.

Multicollinearity proves a serious obstacle to testing these hypotheses. Hence we proceed piecemeal, including only subsets of variables in each equation; variables that appear to be significant may owe their success to others included in the overall model but not in the individual equation. Weighting the variables again amplifies the problem of multicollinearity, and so the following equations are unweighted:[32]

(1) $FI = 1.04^a - 0.000001^b \; TA + 0.01^a \; DB + 0.19 \; DZ + 0.24^c \; DC.$
         (2.69)   (−2.44)   (3.77)   (1.42)   (1.82)

$$\bar{R}^2 = 0.073^c; \; F = 4.02.$$

(2) $FI = 2.91^a + 0.15^a \; DP - 0.0028^c \; DI - 0.01^a \; VS$
              (12.1)   (2.78)   (−1.65)   (−4.96)

                $+ 0.31^b \; DZ + 0.36^a \; DC.$
                  (2.37)   (2.80)

$$\bar{R}^2 = 0.134^b; \; F = 6.11.$$

(3) $FI = 2.21^a + 0.0021 \; CR - 0.0007 \; GR + 0.0083^b \; BL$
             (12.1)   (0.84)   (−0.75)   (2.08)

               $+ 0.07 \; DZ + 0.18 \; DC.$
                 (0.47)   (1.26)

$$\bar{R}^2 = 0.024; \; F = 0.96.$$

32. For all equations the significance levels (two-tailed test) are a = 0.01, b = 0.05, and c = 0.10, keyed to the footnote references on the constants and the coefficients.

(4) $FI = 2.34^a + 0.0019\ CR - 0.0089\ GR + 0.0052^c\ SH$
           $\qquad (14.0) \quad\ (0.78) \qquad (-0.94) \qquad\quad (1.64)$

           $\qquad\qquad + 0.12\ DZ + 0.24^c\ DC.$
           $\qquad\qquad\ \ (0.85) \qquad (1.69)$

$$\bar{R}^2 = 0.017;\ F = 0.67.$$

Both TA and DB in equation (1) are correctly signed and significant. In equation (2) FI is inversely related to DI—repeating the pattern observed previously in DI's relation to PA. There is also a perverse and highly signifiicant relation to VS that defies explanation.

The dummies for zaibatsu membership are positive and sometimes significant. Dummies for the individual groups, when entered instead of DZ and DC, are always positive but not significant. The positive influence of group membership is strongly supported by the significant positive relations of FI to BL and SH in equations (3) and (4)—the two variables showing the extent of firms' indebtedness to and ownership by their groups. We conclude that group firms probably make higher average payments for borrowed capital than do independent companies.[33]

An equation similar to equation (1) of table 4-5 implies that group-affiliated companies earn 1.5 percent less net profit on equity after other factors are taken into account (a larger short-fall for bank affiliates, smaller for zaibatsu affiliates) than do independent companies. At the mean ratio of equity to total assets for firms in the sample, this short-fall could result if the group firms earned the same rate of return on total assets as independent firms while transferring rents to their suppliers of debt capital at a rate of 0.5 percent per annum. The equations explaining FI suggest that the rate of diversion is in fact lower—0.2–0.3 percent. The equations for PA in table 4-5 are consistent with this lower rate of profit diversion, because they place the group firms' rate of profit on total capital below that of independent firms, although the short-fall is less than for profit on equity. Though the regression coefficients of these various equations are not completely consistent in magnitude with one another, they lie within one standard deviation of consistent true coefficients.

It is often observed that the zaibatsu are dominated by firms in the more

---

33. Since borrowed capital (the denominator of FI) is not net of compensating balances, the conclusion would be invalid if group firms are allowed by their affiliated banks to maintain smaller compensating balances than are independent customers, offset in part by higher nominal interest rates. Fortunately, the evidence seems to show that banks' retained balances are in fact larger when loans are made to group affiliates, and that the city banks regard the larger balances and smaller net leakage as a major advantage of the system. See Yao, *Monetary Factors in Japanese Economic Growth*, p. 203.

mature sectors of the Japanese economy turning out intermediate and producer goods, whereas many of the fast-growing consumer-good firms born since World War II are independent.[34] Our statistical model (table 4-5) fails fully to capture this difference, leaving an apparent negative residual effect of group membership on gross profits. But a positive effect might appear in a fully specified model. Thus we cannot rule out the possibility that group membership, ceteris paribus, does raise profitability. Nor have we excluded another possibility: that group-derived excess profits are partly consumed in technical inefficiency. Indeed, the analysis in chapter 6 suggests that excess administrative costs in group firms may consume resources that translate into a reduction of 0.3 percent in profits on total assets or about 1 percent on equity. Thus the rents transferred by group firms in the form of excess finance costs may be derived partly from rents to group coordination not identified in our statistical model and need not result exclusively from exploitation of the holders of the firms' equity shares.

Interdependence among Groups

Members of the various zaibatsu face each other as oligopolistic rivals in industry after industry. Does their behavior in one industry affect their relations in others? This issue arose in the United States as the structures of conglomerate firms began to form parallel lines across industrial markets. In Japan it occurs even more naturally: "Historically, what inhibited competition among the 'majors,' " according to Hadley, "was . . . the highly unusual situation of the oligopolists being the same oligopolists in market after market."[35]

What economic reasoning supports this hypothesis? Suppose a Sumitomo firm considers a move that will raise its profits at the expense of its Mitsui rival. Conventional oligopoly theory holds that the Sumitomo firm will take into account all ways that Mitsui might retaliate in the market that they share. But the zaibatsu connections of both firms mean that Mitsui might retaliate in whatever market affords it the greatest net advantage, and that the Sumitomo firm must take this possibility into account. Group connections thus supply each single-industry oligopolist with an enlarged arsenal of defensive weapons, and the deterrents to independent (versus interdependent) conduct

34. In our sample the correlation between *GR* and *DZC* is negative although not significant. The mean growth rate for the independents in 1961–70 was 13.4 percent, for zaibatsu firms 11.5 percent, for large bank firms 7.8 percent (11.4 percent with one deviant group removed), and for firms associated with other metropolitan banks 9.6 percent.

35. Hadley, *Antitrust in Japan*, pp. 18–19. See also, Bisson, *Zaibatsu Dissolution in Japan*, p. 14.

Table 4-6. *Strength of Three Zaibatsu's Affiliates in 64 Major Concentrated Markets, by Share of Market Held, 1955*[a]

	Number of industries in which market share is			
Zaibatsu group	Under 25 percent	25–50 percent	Over 50 percent	Average share of market, percent
Mitsui	11–26	1–12	0–1	12–21
Mitsubishi	20–28	1–3	1	12–13
Sumitomo	11–31	1–4	0–2	12–15
All three	21–25	5–17	2–10	21–34

Source: Rotwein, "Economic Concentration and Monopoly in Japan," p. 270.
a. The lower number in a range of figures takes account of only the core members of each zaibatsu; the higher includes firms with weak and uncertain relations.

are increased. The simplest response to such a situation would be a division of markets among zaibatsu groups, allowing each a sphere of influence which the others would either shun or enter only in a modest way. If such a division were not employed, group affiliation might reduce collusion. Aggressive moves would be taken only where the principal victims were independent firms rather than members of the zaibatsu clans. When rivalry between group firms did break out in some sector, it would transfer itself to other markets.

For this multimarket interdependence to be important, the zaibatsu firms must be joint oligopolists in a significant number of industries. In sixty-four highly concentrated manufacturing industries in 1955, as table 4-6 indicates, the zaibatsu groups dominated only a minority of industries. But they were a substantial presence collectively in a third of the industries. No recent data are available, but the pattern cannot have changed much.

During the 1930s the zaibatsu were said to have divided industrial markets among themselves into spheres of influence. But Professor Miyazaki and others have argued that the principal banks have more recently sought representation of their affiliates in all major industries, implying parallel sets of nonfinancial companies in the various groups and rivalrous or parallel entry into markets. Professor Miyazaki's data on the groups' shares of sixteen major sectors over three decades permit a crude analysis of their behavior. We have converted his estimates of the shares held by Mitsui, Mitsubishi, Sumitomo, and Yasuda (and its successor Fuji) firms in 1937, 1941, 1946, 1955, 1960, and 1966[36] to reflect changes over the five time periods bracketed by these years. To determine whether these groups' actions were rivalrous or collusive, we asked three questions:

1. Did the groups tend to move into or out of industries at the same time—

36. Miyazaki, *Kasen,* pp. 58–59.

suggesting uncoordinated behavior—or did their shares shift in opposite directions—possibly a recognition of agreed spheres of influence? Opposed movements could, of course, reflect attack and withdrawal. Nonetheless, interpreting such moves as collusive has a logic in the limit because the allotment of spheres of monopolistic influence should provide the ultimate form of group coordination. In the five periods the number of instances in which the groups' shares of their markets changed was as follows:

	1937–41	1941–46	1946–55	1955–60	1960–66
Rivalrous changes	42	60	49	54	54
Collusive changes	54	36	47	42	42

There was a clear positive correlation in the movement of the groups' overall shares of industrial capital—mainly down in 1946–55, up in the other four periods. Therefore, an unbiased test for similarity or opposition in the signs of their changes in individual markets cannot rest on absolute changes but rather those that are above or below each group's median change. On a random basis, 48 of the 96 paired changes (that is, 6 pairs of groups in 16 industries) should be like-signed. Except for 1941–46 we cannot reject the hypothesis that share changes were randomly drawn, suggesting no systematic relationships in the groups' rivalry one way or the other. And the 1941–46 period surely reflects wartime government policy and not parallel rivalrous moves by the groups.

2. Did groups tend to avoid moving into industries where other groups held leading shares, or did they tend to move out of such industries? We counted the number of times when group A increased its share in an industry where B's initial share is higher than B's share of overall industrial capital, or A reduced its share in industries where B's initial share is lower than average. These cases would seem potentially inconsistent with collusion and are classed as "rivalrous." The opposite cases count as potentially collusive. This test embodies a bias, when the movements of shares are predominantly in one direction, toward an equal number of "rivalrous" and "collusive" moves.[37] A result other than 50–50 is thus a strong one. The number of changes in each period was as follows:

	1937–41	1941–46	1946–55	1955–60	1960–66
Rivalrous changes	69	79	87	61	62
Collusive changes	74	80	75	87	109

The data suggest a prevalence of collusive behavior after 1955 but not before—contrary to one's expectations from the weakened structural linkages within the groups.

37. Half of B's initial shares are by definition above B's average. If A's changes are either all increases or all decreases, half must count as collusive, half as rivalrous.

3. Did groups avoid inflicting major losses in shares on each other? When *A* scores a large gain in a sector, is it at the expense of group *B*, or is the loss widely spread or concentrated in independent firms? We identified the three sectors in which each group made the largest gain in each period, and the three in which it took the largest loss, and counted the number of "largest loss" changes coinciding with a largest gain for another group. The relevant question is whether the number of coincidences we observe is greater or less than would appear if the changes in shares were drawn randomly. Because the individual zaibatsu shares of the highly aggregated sectors reported by Miyazaki are quite small and their total never more than one-half, we neglect the constraint that the share changes of all market participants must sum to zero. Then on a chance basis the three largest gains of one group would correspond to just under two "largest losses" for the other three groups taken together; aggregated across the four groups, their largest gains would coincide with 7.8 "largest loss" changes if indeed every group always reports share losses in at least three sectors—not always the case. The number of cases in which gains and losses coincided in this fashion was as follows:

	1937–41	*1941–46*	*1946–55*	*1955–60*	*1960–66*
Coinciding gains and losses	2	2	7	3	6.5

The series moves inconsistently, but for three of the five periods suggests fewer coinciding gains and losses than on a chance basis.

Taken together these tests suggest no very strong conclusions, and even if they did, the limitations of the data impose various qualifications. The two tests that suggest a prevalence of collusive behavior in certain periods disagree on the periods. It is conceivable that the groups had ex ante agreements assigning shares in all markets, and that the share changes we observe are nothing but random disturbances intruding because the agreements could not be completely implemented. Thus it seems best to conclude that no systematic relations among the groups have been revealed.

Conclusions

Before their dissolution after World War II the principal zaibatsu groupings, controlling one-quarter of paid-in corporate capital in Japan, consisted of large nonfinancial and financial companies drawn from different industries and linked through holding-company structures, reciprocal shareholding, and lender-borrower and buyer-seller relations. We advance a model to explain how these group relations could generate profits by eliminating price-cost distortions in intragroup transactions and exploiting collective monopoly-monopsony power against outsiders. Casual evidence supports the application of this model to the old zaibatsu. However, a structural analysis of their weakened successors raises doubts that their internal coordinating mechanisms are now as tight as the model would require. The present-day groups do engage in significant business reciprocity and cooperative financing of enterprises in new industries, and occasionally provide help to fellow firms in difficulty.

The Japanese economy contains other important groupings of firms that are not product-market rivals. The families of firms clustered around the principal banks differ only in extent of coordination from the zaibatsu successor groups, and even in the zaibatsu groups banks now appear to play the central coordinating role. The principal-bank groups are linked through intercorporate shareholding as well as stable lender-borrower relations. Intercorporate shareholding is common generally and increasing rapidly in Japan. Shareholding links are found between horizontal competitors and vertically related firms. They encourage business reciprocity and collusive practices. Large nonfinancial corporations are often surrounded by large numbers of affiliated companies tied through ownership interests, interlocking directorates, and stable buyer-seller relations. Many affiliates function as subcontractors to their parents, thereby increasing the parent's production flexibility and reducing its labor costs.

In order to evaluate the significance of zaibatsu and principal-bank group affiliation we studied the determinants of profitability in 243 large companies. After controlling for other determinants of profitability, we found that profits before interest on total assets were if anything negatively related to group affiliation. Pursuing the financial flows of these companies further, we found a weak tendency for group affiliation to reduce the variability of profit and a significant positive relation between group affiliation and the height of interest payments on borrowed capital. We therefore conclude that rents due to group affiliation are captured by the banks, the central organs of the present-day groups. We are not certain whether this is simply income diverted from other recipients (equity shareholders) or whether the real productivity of group affiliation went undetected in our analysis of profit rates. It remains distinctly possible that rents yielded by group affiliation are consumed in technical inefficiency.

Using the overly aggregated data that are available on groups' shares in individual markets, we tried to discover whether the groups' actions in the various product markets in which they faced one another were consistently coordinated. We found no evidence of such behavior.

CHAPTER FIVE

Allocative Efficiency

SELLER CONCENTRATION in individual industries appears to be no higher on average in Japan than in the United States, but collusive arrangements are more prevalent and tolerated. Has the Japanese economy's structure allowed colluding sellers to distort the allocation of resources among sectors?

Determinants of Efficiency

Statistical research on this question has been concentrated on explaining the variation among industries in profit rates, the usual test for misallocation. The pioneer study in this field, relating average rates of return on equity during 1956–60 to concentration ratios for the largest five firms in 1958 for forty-six manufacturing, mining, and service industries, developed no significant result whatsoever.[1] A replication of that study excluding industries for which problems of classification existed or profit calculations could not be properly made also failed to produce any significant results.[2]

The pattern changed, however, when investigations were focused on the 1961–65 period. Concentration ratios for 1963, whether based on the largest one, two, or three firms, were found to be significantly related to profits for that period at the 1 percent level of confidence.[3] Results were again insignificant, however, when profits were measured for the whole period 1956–66

1. Ryūtarō Komiya, "Nihon ni okeru dokusen to kigyō rijun" [Monopoly and Corporate Profits in Japan], in Tsunejirō Nakamura and others, eds., *Kigyō keizai bunseki* [Economic Analysis of Enterprises] (Tokyo: Iwanami Shoten, 1962).
2. Takehiko Musashi, "Sangyō kan rijunritsu kakusa" [Industrial Differences in Profit Rates], *Kōsei torihiki*, December 1970.
3. Kazuo Matsushiro, "Wagakuni no sangyō shūchūdo to rijunritsu" [Industrial Concentration Ratios and Rates of Profit in Japan], *Sanken ronshū*, March 1970.

and related to concentration ratios for 1964.[4] The profits-concentration relation remained significant for the 1966–70 period (using 1968 concentration data) and for the whole period 1961–70.[5] Obviously, different forces were at work at the various time periods.

One factor differentiating these five-year periods is the real rate of growth. The period 1956–60 was one of significantly faster growth and higher profits than 1961–65, and 1966–70 was one of somewhat better performance for the economy. Musashi first showed that differences in the growth rate of output significantly affected the rate of profit. Regressing profits on both concentration and the rate of growth of output, he found the growth variable positively related to profits and significant for both 1956–60 and 1961–65, but more so for the earlier period (1 percent versus 10 percent confidence, and a larger coefficient). Concentration remained insignificant in the earlier period, significant in the later one. Uekusa added other structural variables to a regression equation explaining profits for the 1961–65 period: a measure of minimum efficient plant scale relative to the size of the market, one of capital-cost barriers to entry, and advertising as a percentage of sales to detect the influence of product differentiation—all defined approximately as in the pioneering study by Comanor and Wilson.[6] In sharp contrast to the American study none of these three additional variables proved significant, and the growth rate became insignificant when they were included. Concentration, however, remained serenely significant through these changes in the other variables.

Differences in Performance

How can these Japanese results be explained and reconciled with the ones reported for other countries? First, apparently, we must distinguish between periods when Japanese industrial growth has been "explosive" and when it has merely been rapid. In chapter 2 we suggested reasons why periods of

4. Hiroshi Niida, "Shūchūdo no henka to rijunritsu" [Changes in Concentration Ratios and Rates of Profit], in Hiroshi Niida and Akira Ono, eds., *Nihon no sangyō soshiki* [Industrial Organization in Japan] (Tokyo: Iwanami Shoten, 1969).

5. Masu Uekusa, "Rijunritsu to shijō kōzō shoyōin—Nihon to Amerika" [Rates of Profit and Market Structure Elements in the United States and Japan], *Mita gakkai zashi*, July 1970; Masu Uekusa and others, *Kasen sangyō niokeru shijō seika no keiryō bunseki* [Quantitative Analysis of Market Performance in the Oligopolistic Industries in Japan], report prepared for Fair Trade Commission of Japan (1973).

6. William S. Comanor and Thomas A. Wilson, "Advertising Market Structure and Performance," *Review of Economics and Statistics,* vol. 49 (November 1967), pp. 423–40.

very fast macroeconomic growth should translate themselves into micro-economic imbalances. When it appears profitable at the margin to expand production in practically every industry, an industry's profit rate may depend primarily on how fast it can enlarge its capacity. In industries that face long planning and construction delays in expanding capacity, substantial short-run windfalls may accrue even if the industry is potentially competitive enough that they will be eliminated in the long run. Industries adjusting more quickly will reap smaller windfalls, even if concentration is high enough to keep prof-its above the competitive norm in the long run. Thus concentration may fail to register a significant influence on profits in periods of explosive growth, un-less we take account of differences in short-run constraints on the expansion of industries' outputs. And interindustry differences in growth should be a more potent determinant of profit rates in periods when growth is on average very rapid than when it is normal, because windfalls then bulk larger in the interindustry variance of profits.[7]

The other major problem of interpretation is posed by the strong perfor-mance of concentration as a determinant of profits (except when growth is explosive), along with the relatively weak performance of statistical variables that serve as proxies for the barriers to the entry of new firms. Studies done in the United States have, generally speaking, shown just the opposite result: entry-barrier variables have proved significant, concentration irregularly so; thus it has been rationalized that entry barriers in the long run determine con-centration; when industries are observed in or near long-run equilibrium, con-centration will be determined by and hence collinear with the entry-barrier variables. How, then, do we explain the reversed results for Japan? Two sets of forces may be at work.

First, entry to Japanese industries is clearly impeded by forces omitted from the standard treatment of the theory of entry barriers[8] and thus from the

7. This hypothesis about the influence of growth on profits predicts a positive effect via the windfall component of reported accounting profits. An alternative hypothesis (explained in chapter 2) suggests that, when intertemporal dependences affect the de-mand for a firm's product, an *expected* rapid rate of growth will encourage entry and the expansion of output in the short run and thus tend to drive profits down; it thus predicts an inverse relation between growth and the "normal" or nonwindfall component of prof-its. The two mechanisms are not inconsistent with one another (or with still other rela-tions one can devise) and could be operating at the same time. They differ in their im-plied time horizons and thus in the appropriate empirical specification in a regression analysis—the one calling for a short-term deviation of actual from expected (or recent past) growth, the other for a longer-run measurement. This distinction in their specifica-tion is never made, and consequently the statistical behavior of the growth variable probably depends on which mechanism is predominant in the period of time under study.

8. Joe S. Bain, *Barriers to New Competition: Their Character and Consequences in Manufacturing Industries* (Harvard University Press, 1956).

statistical tests of that theory. The most obvious of these is government intervention to deter or (occasionally) promote entry. The Ministry of International Trade and Industry has used a variety of formal and informal powers not only to regulate competition within industries but also to control the flow of new entrants. The most important legal basis has been the Foreign Investment Law, designed to regulate imports of foreign technology and control payments made abroad for it. In industries such as petroleum and petrochemicals where new firms required foreign technology, MITI could impede entry. The synthetic fiber industry provides several examples. After Du Pont's patent on nylon expired in 1960, four new companies prepared to enter the market controlled by two incumbent producers; it took MITI more than a year to sanction the four firms' licensing agreements with foreign companies under the Foreign Investment Law. With public authority standing at the gate, a would-be entrant's ability to clamber over the economic barriers is no longer sufficient to assure his entry. The statistical performance of the entry-barrier variables should become less significant. By the same token, with entry impeded by MITI as well as natural forces, actual concentration should become more important in determining the ability of going firms to capture monopoly rents within an industry.

The second set of forces intertwines with the rates of growth. Cross-industry statistical investigations in industrial organization generally assume that industries are observed in long-run equilibrium, or at least in an equilibrium disturbed only by separable fluctuations in the growth rate and profit windfalls. We have argued that these windfalls could obscure the influence of seller concentration; they could even more readily obscure the influence of the condition of entry. A new firm's entry into an industry is surely subject to a longer lag of perception, planning, and execution than is the decision of a going firm to change its level of output or capacity. Hence, whatever the tendency of fast growth to obscure the influence of concentration, it would obscure even more the influence of the long-run structural barriers to entry. If going firms take account of the entry lag in their planning, concentration could in fact be elevated in its significance, because firms in highly concentrated industries are in a position to seize short-run windfalls knowing that entry in any case is apt to occur in the future.[9] Hence, this line of reasoning is consistent with the good performance of the concentration variable in all but periods of explosive growth, as well as with the poor performance of variables for the structural barriers to entry.

9. For evidence of the effect of growth on entry rates, see Dale Orr, "The Determinants of Entry: A Study of the Canadian Manufacturing Industries," *Review of Economics and Statistics,* vol. 56 (February 1974), pp. 58–66.

Statistical Analysis of Performance

We pursued an analysis of the determinants of industry profits based in part on data used to analyze enterprise profits in chapter 4. Industry-level profit figures—the dependent variable in the analysis—were constructed by classifying firms contained in the chapter 4 sample to 35 industries, and for each industry taking a weighted average of the profit figures of all firms classified to that industry (no official figures exist for profits by industry in Japan). Two measures of profit are used once again: average profit after taxes on owners' equity, PE, and profit plus interest on total assets, PA, both for the years 1961–70. Independent variables for concentration, CR, and advertising outlays as a percentage of sales, AD, are defined as in chapter 4. Our measure of market growth, GD, now is the average of annual percentage changes in industry shipments over 1961–70—not the average growth rates in sales for the firms in question.

One reason for including the growth variable in the analysis is to remove from the variance of profits any windfalls due to demand growth that is not as fast or slow as entrepreneurs anticipated when they planned their additions to capacity. We wondered if industries' participation in export markets during the 1960s might also have been an indicator of such windfalls. Undervaluation of the yen evidently made many lines of export sales quite profitable and supported their rapid growth. However, it also appears that some Japanese industries were systematically selling abroad at prices lower than in the domestic market and in general facing greater effective competition abroad than at home. Hence a positive sign is likely but not assured for the variable:

XR = industry exports as a percentage of shipments, 1970.

An a priori case can also be made for including a variable to represent the competition of imports with domestic shipments. A simple measure of imports' share of the domestic market has proved significant as a determinant of the market power of domestic sellers in the United States and United Kingdom, although not Canada.[10] But in Japan, tariffs and exchange control have been used actively to shield many manufacturing industries from import

10. Louis Esposito and Frances F. Esposito, "Foreign Competition and Domestic Industry Profitability," *Review of Economics and Statistics,* vol. 53 (November 1971), pp. 343–53; Javad Khalilzadeh-Shirazi, "Market Structure and Price-Cost Margins in United Kingdom Manufacturing Industries," *Review of Economics and Statistics,* vol. 56 (February 1974), pp. 67–76; J. C. H. Jones, L. Laudadio, and M. Percy, "Market Structure and Profitability in Canadian Manufacturing Industry: Some Cross-Section Results," *Canadian Journal of Economics,* vol. 6 (August 1973), pp. 356–68.

rivalry. For that reason and because reconciling the statistical classification of imports with that of domestic output is quite difficult, we did not attempt to measure the influence of import competition in Japan.

We suggested in chapter 2 that the costs of primary inputs to Japanese manufacturers are fixed to a much greater degree than in Western industrial countries. The practice of permanent employment and the prevalence of high debt-equity ratios contribute to fixed costs and thereby increase the risk to which large enterprises are exposed. They should raise reported profits because they increase the risk exposure of equity capital and thus presumably raise the risk premium demanded by those who supply it. They may also strengthen firms' preferences for collusive and parallel conduct and thus dampen the tendency of rivalrous behavior to undermine monopoly rents in moderately to highly concentrated industries. Neither component of fixed cost is easily subject to a measurement that is both simple and accurate. The proportions of permanent employees vary from company to company, and the wages paid to permanent employees are presumably viewed as a more rigid obligation than their large semiannual bonuses. Likewise, we found in chapter 4 that companies' relations to their banks make debt-service costs a less rigid claim on cash flows than they would be in a Western country. Nonetheless, we made a crude attempt to measure the variations in these fixed charges from industry to industry using the following variables:

WR = wage and salary payments as a percentage of total costs, average of 1963 and 1968 figures for the companies classified to each industry

FC = fixed costs (depreciation, finance costs, lease costs, maintenance) as a percentage of total costs, average of 1963 and 1968 figures for the companies classified to each industry.

Because these two components should be nearly proportional in their effect on business behavior, we generally used their sum as an independent variable.

The statistical results of relating profit rates to the foregoing variables are reported in table 5-1. All signs are correctly positive, and the variables for concentration, CR, advertising, AD, and growth, GD, are always significant determinants of PA and sometimes of PE. The export-share and fixed-cost variables are not significant.[11] The results parallel the analysis of companies' profits in chapter 4 in that PA can be explained better than PE, but the difference is reduced, and the growth variable no longer dominates the equations

11. Equally insignificant was another variable constructed to measure the weight of fixed costs: regular employees in an industry as a percentage of total persons engaged, averaged for 1963 and 1968.

Table 5-1. *Regression Analysis of Determinants of Average Profit Rates, 35 Manufacturing Industries, 1961–70*[a]

Dependent variable	Independent variable					Constant	$\bar{R}^2$
	CR	AD	GD	XR	FC + WR		
PE[b]	0.102[c]	0.698	0.349	0.083	0.110	−4.836	0.580
	(2.40)	(1.57)	(1.64)	(1.20)	(0.84)		
PA[b]	0.054[d]	0.287[e]	0.133[e]	0.002	0.056	2.369	0.636
	(3.54)	(1.80)	(1.74)	(0.06)	(1.21)		
PE	0.119[c]	0.550	0.448[c]	...	...	−3.584	0.562
	(2.92)	(1.29)	(2.18)				
PA	0.059[c]	0.259[e]	0.148[e]	...	...	3.046	0.647
	(4.02)	(1.69)	(1.99)				
PE	0.112[c]	0.913[c]	...	...	...	2.955	0.485
	(2.61)	(2.21)					
PA	0.057[d]	0.378[c]	...	...	...	5.209	0.604
	(3.70)	(2.57)					

a. See text for definition of variables. Values of $\bar{R}^2$ are corrected for degrees of freedom; *t* values appear in parentheses.
b. One industry has been excluded.
c. Significant in a two-tailed test at 0.05.
d. Significant in a two-tailed test at 0.01.
e. Significant in a two-tailed test at 0.10.

for *PE*. Apparently, classifying competing firms to their industries and averaging their profit rates eliminates some noise due to firm-specific factors and thus exposes the influence of concentration and (to a lesser degree) advertising outlays.

We experimented unsuccessfully with other variables. In his study on profit rates for the 1961–65 period, Uekusa detected no influence of two possible entry barriers—minimum efficient plant scale as a percentage of the market, and the absolute capital costs (tangible assets) of the average-size plant in the industry.[12] When values of this variable, constructed for 1963 and 1968 and averaged, were added to the equations reported in table 5-1, the resulting series proved quite insignificant. Economies of scale that persist until the plant or firm occupies a significant share of the market can constitute an entry barrier and source of excess profit, but only to the extent that the costs of inefficiently small units are indeed strongly inflated. Recent studies using U.K. and U.S. data have shown the merits of bundling together these two dimensions of scale-economy barriers into a single measure.[13] A

12. Uekusa, "Rijunritsu to shijō kōzō shoyōin."
13. R. E. Caves, J. Khalilzadeh-Shirazi, and M. E. Porter, "Scale Economies in Statistical Analyses of Market Power," *Review of Economics and Statistics,* vol. 57 (May 1975), pp. 133–40.

similar measure in our analysis failed to detect any influence of scale-economy entry barriers.

This conspicuous failure of capital requirements and scale economics to influence profits accords with our impression of the institutions at work. Rapid growth makes interindustry profit differences depend more on lags and expectations and denies us the possibility of observing industries in equilibrium with respect to entry. Large financial institutions and the collaborative financing of entry by groups of firms defuse the exclusionary power of absolute-capital-cost barriers to entry. And the government has surely obscured the influence of scale-economy barriers through its policies toward entry into certain industries: its rationing of entrants through its control over technology licenses, imported inputs, and favored access to borrowed funds; and its active encouragement of large plants in certain export-oriented industries.[14]

Our study finds an influence of seller concentration on profits that is stronger than that usually reported in multivariate analyses of Western manufacturing industries. This result has two implications. First, although Japan's cultural patterns certainly make interfirm relationships different from those elsewhere, they do not impair the tendency of enlarged numbers to erode sellers' ability to exploit shared market power. Nor is government-sponsored support of collusive action (discussed in chapters 3 and 8) strong enough to void the effect of concentration on profitability. The influence of advertising rates on entry barriers and thus on profitability is weakly significant and somewhat less potent than in Western economies. The public and private institutions that overturn the other entry barriers do not greatly affect the role of advertising (MITI's interest in most consumer-good industries seems relatively limited). Furthermore, our use of profit rates measured over a period as long as ten years reduces the danger that the advertising-profit relation could be due to accounting peculiarities.

It has unfortunately not been possible to undertake a parallel study of allocative efficiency in Japan and the United States. Parallel investigation of the United Kingdom and United States has shown that the same mechanism appears to determine profit rates in both economies.[15] That conclusion prob-

14. The dependent variable in our analysis represents not the profits of all firms in an industry but only selected large firms. Research in progress by Michael E. Porter shows that the structural determinants of profitability differ greatly between the large and medium—"leader" and "follower"—firms in U.S. industries. He finds that capital-cost barriers affect only the medium-size firms, advertising primarily the leaders.

15. J. Khalilzadeh-Shirazi, "Market Structure and Allocative Efficiency: A Comparative Analysis of U.K. and U.S. Manufacturing," *Economic Inquiry* (forthcoming); also

ably would not hold for Japan. Yet a broad similarity of structural forces is apparent despite the imprint of Japan's particular economic structure.

The profit levels reported by about a thousand large manufacturing companies in Japan have been compared with a similar sample in the United States. Because average levels of seller concentration appear to differ little in the two countries, any difference in mean profit levels might be taken to reveal other economy-wide structural differences. The data suggest that mean profit rates for the period 1967–71 were essentially identical for the two countries, with the distributions also very similar except that the United States shows a slightly greater variance.[16] However, accounting rates of return, even averaged over five years, are only rough approximations to economic (or discounted-cash-flow) rates of return. If two firms report equal rates of accounting profit, the one with the faster (steady-state) growth rate will tend to be earning the higher economic rate of return. Because the growth of Japan and her large companies was markedly faster than the growth of the American economy, we cannot rule out the possibility that economic rates of return have been higher in Japan.

Market Structure and Wage-Price Movements

Positions of market power can produce short-run distortions in price movements in addition to long-run distortions in the allocation of resources. The distorting potential of market power received close attention in the United States during the past several decades in discussions over "administered prices" and "price rigidity" in oligopolistic markets. Despite Japan's long-sustained success with wholesale price stability, there have been suggestions that market power was influencing the movement of the price level there.

Let us consider two logically defensible hypotheses. First, prices (and wages) in concentrated industries can be less sensitive to shifts in excess demand than those in more atomistic industries. Oligopolistic prices are apt to exceed marginal costs to a degree comfortable to the sellers, and to be maintained at that level through tacit or clandestine arrangements that are somewhat inflexible. The adjustment of list prices threatens dispute and misunder-

William James Adams, "Corporate Power and Profitability in the North Atlantic Community" (doctoral dissertation, Harvard University, 1973).

16. Industrial Bank of Japan, "Differences in Accounting Practices and Returns on Investment between the United States and Japan, 1000 Industrial Companies, 1967–1971" (paper presented at Sixth Professional Committee Meeting, Japan-California Association, Kanawa, Jan. 26, 1973).

standing. Hence changes come only when price is far enough out of alignment to win the necessary consensus on a change. Second, price-level disturbances can emanate from concentrated sectors even in the absence of any macroeconomic disturbance. Suppose that an oligopoly's price exceeds marginal cost but falls short of maximizing joint profits. An increase in seller concentration, or merely some shift in behavior patterns among the market rivals, can prompt a price escalation. An atomistic industry cannot generate such disturbances unless its market structure shifts into the oligopolistic camp.

The flexibility of wholesale prices has become an issue in Japan because of evidence that the proportion of products showing price declines dropped steadily from the 1957–58 recession through 1961–62, 1963–65, and 1969–71. Kobayashi has shown that the average rate of price decline has been greater the less is seller concentration—at least for industries near the upper and lower limits of seller concentration. He compared measures of the variability of prices to measures of the year-to-year variability of seller concentration, finding a close positive relation between the instability of concentration (whatever its level) and the flexibility of prices.[17] Shinjo has demonstrated that seller concentration's positive influence on annual price increases, particularly evident in periods of recession, becomes apparent only after changes in unit costs and inventories are controlled.[18] A study by the Fair Trade Commission of Japan found the frequency of monthly price changes to be somewhat less in monopoly market structures than in oligopoly, and much greater in competitive industries than in oligopolies. Similar conclusions were drawn when the amplitudes of monthly price changes were related to market structures.[19]

Movements of wage rates have also been examined, in relation to size of firm—a variable that usually shows a high correlation with the firm's market share. The sensitivity of wages to excess demand in the labor market diminishes as size of firm increases, while their sensitivity to the firm's profit rate increases with size.[20]

Other studies have inquired whether the level of seller concentration in-

17. Yoshihiro Kobayashi, "Market Structure and Inflexibility of Wholesale Price" (Hokkaido University, 1974; processed).

18. Kōji Shinjō, "Business Pricing Policies and Inflation: The Japanese Case" (Kōbe University, 1975; processed). Compare Yōichi Shinkai, "Business Pricing Policies in Japanese Manufacturing Industry," *Journal of Industrial Economics*, vol. 22 (June 1974), pp. 255–64.

19. Japan, Fair Trade Commission, *Kanri kakaku* [Administered Prices] (1970), p. 320. This study also reports a relation between changes in ten-firm concentration ratios and average price indexes for 44 industries (p. 322).

20. Japan, Economic Planning Agency, *Economic Survey of Japan, 1970–1971* (Tokyo: Japan Times, Ltd.), pp. 106–07.

fluences longer-run inflation in industries' prices. The Economic Planning Agency noted that the movement of sectoral wholesale prices has the predicted positive relation to the change in concentration (over a five-year period) when products are grouped according to the initial level of concentration.[21] It is highly desirable, however, to control for such factors as the growth of output, change in materials costs, change in labor cost, and change in labor productivity. Studies of the U.S. economy including such factors show that concentration was associated with price increases in the 1950s, but that the relation disappeared later or even reversed during periods of rapid recovery from a slump.[22] Statistical studies of Japan also find a link between market power and inflation during prosperous periods variable at best. Nishikawa reports for 1960–70 a significant negative relation of concentration to industries' price changes.[23] Kobayashi found no significant relation during the 1965–69 boom,[24] and his analysis of other periods ascribed a regularly significant influence only to changes in raw-materials prices. He finds a cross-industry relation between changes in prices and changes in the volume of output that is often negative and significant. This result implies that industry price movements have been dominated by supply shifts, with industries that experienced large gains in productivity able both to increase their rate of output growth and lower their relative prices. For macroeconomic price movements as well as for real-income gains, interindustry differences in productivity growth thus appear very important. We consider them in chapters 6 and 7.

An aspect of macroeconomic performance closely allied to wage-price stability is the stability of capital formation. Concentrated industries might invest at an uneven pace over time because oligopolistic rivalry entails close imitation of each other's actions, or because the same scale economies that cause concentration also force a lumpy course of investment in efficient-size additions to capacity. Iwasaki found a strong positive relation between the instability of investment over 1961–70 and seller concentration in Japanese manufacturing industries, after controlling for the significant influence of the instability of demand and the size of the market (as well as other factors that

21. Ibid., pp. 97–99.
22. See James A. Dalton, "Administered Inflation and Business Pricing: Another Look," *Review of Economics and Statistics*, vol. 55 (November 1973), pp. 516–19, and papers cited by Dalton.
23. Shunsaku Nishikawa, "Kanri kaku *inflation* to kasen" [Administered Price Inflation and Oligopoly], *Contemporary Economics*, Summer 1973.
24. Yoshihiro Kobayashi, "The Determination of Wholesale Price in Japanese Economy," *Hokudai Economic Papers*, vol. 3 (1972–73), pp. 77–91.

proved insignificant). At very high levels concentration ceases to inflate the instability of investment, probably because near-monopolists and tight-knit oligopolists do not imitate each other's increases in capacity.[25]

Conclusions

The allocative efficiency of Japanese industry can be investigated by statistical analysis of the influences on industry profit rates. Previous studies of Japanese manufacturing industries have found seller concentration to increase profits significantly, although not during periods of explosive growth. Our analysis of the profits earned by large firms classified to thirty-five industries finds that concentration, the growth of industry shipments, and advertising outlays as a percentage of sales all wield positive influences on profits. Measures of barriers to entry other than advertising are not significant, confirming our view that entry barriers have been a less important influence in Japan than in the United States: the Japanese economy is well equipped for entry by established firms into industries that would otherwise be protected; rapid growth tends to mute the influence of entry barriers because of the lag with which entrants respond to profit signals; and entry into some industries has been closely regulated by public policy. We found no influence on profits of the levels of industries' fixed costs or of their access to export opportunities.

These statistical results at the industry level can be supplemented from our analysis of the determinants of large firms' profits from chapter 4. Concentration in the firm's principal industry strongly influences its profits on total assets, as do its advertising outlays and rate of growth. After these and other variables are controlled, the large firm's profit rate increases with its size, although only up to a point (a quadratic term has a negative sign). We are not sure whether this represents an influence of capital-cost barriers to entry, the treatment of large enterprise by public policy, or some other set of forces. We did discover that much of the variability of profits can be explained by two simple hypotheses about interacting structural determinants: the highest profits emerge when sellers are both concentrated and specialized; and the highest profits emerge when sellers are both large and spend heavily on advertising. The latter hypothesis deals with the construction of entry bar-

25. Akira Iwasaki, "Market Structure and Stability of Investment in Japanese Manufacturing Industries" (Kōnan University, 1975; processed). Compare Frederic M. Scherer, "Market Structure and the Stability of Investment," *American Economic Review*, vol. 59 (May 1969, *Papers and Proceedings, 1968*), pp. 72–79.

riers, the former with the behavioral determinants of effective collusion. This analysis also provided some indication that firms with market power (high concentration, high advertising) take part of their profit in a quiet life with low leverage and (less certainly) a low variance of profit.

Fears have been expressed in Japan that the selling prices of concentrated industries are inflexible or tend to rise in the presence of excess capacity. There is some evidence of growing downward inflexibility of concentrated industries' prices during recessions, despite high fixed costs that should expand the temptation for Japanese oligopolists to cut prices. Wage rates also seem relatively insensitive to excess demand in concentrated industries. But there is little evidence that concentrated industries have served as independent sources of inflationary disturbances. Thus concentration seems mainly to have decreased the downward flexibility of prices in Japan.

CHAPTER SIX

Technical Efficiency

THE POTENTIAL social gains from improvements in allocative efficiency are widely thought to be small relative to those attainable by improvements in technical efficiency—that is, by lowering the costs of the bundle of resources required to produce a given bill of output. But technical efficiency is elusive because firms may use more resources than are necessary or the wrong bundle of resources (at going factor prices), or produce at scales that do not minimize long-run average costs. These defects are difficult to analyze because there are no satisfying explanations of why technical inefficiency should persist, and because there are few data available from which to determine who is or is not technically efficient.

The most tractable aspect of technical inefficiency for research is inefficiently small scales of operation in the plant or enterprise. That coincides nicely with the Japanese preoccupation with the "small and medium enterprise problem."[1] Thus we examine here small business and efficiency in the manufacturing and distribution sectors, and briefly consider some other aspects of technical efficiency.

Small Enterprise in Manufacturing

A formidable amount of research has been done on small business in Japan. Much of it, however, deals with such issues as the stage of capitalism that the sector has achieved and the degree of its adherence to preindustrial

1. Following Japanese practice, our discussion switches freely between talking about small plants and small firms. The problems they create could be quite different (for example, if large enterprises maintain some of the inefficiently small plants), but the difficulty does not seem great in practice.

technology.[2] Our concern is with small enterprise as a market phenomenon: its relation to conditions in factor and product markets, and the extent to which it presents a problem of poor market performance.

It is widely believed that a uniquely great number of small enterprises is found in the Japanese economy. The same phenomenon appears in other late-industrializing or partially industrialized countries. For instance, International Labour Organisation figures show that the ratio of proprietors plus family workers to total employees (which should be a good measure of the prevalence of small business) tends to fall regularly and sharply as economic development proceeds. In the 1960s it was over 30 percent in Greece, Thailand, and Turkey, 21.6 percent in Japan, less than 10 percent in the United States, the United Kingdom, and Sweden.[3] The proportion of manufacturing establishments with less than a hundred employees shows a similar systematic pattern: it is 27 percent in the United States, only 20.3 percent in the United Kingdom, and 52.8 percent in Japan; but it is also high in small industrial countries—53.2 percent in Norway, 47.2 percent in Denmark.[4]

We sought to explore these relations by means of a cross-country regression analysis. The exercise is necessarily crude, for the data must be taken from national censuses and surveys that vary in accuracy as well as in their definitions and categorizations. Moreover, economic and social theory provides only the roughest guidance to the proper independent variables and forms of the relations. We chose a sample of thirty-four countries in varying stages of economic development, the primary criterion for selection being general comparability in the treatment of proprietors and family workers (especially in agriculture) in the population census.[5] Japan ranks fourteenth among these in gross domestic product per capita (1969). Two dependent variables were constructed:

$Y1$ = employers and own-account workers as a percentage of the labor force

$Y2$ = employers, own-account workers, and family workers as a percentage of the labor force.

2. For a lucid survey see Miyohei Shinohara, "A Survey of the Japanese Literature on Small Industry," in Bert F. Hoselitz, ed., *The Role of Small Industry in the Process of Economic Growth* (Humanities Press, 1968), pp. 1–113.

3. Quoted in Miyohei Shinohara, *Structural Changes in Japan's Economic Development,* Institute of Economic Research, Hitotsubashi University, Economic Research Series, no. 11 (Tokyo: Kinokuniya Bookstore, 1970), p. 305. Also see Seymour Broadbridge, *Industrial Dualism in Japan: A Problem of Economic Growth and Structural Change* (Aldine, 1966), pp. 5–7.

4. Shinohara, *Structural Changes,* p. 306.

5. Detailed information on the data sources and construction of the variables appears in the appendix to this volume.

Family workers are included in $Y2$ to reflect the extent to which the activities of household and enterprise are intertwined, since such enterprises are perhaps less subject to rational calculation than those managed at arm's length. But the usefulness of family workers depends greatly on the activity they are engaged in (compare the farmer to the physician), and hence their number should vary with the mixture of economic activities undertaken in the national economy. And the measurement of family workers in population censuses is surely quite inaccurate.

The first independent variable that we include is:

income = gross domestic product per capita, 1969, expressed in U.S. dollars at the going exchange rate.

The general hypothesis is that the proportional role of small-enterprise and household production declines as a country's level of development rises, and GDP per capita seems as good a measure as any of the real volume of economic activity per person. This inverse relation may not be linear. The shake-out of inefficient family enterprises may be completed at a stage in development already reached by some countries. Indeed, we could imagine a positive relation prevailing over a group of high-income countries, with the richer among them distinguished by a greater density of entrepreneurial talent and hence a larger population of enterprises. To detect this effect we include the squared value of GDP per capita in some regressions.

We also wish to control for variations in the overall size of the national economy. Because the productivity of the national factor endowment is already measured in the *income* variable, economic size should be measured by input rather than output:

size = total economically active population, census year between 1960 and 1970.

This variable is included because considerable evidence suggests a positive correlation between the size of the national market and the size of the enterprise or establishment in the manufacturing, financial, and utility sectors of the economy. If larger enterprises populate larger countries, the proportion of the labor force who are entrepreneurs should decline as the size of the labor force increases. This effect, like that of *income,* may well be nonlinear. We included the square of *size* in some regression equations, expecting a positive sign that would indicate a weakening of the underlying inverse relation as national economies get larger and larger.

The shake-out of a nation's small enterprises leads to the transfer of some factors of production to more productive uses. Japan's case suggests that this transfer can be a lagging feature of economic development, with factors grad-

Table 6-1. Regression Analysis of Determinants of Proportion of Employers and Own-Account Workers in the National Labor Force, 34 Countries, Late 1960s[a]

Equation number	Dependent variable	Independent variable						Regression statistic	
		Income	Income²	Size	Size²	Growth	Farms	$\bar{R}^2$	Japan's deviation
(1)	Log Y1	-0.0666[b] (-4.18)	0.0009[c] (2.19)	-0.0017 (-0.44)	...	0.0139 (0.66)	...	0.71	0.26
(2)	Log Y2	-0.0543[b] (-3.30)	0.0006 (1.49)	-0.0422 (-0.54)	...	0.0558[c] (2.55)	...	0.74	0.31
(3)	Log Y2	-0.0366[b] (-6.45)	...	-0.0261[c] (-2.33)	0.0005[c] (2.48)	0.0592[b] (2.90)	...	0.78	-0.49
(4)	Log Y2	-0.0232[b] (-3.19)	...	-0.0004 (-0.11)	...	0.0494[d] (1.99)	0.0168[d] (1.88)	0.76	0.18

a. See text for definition of variables. Values of $\bar{R}^2$ are corrected for degrees of freedom; t values appear in parentheses.
b. Significant in a two-tailed test at 0.01.
c. Significant in a two-tailed test at 0.05.
d. Significant in a two-tailed test at 0.10.

ually being pulled from the small-enterprise sector as exogenous changes raise their potential productivity in the large-enterprise or modern sector. Consider a group of countries having the same income per capita in a given year. If this shake-out were a lagging feature of the development process for each of them, and growth had proceeded at varying rates, there would be a positive relation between their historical growth rates and the proportional size of their (remaining) small-enterprise populations. Hence we include:

growth = growth rate per annum of general industrial production, 1953–
  70 (or shorter period included within those years).

We expect but are not completely confident about a positive sign, because the elimination of inefficient small enterprises could be a cause rather than an effect of economic development. It thus depends on the development process that has apparently operated in Japan being characteristic of most countries in our sample.

Finally, dependent variables Y1 and Y2 should depend on the mixture of economic activity undertaken in a country. We know that the sizes of enterprises and establishments vary greatly from sector to sector of the economy, probably in a similar fashion from country to country. That similarity would be expected if the size variation largely reflects technical economies of scale in production. Suppose that a country's consumers spend relatively large fractions of their incomes on goods or services that small enterprises can produce efficiently, or that the nation enjoys a comparative advantage in exporting such goods or services. Its values of Y1 and Y2 would therefore be elevated. To control for the most obvious differences in national patterns of economic activity,[6] we include:

farms = percentage of gross domestic product originating in agriculture,
  hunting, fishing, and forestry, 1969.

Though a measure based on the proportion of the labor force in agriculture would probably be more useful than one based on the proportion of output originating there, structural variations in national censuses and labor-force surveys make the labor-force measure less reliable.

The regression equations reported in table 6-1 test indirectly our hypotheses about the large small-enterprise population in Japan. The residuals of each equation also allow us to determine whether the observed dependent

6. Ideally, the dependent variable would be a weighted average of the proportions of employers and own-account workers of the total economically active population attached to each sector of the economy, with a common set of weights used for all countries. Most countries probably do not collect enough census and employment data to compute this index.

variable for Japan in fact indicates a small-enterprise population larger than we would expect given its economic structure. Therefore Japan's deviation in table 6-1 is the difference between the actual and estimated value of the dependent variable for Japan expressed in units of each equation's standard error of estimate. The uncertainty about functional forms that led us to test squared values of some independent variables prompted us to fit the dependent variables $Y1$ and $Y2$ in logarithms as well as in natural units. The semilogarithmic equations reported in table 6-1 generally yielded somewhat higher significance levels of independent variables.

In the table all signs conform to our expectations; most variables are statistically significant, and a large proportion of the variance is explained. The influences of *income* and its squared value are quite robust. Equations (1) and (2) suggest that the negative relation between the dependent variables and GDP per capita flattens out on the average when countries reach the per-capita income levels of Canada and Sweden. The influence of increasing size eventually diminishes also, flattening out for countries whose labor forces reach (approximately) the size of the United Kingdom's or West Germany's. But *size* is not significant in all specifications, especially when the equations are estimated using natural units of the dependent variables. The variable *farms* in equation (4) is weakly significant; it is collinear with *income*[7] and becomes highly significant if *income* is omitted. Evidently both variables serve as reasonably good proxies for the nation's level of economic development. It makes no systematic difference for the significance of the independent variables whether the dependent variable excludes family workers, $Y1$, or includes them, $Y2$. The absolute values of the regression coefficients are generally a little larger when the dependent variable is $Y1$, consistent with our view that the measurement of family workers is subject to copious errors.

Finally, Japan's deviation from each regression plane, expressed as a fraction of the equation's standard error of estimate, is positive in three of the four equations but quite small. If the equations are fitted using natural units of the dependent variables, Japan's residuals are almost always negative and somewhat larger. We therefore agree with Shinohara, Broadbridge, and other observers of the Japanese economy who argue that the small-enterprise population does not represent a unique feature calling for special explanation.

Nevertheless, small enterprises are one of the important structural features of Japan's economic system. Some small manufacturing activities are carried on part time by family workers whose primary occupations—often agriculture—are seasonal. Their persistence reflects the underutilization of labor

---

7. Zero-order correlations are: *income* and *farms*, −0.68; *income*^{2} and *farms*, −0.54; *size* and *income*^{2}, 0.29; *size* and *growth*, 0.19.

in the primary activity, and is a direct manifestation of Japan's "dual economy." Other small manufacturers are essentially the direct descendants of the traditional handicraft industries that existed in the Meiji period. Yet their technology may have changed greatly in the interim. One survey of 95 small-business industries found that 81 of them had existed in the Meiji period, 58 of them (72 percent) as predominantly handicraft industries; as of 1958–59, however, only 16 percent were still classed as handicraft.[8] Another survivor, from pre-Meiji Japan, is small manufacturing done on the putting-out system, with wholesalers or assemblers supplying working capital and distribution services. These are the descendants of relatively large merchant organizations with an abundance of capital. Finally, a large proportion of small manufacturers function as subcontractors of larger (often very large) manufacturing firms. Many subcontractors are wholly dependent on a single buyer and may well have been set up in business by him, but nonexclusive relations are increasingly common.

One feature of small enterprise that bears heavily on its efficiency is the quality of its entrepreneurial talent. If it is family-run, its accounts may be entangled with those of the family and its operation tied in to the family's pursuit of noneconomic objectives. A 1958–59 survey of small enterprises found that relatives of the owners accounted for 43 percent of managerial personnel, promoted employees for 27 percent, and outsiders for 23 percent (with 6 percent of unknown origin). As evidence of increasing professionalism, it observed that over time the number of relatives and descendants of founders was declining and the number of engineers increasing.[9] Nonetheless, the high percentage of family executives continues to be a source of concern.

The imperfections of the factor market are the most important reason for concern about the Japanese small-business sector. Small enterprises pay at least 50 percent more for borrowed funds than do medium-size businesses (see table 2-8 above). Furthermore, there is ample evidence that the small-business sector is cyclically sensitive, the first to feel any squeeze in supplies of funds. This discrimination in the capital market is not easy to explain. There was a rich institutional development of small-scale money-lenders, merchant banks, and mutual loan associations in the first half of the Meiji period. Although the smaller financial institutions have undergone squeezes, as from 1919 to 1932 when the total number of banks declined greatly, there seems now to be a wide array of lenders by size, function, and locality, excepting only merchant capital for the putting-out system, which is in an accelerated decline. True, large and small businesses draw their funds from different

8. Shinohara, "Survey," pp. 58–61.
9. Summarized in ibid., pp. 63–64.

financial institutions: large corporations borrow 43 percent of their funds from city banks, 13 percent from local banks, and 11 percent from long-term credit banks; medium and small enterprises take only 19 percent from city banks, 22 percent from local banks, 20 percent from credit-association banks, and 17 percent from mutual loan and savings banks.[10] But this functional specialization is hardly sinister in itself, and leaves open the question of why arbitrage has not tended to reduce (if not eliminate) the large interest differential. Why in particular have the large banks not grown more active in direct or indirect lending to smaller enterprises?[11] The market power and abundant tangible property of the large industrial borrower entail a potentially lower level of risk, of course, but it is hard to write off a 50-percent differential as a risk premium.[12] Loans to small business are well collateralized by land, and rates of loss to lenders appear very low. It also seems unlikely that transactions costs could explain this differential. In the United States, where interest differentials between large and small business borrowers are much smaller than in Japan, the differences appear to be due mostly to transactions costs.[13]

Discrimination in the labor market of course runs the other way—in favor of small enterprises. The rapid absorption of surplus labor from Japanese agriculture has led to much concern about how quickly the disequilibrium of the "dual economy" will vanish, and how painful the squeeze on the small-business sector will be. Wages for young workers with middle-school or less education are now about the same in small and large establishments, although the seniority gradient remains much steeper in the larger establishments, and hence their average labor costs remain higher. The same general pattern holds for women (but with flatter seniority gradients) and for office workers (steeper seniority gradients). But less than a fifth of the average wage differential between establishments with more than 1,000 employees and those with

10. Data from Bank of Japan for 1969, assembled by Hiroshi Kawaguchi, " 'Over-loan' and the Investment Behavior of Firms," *Developing Economies,* vol. 8 (December 1970), pp. 395–96.

11. It is charged that smaller enterprises do much more business with the large banks as depositors than as borrowers. See Minor Industry Problem Inquiry Committee, *Minor Industries and Workers in Tokyo,* TMG Municipal Library, no. 8 (Tokyo Municipal Government, 1972), p. 99.

12. Shinohara, "Survey," pp. 51–57; Taikichi Itoh, *Structural Analysis of the Problem of Medium and Small Enterprises in Contemporary Japan,* Management and Labor Studies, English Series, no. 21 (Institute of Management and Labor Studies, Keio University, 1972), pp. 16–17.

13. Albert M. Levenson, "Interest Rate and Cost Differentials in Bank Lending to Small and Large Business," *Review of Economics and Statistics,* vol. 44 (May 1962), pp. 190–97. Also see Stephen H. Archer and LeRoy G. Faerber, "Firm Size and the Cost of Externally Secured Equity Capital," *Journal of Finance,* vol. 21 (March 1966), pp. 69–83.

10–99 in 1959 could be explained by such factors as age (as a proxy for experience), sex, and education.[14] If the differential in wage costs between large and small establishments adjusted for the quality of labor disappears faster than the capital-cost discrimination against small enterprises, market pressures will be artificially loaded against the small firms.

How has the small-enterprise sector fared in the face of these pressures? If the elimination of wage differentials is the dominant force influencing costs for different groups of firms, those initially paying high wages ought to be able to hold their share of the labor force at less than the average cost in increased wages. In an analysis of census data, the rate of change in wages between 1955 and 1967 was found to be negatively related to the rate of change in shares of the labor force held by Japanese manufacturing establishments grouped by size.[15] This finding confirms the dominant role of the elimination of labor-market distortions.

In a related test on Japan's two-digit manufacturing industries we used census data for 1951, 1960, and 1970 to compute the average wage for establishments employing from 10 to 99 regular workers and for those employing 100 or more. Wages in the small plants were expressed as percentages of wages in the large plants. We also calculated the share of the labor force in each industry held by the small plants. If there is a disequilibrium between the large- and small-industry sectors, changes in relative wages should be negatively correlated with changes in labor-force shares across these industries. We found no significant correlations for either 1951–60 or 1960–70. We did notice, however, that relatively low wages at the start of each period seemed to help small establishments to hold their share of the industry's work force (presumably giving them room to absorb wage increases). When we divided the industries into those above and below the median ratio of small- to large-establishment wages, the small establishments that fell below the median in 1951 managed on average to raise their share of the industry's labor

14. Ron W. Napier, "The Labor Market and Structural Change in Postwar Japanese Development" (senior honors thesis, Harvard College, 1972), chap. 2.

15. Napier analyzed rates of changes in wages and labor-force shares for the ten size-classes of establishments within each of the twenty two-digit industries in Japan's census of manufactures in 1955–63 and 1963–67; he found a significant negative relation between the two growth rates across these groupings. Ibid., p. 53. Without this force operating, one would expect a positive correlation: wages would rise more in sectors where demand conditions induce firms to bid for increased shares of the labor force. The squeeze is also evident in data on profits or margins in small enterprise; see Japan, Economic Planning Agency, *Economic Survey of Japan, 1967–1968* (Tokyo: Japan Times, Ltd.), table 69, p. 119. Some studies have found small-enterprise profits to exceed those of large, but they are evidently based on samples biased toward profitable companies; see Shinohara, "Survey," pp. 48–51.

force by 0.7 percent over 1951–60. The small establishments that initially paid above-median relative wages suffered a decline of 3.6 percent in their employment share. The same differential appeared in the averages for the 1960–70 decade but was much reduced; the corresponding figures are −4.3 percent and −4.9 percent.

These calculations and Napier's findings suggest that small-large differentials not only have existed throughout Japanese manufacturing, but have varied from industry to industry. Thus the elimination of these differentials goes along with the elimination of interindustry imbalances. We calculated the following measures of dispersion of the large-small differentials among two-digit industries in each of three years:

	1951	1961	1970
Standard deviation	14.4	12.8	8.7
Coefficient of variation	0.21	0.18	0.11

As they show, the proportional variation among industries has been cut in half over two decades.

The questions about distortions in the factor market go beyond how large they are and how quickly they are being eliminated. At least as important for economic performance is the question of how effectively small establishments are adapting to these shifts in cost conditions. Rising labor costs should induce both an increase in investment, to substitute capital for labor, and an effort to reduce "outright" inefficiency or stave off disaster through gains in "X-efficiency." Levels and movements in labor productivity reflect both of these adjustments. The data on productivity differentials certainly suggest that a problem remains for small Japanese establishments. The ratio of value added per worker in the largest Japanese manufacturing establishments (a thousand or more workers) to that for all manufacturing establishments was 1.71 in 1967. In the United States the corresponding figure was 1.16. This productivity differential reflects some combination of lower efficiency and lower capital-intensity in small establishments. What has happened to it over the postwar period? Between 1955 and 1963 the productivity gap fell from 1.80 to 1.69, but then it widened slightly to 1.71 in 1967. Small establishments were increasing their capital per worker in 1963–67 faster than the large ones (reliable data are not available for earlier years). But the productivity gap has not been greatly reduced, and of course the relative growth of the smaller establishments has been retarded.[16] We conclude that small establishments, especially in the 1960s, were not able to raise productivity enough

16. These data from census sources are analyzed by Napier, "The Labor Market and Structural Change," chaps. 1 and 3.

to prevent a sharp decline in their share of economic activity. Efficient allocation of resources in manufacturing appears to call for a continued consolidation.

The relation among the technical efficiency of small establishments, their capital intensity, and the investment necessary to eliminate any small-scale efficiencies is complex. Only explicit information on production functions would tell us how much of small plants' inferior productivity might be explained by low capital intensity. If distortions in Japan's factor markets were eliminated, small plants would raise their capital per worker, and large plants tend to reduce theirs. It is highly doubtful, though, that this reallocation would eliminate the difference between the capital intensity of large and small establishments. The tendency for capital-intensity to increase with size appears in many countries, in both aggregate data and those pertaining to well-defined industries. Therefore any shake-out of Japan's small establishments will be constrained by the country's rate of capital formation, because a significant amount of extra capital would be needed to reemploy their noncapital factors of production in larger establishments.[17]

If Japan's small manufacturers are to be squeezed by a reduction in factor-price distortions, in which industries will the pinch be greatest? Average ratios of capital to labor are significantly less sensitive to rising relative wages in some industries than in others. For instance, a study of Japanese and Korean industries shows a clear division between the assembly industries (including textiles as well as metal products, machinery, and so forth) and the process industries (foodstuffs as well as pulp and paper, chemicals, and so on). The former group's capital-labor ratio is distinctly less sensitive to changes in factor prices.[18] Consider the effects of removing from all industries a distortion that has confronted a subgroup of manufacturers—the small establishments—with a lower ratio of wages to capital cost than the rest. The more the distortion had caused them to substitute labor for capital, the more will its removal leave them stranded with average unit costs higher than those of firms using "efficient" combinations of inputs. Hence we expect Japan's slow departure from the status of a dual economy to force less retrenchment of small plants in the assembly industries and others with limited possibilities for substituting capital for labor. These are the kinds of industries that the Small and Medium Enterprise Agency includes in its list of sectors where

17. Napier (ibid., p. 7) points out that if all of Japan's 1967 capital stock in manufacturing had been concentrated in plants employing 1,000 or more, it would have supported employment of only 5.37 million, rather than the actual 10.55 million, given the capital-labor ratios prevailing in those plants.

18. *Economic Survey of Japan, 1967–1968*, pp. 91–92. Also see Shinohara, "Survey," p. 45.

Table 6-2. *Utilization of Subcontractors in Japanese Manufacturing Industries, by Size of Principal Enterprise, 1973*

Size of principal enterprise, by number of employees	Percentage of enterprises using subcontractors	Average number of subcontractors per enterprise
1–3	11.5	3
4–9	33.9	4
10–19	48.4	7
20–29	58.9	9
30–49	64.0	11
50–99	69.3	18
100–199	75.8	23
200–299	77.6	28
300–499	80.3	36
500–999	82.3	84
1,000 or more	83.3	160

Source: Japan, Ministry of Small and Medium Business, *The Fourth Fundamental Survey on Industrial Structure* (1973).

small firms continue to enjoy relative success. They include industries "where demand is diversified, fashionable, seasonal, or regional and in which demand is dispersed because the product is new" (neckties, curtain lace, concrete blocks, packaging machinery); activities in which the raw-material supply is localized or heterogeneous (leather goods, canned fruit, sawmills); "fields in which the mechanization of the technology is difficult" (needlework products); and labor-intensive industries (plastic cups, simple machine processing).[19]

Many small and medium manufacturing firms produce under subcontract to another firm. Traditionally the subcontracting relationship has been a highly dependent, long-lived connection although based on annual contracts. The firm offering the contract takes complete charge of design, specification, and approval of quality, generally paying the subcontractor cost (with 5 percent leeway) plus a processing fee, and expecting continual cost-reducing productivity gains. Most subcontractors are very small, although some have as many as a thousand employees.[20] More than three-fourths of all but the smallest manufacturing companies use subcontractors, as table 6-2 indicates,

19. Japan, Ministry of International Trade and Industry, Small and Medium Enterprise Agency, "White Paper on Small and Medium Enterprises," *White Papers of Japan, 1969–70: Annual Abstract of Official Reports and Statistics of the Japanese Government* (Japan Institute of International Affairs, 1971), pp. 295–96.

20. James C. Abegglen, ed., *Business Strategies for Japan* (Tokyo: Sophia University, 1970), pp. 162–63.

Table 6-3. *Number of Small and Medium Enterprises and Proportion Engaged in Subcontracting, by Principal Japanese Manufacturing Industry, 1971*

Industry	Small and medium enterprises	
	Number	Percentage engaged in subcontracting
Food and kindred products	93,181	30.2
Textile mill products	110,226	75.4
Clothing and apparel	27,766	71.7
Lumber and wood products	53,920	43.7
Furniture and fixtures	33,644	49.7
Pulp, paper, and paper products	16,102	43.8
Publishing and printing	30,433	51.0
Chemicals and related products	3,712	38.4
Petroleum and coal products	241	29.5
Rubber products	3,829	53.4
Leather and leather products	6,826	64.5
Ceramic, stone, and clay products	24,221	33.7
Iron and steel	5,015	65.0
Nonferrous metals	2,943	69.2
Fabricated metal products	65,515	71.5
Machinery	34,621	75.5
Electrical machinery, equipment, and supplies	16,125	78.9
Transportation equipment	20,518	77.2
Instruments and related products	6,574	70.5
Miscellaneous products	52,299	57.8

Source: Japan, Ministry of Small and Medium Business, *The Fourth Fundamental Survey on Small and Medium Enterprises* (1973).

and even tiny ones often do. The number of subcontractors rises steadily with the size of the parent, with large companies sometimes subcontracting more than 50 percent of the direct labor going into their product. The industries that undertake assembly or discrete processing operations contain numerous small enterprises, and large proportions of their small-enterprise populations are engaged in subcontracting. The distribution of small enterprises and sub-contracting activity shown in table 6-3 confirms their dominance in sectors whose output can feasibly pass in stages under a number of factory roofs.

Subcontracting is prevalent in part because it allows the parent enterprise to reduce its labor costs and, where "tapered integration" is present, to shift part of the risk of demand fluctuations and keep its own permanent labor force busy. It also provides a selective way to reward (and retain the use of) able employees after they are retired at fifty-five, by shifting them to or setting them up in business as subcontractors. Because consolidated financial state-ments are not required by Japanese commercial law, subcontractors can provide a method of concealing the parent firm's unprofitable activities.[21] And in industries such as plastics and synthetic fibers where large manufacturers of raw materials subcontract their fabrication into finished products, the manufacturer's influence over price is extended one step farther along the chain of markets. This approximates vertical integration into a stage where product differentiation starts to appear, and where a given level of seller concentration may yield the parent raw-material producer (and his oligopolistic rivals) more market power or the easier maintenance of consensus.[22] Subcontracting seems also adroitly to avoid some of the uncertainties of arm's-length transactions that are held to be a principal basis for vertical integration.[23]

Does the subcontractor also benefit from the relationship? Exploitation has been a matter of much concern in Japan, and the subcontractor tied to a single large company with no alternative is clearly vulnerable to an all-or-nothing offer. Probably the typical subcontractor does have alternatives, though, and is better described as a pure competitor who in the long run must be paid his opportunity cost to keep him at work. Supporting this view is the evidence of cyclical sensitivity in the processing fees paid to subcontractors; their familial relation to their parents neither denies them profit from excess demand nor protects them from dark days of excess supply.[24] Yoshino suggests that in the 1950s as rapid growth set in, the treatment of subcontractors significantly improved because of the need to encourage expansion of their capacities along with those of the parent firm.[25] For the same reasons parents have been concerned about technological change among their subcontractors and their ability to finance investment. There is an increasing tendency for subcontractors to secure business from more than one parent,[26] which clearly affords a potential improvement in their bargaining power even if it costs some forms of assistance that a single parent would render.

Is the extensive practice of subcontracting an efficient one? There is no doubting its private rationality, but much of that turns on advantages that

21. See M. Y. Yoshino, *Japan's Managerial System: Tradition and Innovation* (MIT Press, 1968), pp. 150–55.

22. Ibid., p. 157. Compare William S. Comanor, "Vertical Mergers, Market Powers, and the Antitrust Laws," *American Economic Review,* vol. 57 (May 1967, *Papers and Proceedings, 1966*), pp. 254–65.

23. Oliver E. Williamson, "The Vertical Integration of Production: Market Failure Considerations," *American Economic Review,* vol. 61 (May 1971, *Papers and Proceedings, 1970*), pp. 112–23.

24. Shinohara, "Survey," p. 65, and *Structural Changes,* pp. 327–28.

25. Yoshino, *Japan's Managerial System,* p. 156.

26. Shinohara, "Survey," pp. 76–77; and Shōkō kumiai chūō kinko, *Shitauke chūshō kigyō no jittai* [The Actual Conditions of Subcontracting Medium and Small Industries] (1971).

may not minimize social costs. Wage differentials by plant size could make subcontracting profitable even where the subcontractor is not efficient in real terms. The use of retired employees merely reflects the perversity of the retirement system and the practice of permanent employment. Critics have held that subcontracting can impair the parent's flexibility, precludes an arm's-length make-or-buy decision, and delays the development of independent large-scale component producers who might enjoy greater economies of scale.[27] Its chief social advantage is probably to serve as an alternative to vertical integration, assuming that formal integration can raise barriers to entry into an industry by forcing the entrant to choose between the capital commitment of integrated entry and the uncertainties of a thin spot market if he enters unintegrated. To the extent that subcontractors are not fully captive, they broaden the entrant's options.

A final aspect of small and medium manufacturing business is its relation to regional economic imbalances and adjustments in Japan. As one would expect, growth in productivity of small and medium enterprises is greater in the six largest cities than in small centers or rural districts. Presumably this is due to the pressure that increasing labor and other input prices bring for cost-reducing innovations.[28] Shipments of the 313 industries that the Ministry of Small and Medium Business identifies as local industries account for one-fifth of all shipments by small enterprises. Ninety-eight of these industries are classed as export-oriented, making them (and their localities) vulnerable to international market fluctuations. No doubt a significant number also compete closely with imports. Shinohara's work on regional disparities in income and productivity also suggests that variations in size of enterprise are associated with variations in income per capita between prefectures.[29] These bits of evidence suggest that there is some association between the prevalence of small enterprise and the level and stability of regional incomes.

Small Enterprise in the Distributive Sector

It is widely agreed that technical efficiency is a major problem in Japan's distribution system. For instance, Japan has 2.2 times as many grocery outlets as the United States but half the population. Specialized by product line, their average daily sales in 1968 were less than $60. Abegglen calculated that the net income of the average owner was surely less than half what a worker

27. See Yoshino, *Japan's Managerial System*, pp. 159–61.
28. Shinohara, "Survey," pp. 58–61, citing evidence from General Survey of Technological Progress in Small-Medium Industry, 1958–59.
29. Shinohara, *Structural Changes*, pp. 383–90 and 413–19.

in a large factory could earn.[30] The pattern prevails throughout the retailing sector; 64 percent of establishments had only one or two employees in 1970, only 3.7 percent ten or more. Productivity varies so markedly with scale that sales per employee in small stores are perhaps one-third of those in large outlets.[31] The wholesalers are also relatively small (average 10.8 employees in 1968) and numerous, and transactions wind through long chains of wholesalers. In 1964–66, 40 percent of Japanese wholesalers' sales were to other wholesalers, whereas for the United States only 23 percent were as long ago as 1947.[32] There is no clear evidence of recent consolidation of this elaborate structure.

A number of causes share blame for the manifest inefficiency and low productivity of distribution. The mere fact that the distributive sector is much older than manufacturing and once contained the dominant (wholesaling) enterprises contributes to its rigidity. Until the end of the Tokugawa period the country was regionally fragmented, deterring large-scale distributive transactions. Until recently, road transport facilities (especially for larger trucks) were poor. Nowadays the congestion of the large cities and high land costs discourage increases in the size of establishments. The inadequate pensions that retirees receive at fifty-five generate a supply of "cannon fodder" entrepreneurs who have few alternatives to opening a small shop as an income supplement. The heavy use of resale price maintenance has deterred growth through aggressive pricing. And, in Japan as elsewhere, the organization of the distribution sector conforms to household shopping patterns. The low mobility of housewives has impelled many neighborhood stores that are necessarily small. Low household income and a lack of consumer durables (especially refrigerators) has meant frequent shopping and small-scale transactions—hostile to scale economies in store operation. The importance placed by shoppers on the proprietor's judgment and reputation argue against many employees. Affluence is relaxing these constraints, but ingrained shopping habits linger on.

These forces keeping the retail outlets small have made wholesale transactions small as well, frustrating the pursuit of scale economies farther

30. Abegglen, *Business Strategies*, p. 145. Also see M. Y. Yoshino, *The Japanese Marketing System: Adaptations and Innovations* (MIT Press, 1971), chap. 1.

31. This figure pertains to Tokyo, where labor-market pressure on small enterprises is greater than in most parts of Japan. Assign an index of 100 to annual average sales per employee in all Tokyo retail stores with more than 50 employees. Average sales per employee in stores employing 5 to 50 are 38.5, and in stores employing under 5 the index is 29.6. (See Minor Industry Problem Inquiry Committee, *Minor Industries and Workers in Tokyo*, p. 25.)

32. *Economic Survey of Japan, 1967–1968*, pp. 131–33. Figures on the size of wholesalers' staffs are from Yoshino, *The Japanese Marketing System*, p. 11.

upstream. The subnormal returns to many enterprises have discouraged investment in productivity-raising improvements. The only long-standing distribution enterprises of large scale are the department stores, which have been content with maintaining a traditional image of high quality and personal service.

The absence of large-scale manufacturing of consumer goods in Japan until after World War II probably helped to sustain the complex and inefficient distribution system. Since then some manufacturers have tried to seize the initiative in improving the organization of the distribution channels simply to serve their self-interest.[33] Generally, however, it is not rational for one manufacturer to take the lead in reorganizing distribution, because of the heavy administrative costs. Since the gains accrue partly to his rivals, the rents he can collect for his efforts will be much less than the total productivity increase if he succeeds.[34] The Japanese' obsessive fears about admitting foreign enterprises into their consumer-goods sector are tied to a concern that the American would take on the distribution problem and succeed—"seek out the most direct channel and direct his product toward the high volume customer"—while his Japanese competitor remained tied by tradition and complex financial arrangements to the existing trading companies and wholesalers.[35]

What does statistical evidence reveal about productivity gains in distribution? The wholesaling sector is more attractive for analysis than the retailing sector because its fate is less tied to population and locational patterns. The growth of productivity in wholesaling (measured by annual sales per employee) could be associated with at least two forces—reduction in the number of enterprises and their consolidation into larger units, and the general growth of final demand allowing the expansion of individual enterprises and speeding the construction of more efficient premises and facilities. Using data on ten broad classes of wholesaling enterprises, we calculated the following measures of change for each sector over 1964–68:

X_1 = percentage increase of total annual sales of wholesaling establishments

X_2 = percentage increase of annual sales per regular employee

X_3 = percentage increase of number of wholesaling establishments.

The zero-order correlations among these series are: $r_{12} = 0.754$; $r_{13} = 0.610$; and $r_{23} = 0.436$. The first two are significant at the 0.05 level. Thus produc-

---

33. For an example, see Yoshino, *The Japanese Marketing System*, p. 96. These initiatives can have the incidental effect of increasing the manufacturer's market power and the barriers to entry into competition with him.

34. Abegglen, *Business Strategies*, pp. 139–41.

35. Ibid., pp. 79–80.

tivity growth is significantly related to total growth in these wholesaling activities. The direction of causation is not wholly clear, of course, because general growth in productivity tends to raise the level of activity in all sectors. The relation between productivity growth and the number of establishments is positive although not significant, so there is no evidence (in this simple test) that productivity gains in wholesaling are closely associated with the consolidation or elimination of enterprises. The correlation between productivity growth and total growth remains significant when we hold constant the number of establishments: $r_{12.3} = 0.684$.[36]

Change is now coming to the distributive sector.[37] Retail establishments with fifty or more employees raised their share of sales from 13.1 percent in 1960 to 17.8 percent in 1966. Conventional chain-store organizations (mostly associations of existing stores) are starting to appear, as are innovative mass merchandisers—"supermarkets" that handle high-volume foodstuffs, household goods, kitchen utensils on a discount basis; and department stores specializing in installment sales. The 112 retailing firms with annual volumes exceeding ¥5 billion in 1969 (there were 31 in 1960) included 46 department stores, 52 supermarkets, 5 installment credit stores, and 9 specialty stores. Supermarkets have successfully appealed to lower-income buyers, and in large cities over half of total sales of some popular food products are self-service.

There is good prospect that these innovations will spread. Manufacturers of major brands are taking a warmer view toward mass distributors rather than insisting on trading through their traditional channels. So are the general trading firms, which have otherwise been a passive force. In many classes of products, mass merchandising firms are attempting to bypass the labyrinthine wholesale sector and deal directly with the manufacturer, and some large mass-merchandising firms have gone into private branding. The pressure from these larger retailers has not only tended to compress wholesaling into a smaller number of vertical stages, but it has also induced some lateral consolidation by discouraging an apparently excessive commodity specialization in wholesaling.[38] The relative productivity of the distribution system is improving but it is late and slow in coming. Its arrival has a few negative side

36. Data for this analysis (originally from census sources) are taken from Distribution Economics Institute of Japan, *Outline of Japanese Distribution Structures* (Tokyo: Distribution Economics Institute of Japan, 1971), pp. 17–18.

37. Most information in this paragraph is taken from Yoshino, *The Japanese Marketing System,* chap. 4; and Distribution Economics Institute, *Outline,* chaps. 3 and 4. Also see Kōichi Tanouchi, "Voluntary Chains in Japan," *Hitotsubashi Journal of Commerce and Management,* vol. 8 (July 1973), pp. 1–8.

38. Yoshino, *The Japanese Marketing System,* pp. 158–59 and 170–71; and Distribution Economics Institute, *Outline,* pp. 40–41.

effects: the economic and social costs in the displacement of small enterprises, and the development of product differentiation and elevation of entry barriers in some consumer-good industries.[39] Only recently has government policy come actively to support changes that improve productivity in distribution; formerly it actively discouraged change and intersectoral competition.[40]

Other Sources of Inefficiency

Sharply limited evidence is available on other possible sources of technical inefficiency in the Japanese economy. Shortfalls in efficiency can occur not just because firms are too small, but also because inefficient firms of any scale are under too little pressure to mend their ways. Oligopolistic price-fixing and other collusive practices are often held to nurture inefficiency, because they allow the inefficient firm to soldier on, earning at least normal profits.[41] The price collusion commonly found in Japanese manufacturing is said to have had this effect.[42] And the production curtailments (under MITI's "guidance," for example) that are devised to leave all firms utilizing the same percentage of their capacity create an incentive for building in excess capacity when the opportunity arises. While increasing total cost, this practice also increases the firm's expected volume of sales at prices in excess of marginal cost.

The rapid growth of productivity and conspicuous success in international markets of the large-enterprise sectors of the Japanese economy easily generate the impression that they deserve high marks for technical efficiency. Yet the permanent employment system, the distorted incentives for addition to capacity, the prevalence of collusion and reciprocity arrangements, and the abundance of last-resort protection for a firm in trouble all provide umbrellas that could shelter some technical inefficiency. Though it is very difficult to test the hypothesis that *all* firms in an industry are inefficient, it is possible to test whether inefficiency varies among firms with the prevalence of conditions that shelter or encourage it.

Technical inefficiency could appear as distortions of various sorts in the level and composition of a firm's costs. Administrative costs, for example, might conceal inflated staffs and levels of executive pay, which Williamson has argued could serve the interest of utility-maximizing corporate man-

39. See Michael E. Porter, "Consumer Behavior, Retailer Power and Market Performance in Consumer Goods Industries," *Review of Economics and Statistics*, vol. 56 (November 1974), pp. 419–36.

40. Yoshino, *The Japanese Marketing System*, chap. 7.

41. For statistical evidence on the United Kingdom, see Jack Downie, *The Competitive Process* (London: Duckworth, 1958).

42. Yoshino, *Japan's Managerial System*, p. 168.

agers.[43] Data on the 243 large enterprises described in chapter 4 permit analysis of the determinants of administrative costs as a percentage of total costs (defined as sales minus profits).[44] Several independent variables explained in chapter 4 might reflect conditions that allow or encourage the inflation of administrative costs. One is the presence of high seller concentration and entry barriers, which together can shelter the inefficient firm from incursions by either new or current rivals. Hence we include seller concentration, CR, and the advertising-sales ratio, AD, the latter because of its strong association with entry barriers. The advertising variable unfortunately is connected to administrative costs in another way, because that category of course includes most outlays on sales promotion related to advertising. Does absolute size of the firm permit economies in administration or does it encourage the diseconomies of bureaucracy? Lacking confidence in either a priori argument, we simply include total assets, TA, and a quadratic term TA^2 to determine the shape of this partial relation empirically.

Several other variables might affect administrative costs. The diversification of a firm's output, even if it brings economies elsewhere, should increase the costs of coordination. The variable DI, based on the specialization ratio, provides a weak inverse measure of diversification by all sellers in the firm's primary industry. Administrative expenses should increase when the firm's environment is changing rapidly. Hence we include the rate of growth of the firm's sales, GR, and the coefficient of variation of sales, VS, expecting a positive relation of both variables to administrative costs. Finally, the possibilities of mutual assistance and the prevalence of reciprocity among the zaibatsu and other affiliated groups prompt us to include dummy variables DZ, DC, and DZC for the firm's group membership status. We assume the many firm-specific factors we have omitted to be random.

When all observations are weighted by the square root of total assets, to correct for heteroscedasticity, we get the following results:[45]

$$(1) \quad AM = \text{constant} + 0.0084^b \, TA - 0.97*10^{-8} \, {}^a \, TA^2 + 0.0026 \, CR$$
$$(2.11) \qquad\qquad (2.88) \qquad\qquad\qquad (0.15)$$

$$+ 1.88^a \, AD + 0.027 \, GR + 0.024^c \, DI + 0.051^c \, VS + 0.636 \, DZC.$$
$$(9.35) \qquad (0.28) \qquad (1.87) \qquad (1.74) \qquad (0.67)$$

$$\bar{R}^2 = 0.764^a.$$

43. Oliver E. Williamson, "Managerial Discretion and Business Behavior," *American Economic Review*, vol. 53 (December 1963), pp. 1032–57.

44. Advertising has been excluded from administrative costs. Ideally, the denominator would be sales minus *excess* profits. In light of the peculiar capital structures of large Japanese firms exposed in chap. 4, above, it did not seem wise to pursue this refinement.

45. For both equations the significance levels (two-tailed test) are a = 0.01, b = 0.05, and c = 0.10, keyed to the footnote references on the constants and the coefficients.

(2) AM = constant + 0.0023 TA + 0.011 CR + 1.94^a AD + 0.062 GR
                    (1.59)   (0.61)   (9.48)   (0.63)
         + 0.029^b DI + 0.082^a VS + 2.05^b DZ + 2.31^a DC.
              (2.23)   (2.94)   (2.39)   (2.62)

$$\bar{R}^2 = 0.755^a.$$

The signs are correct for all variables carrying unambiguous sign predictions except diversification, DI. Concentration, CR, is not significant.[46] Advertising, AD, is formidably significant. That fact is not surprising because some administrative expenses are devoted to sales-promoting activities that complement advertising outlays. The size of the coefficient gives pause, however, because it suggests that an extra percent of sales spent on advertising is associated with nearly an extra 2 percent spent on administration. That certainly leaves room for suspicion that higher product-differentiation barriers to entry promote technical inefficiency. Group membership, DZ, DC, and DZC, is statistically significant only when TA^2 is omitted but the magnitude of the coefficient suggests a relatively large inflation of costs.

A firm facing a highly variable rate of sales, VS, does incur higher administrative costs, although rapid growth does not significantly inflate these outlays. The measures of total size suggest that administrative costs increase with scale only up to a point, with economies setting in for the largest firms. Indeed, when TA^2 is excluded from equation (2) the relation of TA to AM is positive but not significant, suggesting that those economies dominate for the larger firms included in our sample.

Our sample contains enough degrees of freedom to allow examination for possible interactions among the independent variables. We would expect concentration and entry barriers to permit lower levels of efficiency when in fact the position of market power yields more excess profits. That is, extra monopoly profits when protected by concentration and entry barriers should be consumed partly in inflated administrative costs. This hypothesis predicts a positive sign for the interaction term $CR*PE$, the product of the concentration ratio and the firm's profit rate on equity capital. Another relation of interest is between administrative costs and the capital- or asset-intensity of an enterprise, measured by the ratio of total assets to sales, TA/SL. Management costs presumably increase with the relative size of the asset stock when flows of other inputs are held constant, so this variable is designed to remove

46. Masao Baba and Akira Iwasaki, in "The Relation between Industrial Concentration and Technical Efficiency in the Japanese Manufacturing Industries: A Note," discussion paper no. 079 (Kyoto Institute of Economic Research, 1974), find that industries' shortfall from an estimated technical frontier decreases as concentration increases for relatively unconcentrated sectors but increases with increasing concentration in relatively concentrated ones.

an unavoidable component from administrative costs. When we recompute equation (1) with these terms added, the ratio of total assets to sales proves significant. The sign of the interaction $CR*PE$ is correct but the variable is not significant.

We conclude that there is modest support for the hypothesis that secure market power is hostile to technical efficiency. And we are only modestly confident that group affiliation allows the inflation of administrative costs, although our best guess is that the magnitude is large. There is no evidence that economies in administration accrue endlessly as companies are enlarged. Finally, we find some evidence that administrative costs rise when a firm holds a relatively large stock of assets or experiences large fluctuations in its rate of sales.

Conclusions

The technical efficiency of Japanese industry depends on its production of goods at minimum cost. Thus the possibility that the prevalence of small and medium enterprises in many industries causes inefficiency is of much concern to the Japanese. Small enterprises are indeed numerous—though not abnormally so given the level and speed of Japan's development and the size of her economy. Distortions in markets are most likely to affect efficiency in this sector. Small firms are sustained by the low cost of the labor they employ, but are disadvantaged by the high cost of capital and constrained from growth by limitations on its supply. The favorable distortion in the labor market is disappearing with no apparent corresponding elimination of the discrimination in the capital market. The small-enterprise sector's rates of capital formation and productivity gains in the 1960s were insufficient to prevent loss of its share of business activity.

Many small and medium enterprises produce under subcontract to larger firms. This device reduces risk for the parent enterprise and allows it to take advantage of the lower labor costs of small-scale enterprises. The subcontractor is somewhat dependent, but subcontractors increasingly are dealing with a number of parent firms. The subcontracting relation largely compensates for the distortions in Japan's factor markets (including the practice of early retirement), but it may also offer the advantage of lower entry barriers into the parent enterprises' activities.

Inefficient, small-scale operations have been a problem particularly in Japan's distribution sector. They are caused by the same structural forces responsible for small-scale manufacturing as well as by the locational factors and shopping habits that have dictated small-scale retailing establishments. Wholesaling activities have perforce been small-scale and vertically disintegrated. Mass distribution and associated productivity gains are now appearing, but they have been slow in coming and have received no encouragement from public policy.

In the manufacturing sector, collusive practices have sometimes promoted the maintenance of excess capacity and could serve to protect inefficient firms, regardless of size. Our analysis of the determinants of administrative costs in 243 large companies uncovered some influences on inefficiency. Administrative costs as a percentage of sales increase with size except for very large companies and are highly sensitive to rates of advertising outlay—a source of entry barriers and market power. Both results create a suspicion of technical inefficiency in large companies. Our results also show administrative costs increasing, as we expect they would, with companies' capital intensity and with the variability of their sales. They are also positively related to group affiliation, supporting the hypothesis that any rents from that source are consumed partly in technical inefficiency.

In short, we find that the Japanese economy harbors several types of substantial technical inefficiency despite the remarkable productivity gains it has achieved. Public policy could be used to attack these inefficiencies.

CHAPTER SEVEN

Imported Technology and Industrial Progress

A KEY ELEMENT in the postwar growth of Japan has been the rapid import of foreign technology, ending a period of near-isolation from developments in international technology that ran through the period of military preparation for World War II and the war.[1] The rapid absorption of Western technology reflects the ability of the Japanese to imitate foreign modes and their openness to accepting new and useful ideas, themes that run through the country's modernization.

Research and Economic Growth

Convincing evidence of Japan's postwar economic performance appears in estimates prepared by Denison and Chung.[2] Over the years 1953–71 growth in the stock of knowledge (estimated as a residual) contributed 2.30 percentage points annually to the growth of nonresidential business output. The contribution actually accelerated through the period—1.76 for 1953–62, 2.91 thereafter. If, as Denison and Chung suggest, the expansion rate of the world's stock of productive knowledge equals that in the United States— 1.43 percentage points for 1948–69—nearly 1 percentage point of Japan's annual expansion rate during this period was due to the absorption of knowl-

1. Because this chapter will deal in detail with only parts of that story, we draw upon evidence from other studies to supply the larger picture.
2. Edward F. Denison and William K. Chung, "Economic Growth and Its Sources," in Hugh Patrick and Henry Rosovsky, eds., *Asia's New Giant: How the Japanese Economy Works* (Brookings Institution, 1976), chap. 2.

124

edge from abroad. Denison found no comparable catch-up among the European countries during the 1950–62 period.[3] Furthermore, the *level* of residual productivity in Japan fell 17 percent short of that in the United States in 1970, while the level in Northwest Europe was 28 percent below the U.S. level in 1960 (with individual countries ranging between 23 percent and 34 percent).

The process of technology transfer and its relation to resources committed to research within Japan have been examined by Peck and Tamura.[4] Although the country absorbs technology from abroad through many channels, a vitally important one has been technology agreements between Japanese and foreign companies. These have followed a shifting pattern since World War II. At first major new technologies not available in Japan were imported by dominant firms. Gradually these gave way to less significant but more numerous imports of technology representing improvements in techniques already used in Japan, or duplicating technologies already licensed on an exclusive basis by competing firms. Emphasis has shifted from producer to consumer goods, although the same broad industry groups have remained the chief importers throughout. Most of the technology agreements include know-how and other forms of technical assistance, not just patent rights: technology transfer generally involves more than disembodied knowledge. The term of the agreements between Japanese and foreign firms generally is long—a median of ten years—and the royalty rate preset and unchanging. Average royalty rates have fluctuated, falling in the early 1960s but rising recently despite the larger number of sellers of most major lines of technology. Peck and Tamura suggest that the rise in price reflects sellers' recognition that their international customers for technology can become their competitors in product markets—an aspect of increased recognition by oligopolistic firms that their mutual dependence extends across national boundaries. In Japan's case, the rising price of technology may also reflect the bargaining pressure of foreign sellers who but for administrative restrictions would invest directly in the Japanese market.

Until recently, the Ministry of International Trade and Industry has had a major influence on the inflow of technology, having had an active hand in promoting technology imports in favored industries and also in beating down the price paid by Japanese buyers. The ministry was probably responsible for declining royalty rates in the early and mid-1960s, according to Peck and

3. See Edward F. Denison, assisted by Jean-Pierre Poullier, *Why Growth Rates Differ: Postwar Experience in Nine Western Countries* (Brookings Institution, 1967), chap. 21.

4. Merton J. Peck with the collaboration of Shūji Tamura, "Technology," in Patrick and Rosovsky, eds., *Asia's New Giant*.

Tamura. It has fought exclusive licenses to Japanese partners in order to minimize payments abroad for duplicating technology (although would-be Japanese duplicators often find it cheaper to license from abroad than from their domestic competitor, whose asking price will reflect his reluctance to face rivalry at home). The ministry has controlled the market structures of new industries by denying follower firms access to technology until assured that excess capacity and "excessive competition" would not result.

The level and pattern of research and development within Japan are closely related to the import of technology from abroad. Firms must maintain some research capacity in order to know what technology is available for purchase or copy, and they must generally modify and adapt foreign technology in putting it to use—a 1963 survey of Japanese manufacturers showed that on average one-third of the respondents' expenditures on research and development went for this purpose. A leading technology importer thus should carry out substantial research, though less than would a leading exporter. Japan's rate of nonmilitary R&D spending (as a percentage of GNP) is only slightly behind that of the leading Western industrial countries. In real terms the total amount spent on research and development is one-half to two-thirds that of the United States. The distribution of research activity among industries is generally similar to that of the United States. Although rates of R&D expenditure are lower in Japan for firms of all sizes than for their U.S. counterparts, the concentration of research outlays in large firms is lower in Japan than in the United States. Much of it apparently is allocated to short-term and low-risk projects; there are close links between large companies and university researchers, but little involvement by the companies in basic research. The moderate level, wide diffusion, and applied character of Japan's research effort are consistent with a facility for securing new knowledge from abroad.

The consequences of Japan's success as an importer and developer of technology are evident in its industrial activity as well as in its aggregate performance. Those industries most dependent on advanced technology have expanded their shares of Japan's exports and output, and also their shares of total exports among such industries by all member countries in the Organisation for Economic Co-operation and Development. As expected, the number of technology imports by Japanese industries is correlated with the increases in their shares of total exports. Also, Japan has become a significant seller of technology abroad, and in numbers of new agreements now ranks as a *net* seller.[5]

This impressive performance raises various questions about industrial or-

5. Ibid.

ganization. Now that domestic R&D expenditure has risen to a level substantial by international standards, its relation to the structures of Japan's industries and their performance takes on great interest. So do the policies of the Japanese government, especially its effort to control the concentration of industries and the scale of establishments in order to improve market performance.

Market Structure, Innovation, and Diffusion of Knowledge

Market structures can affect an industry's performance in both innovation and the diffusion of knowledge, as extensive research on the U.S. economy has shown. Economists have presumed that the amount of expenditure on research tends to be suboptimal because the individual discoverer generally cannot capture all the quasi-rents due to his innovation. Because there is apt to be less leakage in more concentrated markets, and because funds for speculative investments are more readily available in concentrated markets, some economists have hypothesized that the more concentrated is an industry's structure and the larger its firms, the more nearly optimal will be its research performance. Others have found this reasoning to support only a preference for somewhat concentrated as against completely atomistic market structures. To settle the question the ceteris paribus relation between R&D activity and both concentration and firm size must be determined empirically.

Imai has examined the relation between firm size and research effort for large Japanese firms within each of fifteen two-digit manufacturing and construction industries in 1967.[6] His measures based on inputs are R&D staff and R&D expenditure, his output-based measure patents; he uses values of sales squared and cubed to detect nonlinearities. His results show no particularly clear-cut association of firm size with research in these fifteen industries. In only three industries do all three measures lead to the same conclusion: in textiles, R&D activity increases proportionally with firm size; in steel and nonmetallic minerals it increases less than proportionally. In three more industries, two of the measures point in the same direction: R&D rises less than proportionally with size in electrical machinery and metal products; it rises first less than proportionally but then more than proportionally in construction. Imai's study certainly gives no support to the policy prescription that the enlargement of firm sizes in most industries would raise the total amount

6. Ken'ichi Imai, "Jōhō-gijutsu-kigyō kibo" [Information, Technology, and Firm Size], in Ken'ichi Imai, Yasusuke Murakami, and Jinkichi Tsukui, *Jōhō to gijutsu no keizai bunseki* [Economic Analysis of Information and Technology], research report no. 24 (Tokyo: Japan Economic Research Center, 1969), chap. 10.

of R&D activity, but the study applied only to firms large enough to undertake research.

Uekusa has also analyzed the relation between R&D expenditures and size of firm (measured by sales) for a sample of nearly three hundred large firms in manufacturing and construction.[7] For the whole sample, regression analyses for three separate years (1965, 1967, 1969) imply that R&D expenditures rise more or less proportionally with size to a certain point but then decrease absolutely (the estimates of this critical size differ considerably from year to year). The results change sharply, however, when the firms are sorted by their basic industry affiliation into those belonging to highly innovative industries (chemicals and allied products and electrical machinery), moderately innovative industries (transportation equipment, machinery, and instruments and related products), and less innovative industries (all others). In the highly innovative industries, R&D expenditures indeed do increase more than proportionally to firm sales. In the moderately innovative industries the increase is more than proportional only up to a point, then becomes less than proportional and ultimately declines absolutely. In the less innovative industries the increase becomes less than proportional for those with more than a modest volume of sales, and again an absolute decline ultimately sets in.

Uekusa also analyzes the relation of R&D activity to seller concentration, for a sample of twenty-one two- and three-digit industries. Whether input or output measures of R&D activity are used, the regression coefficient of the five-firm concentration ratio is negative although not statistically significant. The coefficient of the size variable is of course positive and significant. Thus there is no support for the proposition that higher concentration itself is favorable to improved R&D performance, although in the highly innovative industries, size of firm itself seems favorable without limit to improved R&D performance (in other industries it is favorable only up to a point).

Less is known about what determines the rate of diffusion of new knowledge within and between industries. We generally expect faster diffusion in industries organized more competitively. Firms that are asymmetrically placed or vulnerable in their market positions are more likely to risk placing innovations on the market, and firms with more rivals fear the consequences of tardy adoption of an innovation. But small firms may be deterred by the fixed cost of carrying on enough R&D activity to maintain the necessary listening post, and may lack managerial capacity to keep up with best practice. Thus, the predicted effects of concentration and size on diffusion conflict

7. Masu Uekusa, "Sangyō soshiki to inobēshon" [Industrial Organization and Innovation], in Bun'ichirō Hijikata and Kimio Miyagawa, eds., *Kigyō kōdō to inobēshon* [Firm Behavior and Innovation] (Tokyo: Nihon Keizai Shinbunsha, 1973), chap. 3.

with one another to some extent—once we stipulate that average firm size and overall concentration must be negatively related in a given industry.

These propositions should bear both on the diffusion of technology within an industry and its absorption from outside—whether outside the industry or outside the country. Uekusa found no relation between seller concentration in Japanese industries and the volume of their payments for technology imports; the absolute level of firms' payments was related to the size of their sales.[8] Surveys of small businesses to determine what channels they use to acquire new scientific and technical information (whether from domestic or foreign sources) shows the following percentages of firms that used each of the principal channels:[9]

Machinery manufacturers	47.7
People in the same trade	36.5
Domestic newspapers, periodicals	35.7
Material makers	33.5
Information via cooperatives, trade associations	33.3
Products of other firms	33.3
Training courses, workshops	32.5
Exhibitions	29.5
Parent companies	22.6
Scholarly sources (universities, learned societies)	22.2
Overseas periodicals	17.0
Public guidance institutions	16.6

Self-interested sales promotion by makers of producer goods appears quite important, as do industry associations. Because about half of small firms are subcontractors, it is perhaps surprising that the percentage of respondents citing parent companies is no larger than it is. The small dependence on sources of new basic scientific advances (universities, learned societies) confirms that this information must be converted elsewhere into forms usable by industry. The unimportance of foreign relative to domestic information channels is noteworthy.

Determinants of Productivity Growth

Many gaps remain in our evidence about innovation and growth in Japanese industries. Our measures of R&D inputs and outputs do not get at the variable of ultimate concern—the increase in output due to resources com-

8. Ibid.

9. Kazuhiko Ōtsuka, *Balanced Industrial Structure and Transfer of Technology: A Study of Technology Transfer in Small-Scale Industries,* Japan, Ministry of International Trade and Industry (1972), chart 4.

mitted to innovation. Nor does the evidence at hand permit a direct test of the effectiveness of Japan's policy to foster the development of technology-intensive industries by promoting large scale in plants and companies. Therefore we carried out a statistical analysis of the determinants of rates of productivity growth in manufacturing industries, including as independent variables measures of technology import, domestic research, and elements of industry structure (levels or changes) that might affect productivity growth. The fundamental difficulty in any study of technological advance is to ascertain how an industry performed relative to the technological frontier that was available to it, when the location and rate of change of this "best attainable" frontier are never known. To solve this problem we used the rate of productivity growth in a given U.S. industry as a proxy for the rate of outward movement of the world technology frontier available to its Japanese counterpart.

Cross-section statistical analysis is an attractive method of approaching the determinants of technological change that has been used repeatedly on data for the United States and other countries.[10] It can capture the long-run effect of varying the structural environment that determines an industry's rate of productivity advance. But the method must be used carefully lest one impose the assumption that the same microeconomic mechanism is at work in all the industries included in the sample. Would a given rate of research outlay generate the same rate of advance in clothespins as in pharmaceuticals? Probably not.

Our measure of productivity growth is the only one readily available for a large sample of industries—the increase of labor productivity measured by value added per employee. Specifically, the dependent variable *JPROD* is the increase in value added per regular employee in the Japanese industry between 1958 and 1967 divided by the 1958 figure and expressed as an annual rate of change.[11] No adjustment is made for the effect of price changes on the movement of value added. General price movements will show up in the constant term of a regression equation. World movements in the prices of particular inputs or outputs will be reflected in the independent variable—productivity growth in the United States. Price movements falling in neither of these classes are assumed to be random disturbances.

10. See, for example, F. M. Scherer, "Firm Size, Market Structure, Opportunity, and the Output of Patented Inventions," *American Economic Review,* vol. 55 (December 1965), pp. 1097–1125; and Edwin Mansfield, *Industrial Research and Technological Innovation: An Econometric Analysis* (Norton, 1968).

11. Details on sources of data and the construction of variables appear in the statistical appendix to this volume. Japanese census data do not supply a measure of total labor input. However, its changes should be closely correlated with changes in the number of regular employees.

As indicated, the first independent variable that we include is:

USPROD = increase in value added per worker in counterpart U.S. industry, 1958–67, expressed as an annual percentage of value
added per worker in 1958.

This variable serves as a proxy for the rate of outward movement of an industry's technologically attainable production frontier during those years.
We do not assume that U.S. industry is perfectly efficient, but rather that the
United States is still the source of more innovations than any other country,
and that new discoveries are put to work more promptly in the country where
they are made than in the rest of the world. We also assume that actual productivity movements in U.S. industries differ from the movements of their
respective technology frontiers only by a random factor—that is, that no systematic lagging or catching up was taking place during this period. If innovations were Hicks-neutral and transmitted instantly, there should be a close
relation between *USPROD* and the dependent variable. (Industries' depar-
tures from Hicks-neutrality must be assumed random.) If the transmission
process is weak, or if productivity growth depends heavily on factors other
than the international movement of intangible knowledge, *USPROD*'s explanatory power may be reduced and other variables come into play.

Technical change and invention abroad might affect productivity growth
in Japan through numerous channels—the free movement of public scientific
information, the licensing of proprietary technology, the imitation of innovations made by other companies (including foreign subsidiaries or joint ventures operating in Japan), internationally traded capital goods embodying
new technology, and so forth. Ideally we would control for each industry's
access to each of these flows. In fact the statistical resources at hand afford
only a glimpse at one of them, imports of licensed technology:

TIM = total number of technological imports by the Japanese industry,
1958–67, expressed as a percentage of value of shipments, 1967.

We were unable to secure industry-level data on technology payments, so
settled for the number of licenses granted. Technology licenses are usually
granted for a fee representing some fixed percentage of the licensee's sales or
factory cost, and the percentage seems to be set rather mechanically at a small
round number. If these fees are set on a simple conventional basis, data on
payments themselves would measure the net productivity of technology imports little more accurately than would the number received by an industry.
Basing the variable on the cumulated number of imports implies that each
import makes a permanent addition to an industry's productivity; unfortunately there is no way to normalize this number by the initial stock of tech-

nology, so our denominator (the value of shipments at the end of the period) provides only the roughest correction. Furthermore, the disaggregation of technology imports by industry is much less fine than the industry classification of the dependent variable, and so we assumed that technology imports by an aggregate of industries are divided among them in proportion to their value added.

Among the other variables that might affect an industry's rate of growth of labor productivity is the change in inputs other than labor employed by the industry. The only one of these on which data are available is capital:

JKL = annual percentage growth rate of capital per regular employee in the Japanese industry, 1958–67.

For this variable to capture accurately the influence of varying rates of investment on industries' productivity, it can be shown that they would all have to be operating on the same Cobb-Douglas production function. Obviously this assumption is unrealistic. Yet some control for other factors is necessary, and in a cross-section analysis anything more subtle is much more complicated. We report some tests for violation of the Cobb-Douglas assumption.

As an alternative to JKL we computed:

$USKL$ = annual percentage growth rate of capital per man in the U.S. industry, 1958–67.

Increasing the capital intensity of an industry might raise labor productivity simply by providing more capital equipment per worker or by advancing the level of productivity through embodied technological change. If the latter process is important and new capital goods are freely traded internationally, productivity growth in Japanese industries might be related about as closely to the rate of capital formation in counterpart U.S. industries as to their own rates of capital formation. Therefore we include $USKL$ in order to compare its statistical performance to that of JKL.

Whether or not high seller concentration is favorable to innovation and progressiveness is a much debated question. Was Schumpeter right that monopoly is needed to provide the entrepreneur with the breathing space for the really significant innovation and the resources to invest in the necessary research? Or is competition needed to induce firms to take the risk or expend the entrepreneurial effort to innovate? Without firm expectation as to sign, we include:

$JC4$ = proportion of shipments accounted for by the largest four firms in the Japanese industry, 1963

$JC8$ = proportion of shipments accounted for by the largest eight firms in the Japanese industry, 1963

$JC58$ = marginal concentration ratio—difference between $JC8$ and $JC4$

$JC820$ = marginal concentration ratio—difference between the proportion of shipments accounted for by the largest twenty firms and $JC8$.

The alternative cut-offs and the marginal concentration ratios are included because of our uncertainty about what level of concentration is appropriate to these hypotheses. For instance, a core of dominant firms might favor an industry's productivity growth for Schumpeterian reasons (positive relation to $JC4$) and yet numerous small firms on the fringe might also help to speed diffusion by giving the leaders an incentive for continuing innovation (negative relation to $JC58$).

Productivity growth in Japanese industries should be affected by their own outputs of inventive activity, measured either directly or by the inputs needed to secure these outputs:

RDS = average annual industry expenditure on research and development as a percentage of sales, 1958–67

RDE = research and development employment as a percentage of total employment, fiscal 1968

PAT = average number of patents held per firm by companies with more than ¥500 million paid-in capital, fiscal 1968.

The widely recognized weaknesses of these measures dictate that a positive statistical influence of research activity on productivity growth be cautiously interpreted. A positive result might mean that increased research outlays in the typical industry are rewarded with accelerated productivity growth. Or it might mean that, in those industries with a high potential for technological development and productivity growth, entrepreneurs rationally choose to invest in research activities. It is important to note that PAT includes patents licensed from foreign sources.

Industrial policy in Japan (notably that of the Ministry of International Trade and Industry) has often placed great emphasis on the need to enlarge the size of manufacturing establishments and firms to make them efficient and competitive in the international market. If the hypothesis is correct that the nation's manufacturing units are typically too small for efficiency, some positive relation should exist between industries' rates of productivity growth and the rates at which their manufacturing establishments are being enlarged. But do these gains depend on the construction of very large establishments? Or do they depend on the displacement (absolute or relative) of small establishments? Because these hypotheses call attention to different parts of the distribution of plant sizes, we constructed two variables:

PSZ = average value added in 1967 of establishments in the Japanese industry employing 50 or more workers, divided by average value added in 1958 of establishments then employing 50 or more workers

PLG = average value added in 1967 of the largest establishments in the Japanese industry accounting for (approximately) 50 percent of its total value added, divided by average value added in 1958 of the largest establishments accounting for (approximately) 50 percent of its value added in that year.

The relative significance and the size of the regression coefficients of these two ratios should indicate what segment of the distribution of plant sizes makes the greater difference for increases in productivity. It has been shown that in the usual case where small plants are far more numerous than large plants, a measure like *PSZ* is very sensitive to the number of small plants. That is, any variance in *PSZ* between industries is likely to reflect changes in the number of small plants and not in the average size of the (less numerous) larger plants.[12] Thus, superior statistical performance of *PSZ* would support the importance of proportionally reducing the population of inefficiently small plants rather than of encouraging the construction of giant establishments.

Finally, we should allow for the possibility that Japan's industries in this period were in varying degrees catching up to their potential level of technical performance. The destruction and capital consumption of World War II and the nation's isolation from outside sources of innovation during that period surely left her industries varying distances behind the world's best in technological competence. And the recovery process was surely incomplete in 1958, the beginning year for our measure of productivity growth. Thus we expect that the variance of industries' rates of productivity growth is partly explained by their speeds of catching up. Economists commonly suppose that the speed of such adjustments is proportional to the distance between the actual and the target (or optimum) productivity. This implies that rates of productivity growth have been higher in industries with initially lower productivity, a hypothesis that is tricky to test because regressing the change in a variable on its initial level is to commit the regression fallacy plain and simple.[13] Instead, we test a stronger hypothesis: if a catch-up process was

---

12. Frederic L. Pryor, *Property and Industrial Organization in Communist and Capitalist Nations* (Indiana University Press, 1973), chap. 5.

13. S. J. Prais, "The Statistical Conditions for a Change in Business Concentration," *Review of Economics and Statistics*, vol. 40 (August 1958), pp. 268–72.

going on and *remained* incomplete in 1967, the change in productivity over the period 1958–67 would be inversely related to:

JP67 = value added per worker in the Japanese industry, 1967.

The null hypothesis could be confirmed for this variable even if a catch-up process was under way in 1958 but essentially completed by 1967.[14]

Our statistical analysis covers ninety-nine Japanese manufacturing industries that can be matched to manufacturing industries in the U.S. standard industrial classification (the two countries' classification schemes are largely parallel, and neither was revised during this decade; both countries took censuses of manufacturing sector in the same years). Both economically and statistically it seemed fitting to weight all observations for each industry by that industry's value-added per worker in 1967. Statistically, this procedure is appropriate if, as we assume, the standard deviation of an industry's productivity growth tends to be proportional to its size. Economically, if we are concerned with Japan's overall technological performance, it is appropriate to treat industries not as equally important but to weight them by their contributions to national income—approximated by value added. We also experimented with the square root of value added as a weight; the significance levels of the variables drop slightly, but the interpretation of the results is otherwise unaffected.

The principal results of the analysis appear in table 7-1. In equations (1) and (2), *JP67* is positive and highly significant. The positive sign rejects the hypothesis of a catch-up process and suggests instead that the estimated relation reflects nothing but the regression fallacy.[15] When *JP67* is dropped from equations (3)–(5), multicollinearity is reduced and the performance of other variables is significantly affected. In particular, the influence of *USPROD* becomes significant, though not highly so. Its zero-order correlation with the dependent variable is only 0.171, although its partial correlation after allowing for the variables included in equations (3)–(5) is about 0.30.

14. The size and the growth of the Japanese market were rejected as independent variables, although the size is correlated with the level of Japanese relative to American productivity and the growth with the rate of growth of productivity in Japan (see Kenzō Yukizawa, "A Comparison of Labour Productivity in Japanese and American Manufacturing Industry," *Kyoto University Economic Review,* vol. 38 [April 1968], p. 48). The direction of causation in both instances is ambiguous; perhaps a large market encourages productivity growth, but exogenous productivity growth certainly enlarges the market.

15. The catch-up of Japanese to American productivity levels is documented from fitted constant-elasticity-of-substitution production functions in Japan, Economic Planning Agency, *Economic Survey of Japan, 1967–1968* (Tokyo: Japan Times, Ltd.), pp. 94–95. The study suggests that the remaining shortfall is due to the relative inefficiency of small enterprises in Japan.

Table 7-1. *Regression Analysis of Determinants of Growth of Labor Productivity in Japanese Manufacturing Industries, 1958–67*[a]

Independent variable	Dependent variable, JPROD; equation number				
	(1)	(2)	(3)	(4)	(5)
USPROD	0.249 (1.15)	−0.011 (−0.04)	0.571b (2.98)	0.432c (2.33)	0.572b (3.06)
JKL	0.0701 (1.51)	...	0.0534 (1.12)	−0.0214 (−0.44)	0.0407 (0.85)
USKL	...	−0.102d (−1.86)	...	...	...
JC4	−0.000154 (−0.85)	−0.000503c (−2.31)	0.0000701 (0.41)	...	...
JC58	−0.000905d (−1.88)	−0.000767 (−1.15)	−0.000629 (−1.28)	...	...
JC8	...	...	...	0.0000947 (0.87)	−0.0000252 (−0.22)
JC820	...	−0.00178b (−2.82)	...	−0.000764c (−1.74)	−0.000681 (−1.50)
JP67	0.00890b (2.84)	0.0150b (4.12)	...	...	...
RDS	...	...	...	−0.0118b (−2.70)	...
PAT	0.0000433c (2.04)	0.0000292 (1.20)	0.0000440c (2.00)	...	0.0000391d (1.78)
TIM	−0.00284 (−0.83)	−0.00068 (−0.17)	−0.00449 (−1.29)	0.00063 (0.18)	−0.00413 (−1.26)
PSZ	0.0096b (5.16)	...	0.0109b (5.81)	0.0126b (7.04)	0.0107b (6.01)
PLG	...	0.00185b (4.00)	...	...	...
PLG − PSZ	−0.000222 (−0.43)	...	−0.000303 (−0.57)	...	...
Constant	0.064b (5.04)	0.123b (8.69)	0.053b (4.23)	0.078b (5.93)	0.061b (4.25)
R^2	0.469	0.302	0.428	0.462	0.439

a. See text for definition of variables. Values of R^2 are corrected for degrees of freedom; t values appear in parentheses.
b. Significant in a two-tailed test at 0.01.
c. Significant in a two-tailed test at 0.05.
d. Significant in a two-tailed test at 0.10.

The variable *USPROD* alone can explain only about 3 percent of the variance of the productivity growth rate among Japanese industries. Domestic variables in equations (3)–(5) account for about 40 percent more when added to *USPROD*. Statistically the strongest by far is *PSZ*, the change in the average size of plants employing more than fifty workers. In particular, its performance in all specifications of the model is stronger than the competing variable *PLG*, which measures the change in the average size of an industry's larger plants. The coefficient of *PSZ* is always six to eight times as large as that of *PLG*, and its t value is in the range of 5–7 rather than 3–4. Furthermore, the difference term *PLG − PSZ* is never significant and always negative in sign, revealing no evidence that changes in the size of the larger plants contribute to productivity gains after we allow for the contribution of changes in the size of the average plant. This implies that consolidating or eliminating inefficiently small-scale plants may promote significant productivity gains in many industries, but there is no evidence that promoting plants of extremely large scale carries similar promise of productivity gains. Some care is required in drawing policy conclusions from the role of *PSZ*. Small firms in Japan may exhibit low labor productivity both because of distortions in factor prices and because they are technically inefficient *given* the factor prices that they face. The displacement of small enterprises should (ceteris paribus) raise welfare in either case, but the policies appropriate to correct the low productivity vary according to the source of the weakness (see chapter 8).

Several variables reflect the input or output of inventive activities in Japan or the magnitude of international transfers of technology. Our measure of an industry's patent holdings, *PAT*, is positively related to productivity growth and usually significant. The input measures of productivity-raising activities, *RDS* and *RDE*, perform curiously, their signs being perverse and their regression coefficients usually significant, as in equation (4). This may be due to their collinearity with other variables in the model. Consider the following portion of the matrix of zero-order correlation coefficients (variables weighted by each industry's value added in 1967):

	RDS	*RDE*	*PAT*	*TIM*
JC4	0.420	0.248	0.416	0.206
RDS	...	0.733	0.655	0.389
RDE	...	...	0.499	0.285
PAT	...	...	...	0.212

In Japan as elsewhere, the industries in which firms find innovative outlays profitable are also industries in which concentration is high. And the correlations connecting *RDS*, *RDE*, and *PAT* are high enough that we cannot expect to disentangle the influence of one from that of the others. Still, the zero-order correlations between the dependent variable and these measures of inventive activity are not statistically significant, and indeed are negative in the case of *RDE* (-0.017) and *RDS* (-0.117). We cannot rule out the possibility that research outlays in Japan make an insignificant contribution to productivity growth after we allow for industries' access to foreign technology and other influences represented in the model. The normal performance of *PAT* could then be explained by inclusion of licensed foreign patents as well as the fruits of domestic invention in that variable. Still, research and productivity growth *are* positively related among U.S. industries, and U.S. evidence shows that productivity gains from research often turn up primarily in an industry other than the one that does the research (for example, through embodiment in capital goods). Therefore we believe that the performance of the variables *RDE* and *RDS* would have little value for policy decisions.

Our measure of technology imports, *TIM,* is insignificant throughout, probably because of defective measurement rather than the absence of an economic effect, for case studies amply demonstrate its importance. Possibly it is due, however, to MITI's success in keeping the rents from technology transfer out of foreign hands.

Seller concentration is generally not a significant influence on productivity growth in Japan, according to these data. With the discredited variable *JP67* included, the coefficients of *JC4* and *JC58* are always negative and sometimes significant. With *JP67* removed, they and *JC8* are simply insignificant with no regular pattern of signs. The coefficients of our two measures of marginal concentration, *JC58* and *JC820*, are always negative and exceed their standard errors; they are sometimes significant. Thus there is limited support for the hypothesis that a relatively large number of medium-sized firms provides a useful spur to all sellers in an industry to raise productivity.

The change in an industry's capital intensity, *JKL*, was included to avoid a distortion due to measuring productivity growth in terms of labor productivity. The variable is usually correctly signed but not significant. The variable *USKL*, included as a rough test of the role of embodied technical change, performs perversely. The insignificance of *JKL* may be due to its collinearity with the variables measuring changes in average plant size, *PSZ* (0.511) and *PLG* (0.367). This correlation is no surprise, because large plants are generally more capital-intensive than small ones. Hence an industry in which average plant size is increasing will become more capital-intensive overall even if no capital-deepening occurs in plants of a given size class. Note that we cannot identify the direction of causality: increased investment might promote the consolidation or replacement of small plants, or expanding the proportional role of large plants could raise the industry's average capital intensity. If the dependent variable is regressed on *JKL* alone, we get:

$$JPROD = 0.095 + 0.173\ JKL.$$
$$(10.6)\qquad (3.46)$$
$$\bar{R}^2 = 0.101.$$

The functional forms of the equations in table 7-1 enjoy no rigorous support from the underlying theory, and possible interactions and nonlinearities can be contrived without limit. We sought to screen the more likely of these possibilities by subdividing the sample of ninety-nine industries into halves with high and low values of several variables—capital intensity in 1967, the growth of capital intensity 1958–67 (*JKL*), the level of value added per worker in 1967, and the growth of value added per worker 1958–67 (*JPROD*, the dependent variable in table 7-1). On the test of goodness of fit these bifurcations were generally helpful, with the value of $\bar{R}^2$ corrected for degrees of freedom in the two halves higher than in the corresponding pooled equation.

The dubious assumption, followed in table 7-1, that all industries operate off the same Cobb-Douglas production function can be tested by splitting the sample into more and less capital-intensive industries. Indeed, the coefficients of *JKL* tend to differ substantially, being much higher for the industries with high capital intensity (this difference, like most others discussed here, is robust but not statistically significant). The coefficient of *JKL* is also affected by other bifurcations, being much lower (negative, in fact) for industries in which capital intensity is growing fast. It is much higher and more significant in industries with faster-growing productivity.

In table 7-1 top-end concentration (*JC4*) was insignificant, but high marginal concentration tended to be hostile to productivity growth. In industries where the growth of value added or capital per worker is slow, the influence of concentration on that rate tends to be negative and to approach significance. For the industries with fast-growing capital or value-added per worker, *JC4*'s influence is positive and approaches statistical significance. This pattern is quite a plausible one: slow-growing and settled oligopolies could easily behave in ways hostile to progressiveness, whereas oligopolistic rivalry in research under less settled conditions could on balance play a constructive role. The same difference in the behavior of the marginal concentration ratio, *JC58,* appears in equations for industries with slow-growing and fast-growing capital intensity, but not for those exhibiting slow-growing and fast-growing value added per worker.

Subdividing the sample of industries strongly affects the coefficients of our measures of change in average plant size, especially *PLG*. Its coefficient is always significant, but much larger and more significant in the less capital-intensive half of the sample and the half with slower growth of productivity or capital intensity. That is, enlargement of plant scale provides a larger and more reliable source of productivity gains in those industries where productivity gains from all sources together are relatively limited.

The stock of patents, a measure of an industry's productivity-raising intangible capital, is a significant determinant of productivity growth only in industries with high levels of productivity and capital intensity, and those in which capital per worker and productivity are growing fast. This pattern, which cannot be explained by multicollinearity, suggests in a general way that the domestic stock of intangible capital is important in those industries with the potential for quite rapid growth; in those with slow potential growth rates, intangible capital has no systematically important role to play. The perverse relation of productivity growth to technology-input measures *RDS* and *RDE* remains for all subdivisions of the sample. We cannot rule out the possibility that research and development activity in Japan serves mainly to realize the possibilities for productivity growth inherent in new discoveries made abroad, and that it therefore reveals no independent influence once we allow for the expansion of worldwide production possibilities via *USPROD*.

Conclusions

An economy's progressiveness depends on its own research and development activities, its ingestion of new developments from abroad, and the internal diffusion of innovations to all who can use them productively. Japan's overall performance appears generally good in all respects and has clearly been superior in the second dimension. Her economy is well suited to import technology from abroad, and her large domestic R&D effort is consistent with heavy reliance on foreign sources.

Earlier studies have shown that rates of R&D spending in Japanese industries behave rather similarly to those in the United States. Among the larger firms that carry on some research the rate of expenditure (percentage of sales) does not generally increase with firm size, although it does in the more highly innovative industries. It is unrelated to concentration once we control for firm size. The diffusion of technology to smaller enterprises operates through various channels, with capital-goods makers and general trade information especially important; the subcontracting relation does not appear particularly vital for disseminating new techniques.

Our own statistical study of the determinants of productivity growth seeks to separate the influence of domestic and foreign sources of new knowledge. The technology improvement potentially available to each Japanese industry, with the rate of productivity growth in the United States used as a proxy, is statistically significant although not highly so. A very strong influence on productivity is a measure of changes in the average size of establishment that heavily reflects changes in the numbers of relatively small plants. This variable is much more significant than a measure of change in size of the larger establishments. We conclude that shifts in capacity away from very small plants are in the aggregate more important than promotion of very large plants—a favored policy of the Japanese government—for raising productivity. Productivity growth is unrelated to seller concentration. We found no relation to the flow of technology imports, probably because the flow is poorly measured. Measures of R&D activity in Japanese industries surprisingly proved unrelated or negatively related to productivity growth. Patents held by Japanese industries—of both domestic and foreign origin—are positively related. We conclude that the evidence does not support a *general* expansion of research in Japan for the purpose of increasing productivity growth. Japan, like most countries, will depend for the bulk of its productivity gains on flows of new technology from abroad.

CHAPTER EIGHT

Government Policy toward Industry

THE CLOSE RELATIONS between business decisionmakers and government officials in Japan have stirred both fear and envy in Western observers. Indeed, some overheated accounts imply that the performance of the Japanese economy depends not on market structure and competitive forces, but on these informal government-business relations. The statistical analyses of this study, however, provide strong evidence of the power of the economic environment to determine market performance. Whether via the general environmental forces of the competitive marketplace or the special structural forces found in Japan, market structure and rivalrous market behavior do influence performance—if not in quite the same way as in Western economies.

Nonetheless, public policy toward industrial structure and behavior has been diverse and continuously active. Have these policies played an important part in Japan's "economic miracle"? Or has it occurred in spite of them?

Antimonopoly Legislation

Antimonopoly legislation in Japan is a legacy of the occupation following World War II.[1] The chief statute, the Antimonopoly Law, was imposed on the country in 1947 by the Supreme Commander for the Allied Powers.

1. For detailed analyses of antimonopoly legislation, see Eleanor M. Hadley, *Antitrust in Japan* (Princeton University Press, 1970), especially chaps. 15 and 16; Kōzō Yamamura, *Economic Policy in Postwar Japan: Growth versus Economic Democracy* (University of California Press, 1967); Hiroshi Iyori, *Antimonopoly Legislation in*

Based largely on U.S. legislation, it employed novel terms such as "public interest," "substantial," and "competition" that conveyed no clear meaning to the Japanese public who would have to comply with it. The quasi-judicial Fair Trade Commission of Japan (FTCJ), created to enforce the act, was likewise without precedent. Furthermore, no self-recognized interest group in Japan stood ready to benefit from the law and embrace it.

Private monopolization is prohibited absolutely. It is defined as individual or collective actions to exclude or control the activities of others and thereby to cause a substantial restraint of trade contrary to the public interest. Thus, it is illegal to *seek* a monopoly or bolster a monopoly position, but not to *have* a monopoly—a point long ambiguous in the Sherman Antitrust Act of the United States.

Since any substantial restraint of competition is held to contravene the public interest, the public-interest qualification does not effectively limit the force of the prohibition. No precise structural definition has emerged for "substantial restraint of competition," which depends on the facts of the individual case.

In parallel with this emphasis on conduct, the regulation of mergers and other combinations appears fairly strict. The formation of a holding company is prohibited—a reflection of its role in cementing the old zaibatsu structures. Also, financial institutions cannot hold more than 10 percent of the total outstanding shares of the issuing company without special permission from the Fair Trade Commission. Any merger or acquisition must be reported to the commission thirty days in advance, and is prohibited where the effect may be substantially to restrain competition in any particular field of trade, or where unfair business practices have been employed. Controlling acquisitions of stock are banned on the same bases, and all companies of appreciable size must file reports on their acquisitions of shares of other companies. Interlocking directorates, which were prohibited between competing companies until 1953, must be reported.

Unreasonable restraints of trade are prohibited, meaning those that substantially restrain competition in any particular field of trade by fixing or raising prices, limiting production, technology, or facilities, or dividing the market. The effect of this provision is to prohibit cartels and related horizontal agreements. To establish a violation it is necessary to show not just uniform conduct but also "a liaison of wills." Certain practices of trade

---

Japan (Federal Legal Publications, 1969); Yoshio Kanazawa, "The Regulation of Corporate Enterprise: The Law of Unfair Competition and the Control of Monopoly Power," in Arthur T. von Mehren, ed., *Law in Japan* (Harvard University Press, 1963); and Michiko Ariga and Luvern V. Rieke, "The Antimonopoly Law of Japan and Its Enforcement," *Washington Law Review,* vol. 39 (August 1964), pp. 437–78.

associations are proscribed: substantially restricting competition, limiting entry, unduly restricting members' activities, or promoting unfair business practices. International contracts and agreements are prohibited where they constitute unreasonable restraints of trade or unfair business practices, and all international agreements of Japanese entrepreneurs (including technology licenses) must be reported to the FTCJ.

The act prohibits six categories of unfair business practices. As elaborated in a 1953 notification by the Fair Trade Commission, they include: boycotts and refusals to deal; discrimination in prices, terms, or access to concerted activities; unreasonably high or low prices intended to injure a competitor or coercive inducement of customers; exclusive dealing; vertical restrictive agreements including tying and (generally) resale price maintenance; and "abuse of a dominant bargaining position" or interference with the business activities of competitors. In addition the commission can designate business practices as unfair within particular industries, and specific designations have been made in thirteen industries.

Certain exemptions are built into the Antimonopoly Law, and many others have been enacted independently. There are general exemptions for natural monopolies (public utilities), regulated industries, and rights in intangible industrial property. Resale price agreements with individual dealers are exempted for copyrighted works, and the FTCJ may exempt them for other products; since 1974, agreements "within a certain price range" have been authorized on low-priced cosmetics and certain specified drugs.[2] Two types of cartels are permitted. Depression cartels can be approved in advance by the FTCJ, under certain conditions, if supply exceeds demand, prices fall below average costs, and a number of producers are likely to go out of business; approval is usually for no more than one year, and membership is voluntary. Rationalization cartels likewise can be formed with prior approval to carry out concerted efforts to exchange or restrict technology, standardize goods produced, work out specializations by product line, or make common use of transportation or storage facilities.

The Fair Trade Commission is empowered to issue cease and desist orders or to impose any other measure necessary to eliminate a violation that has been found. It can order the termination of illegal stockholdings, sue for nullification of illegal mergers, and so forth. It can make recommendations advising correction of an alleged violation as an alternative to the formal issuance of a complaint followed by a hearing and decision. Decisions can be appealed to the Tokyo High Court, which has sustained the commission in

2. Until 1974 they were permitted on cosmetics, toothpaste, soap and detergents, alcohol, and drugs, and until 1966 also on hair dye, caramel, cameras, and shirts. The commission now restricts "sales by unreasonably cheap prices in retailing."

most cases. The commission has depended heavily on its less formal means of enforcement. Between 1947 and 1971 it issued 292 recommendations and reached 149 decisions after formal hearings—and 99 of those were consent decisions (analogous to consent decrees).[3]

The Fair Trade Commission's enforcement has gone through several phases and has concentrated on certain provisions of the act. Antimonopoly policy was largely inoperative until 1949 while the economy remained under comprehensive economic controls, but between 1949 and 1951 a series of cases was brought dealing with trade associations (under a stronger separate law then in force) and with exclusive dealing arrangements built into international technology agreements. During the next decade (1952–62) pressures were continually applied to weaken or eliminate features of the Antimonopoly Law. Enforcement was correspondingly reticent and passive, with the FTCJ bringing only a few cases against cartels. Support for the legislation and determined efforts to prevent its being weakened, especially during 1958–62, ultimately gave heart to the commission. Price-fixing cartels, especially in consumer goods, came under extensive attack in the 1960s and cases dealing with unfair business practices became more numerous.[4]

Cartel and trade-association cases involving price-fixing and related activities have accounted for a dominant share (84 percent) of the violations of the Antimonopoly Law, as table 8-1 shows. This may be due to the ease of investigating cartels based on trade associations. The only other large category of cases brought is on unfair business practices, which have dealt mainly with boycotts and refusals to deal—means of maintaining control over distribution channels. In the sensitive areas of price discrimination, merger, and monopolization, the FTCJ has made little headway in enforcing the law, although some mergers have been discouraged by informal objections. Critical tests of the merger provisions came in 1968 when plans were announced for mergers of the three largest paper companies, who controlled 60 percent of newsprint production, and the two largest steel makers, who shared 35.6 percent of crude steel production. Both mergers exceeded the 30-percent market share that the FTCJ had established as a criterion for disapproving mergers. The steel merger, backed by the Ministry of International Trade and Industry, went to a formal hearing and was finally approved by the FTCJ under pressure. The paper merger was dropped, however, in anticipation of rejection by the FTCJ.[5]

3. Iyori, *Antimonopoly Legislation*, p. 126; and Japan, Fair Trade Commission, *Annual Report, 1971*, p. 223.

4. Iyori, *Antimonopoly Legislation*, pp. 22–23, 26, and 124–31.

5. Ibid., pp. 31–32, 58, 67–68, 72–73, and 125; Eugene J. Kaplan, *Japan—The Government-Business Relationship: A Guide for the American Businessman*, U.S. Department of Commerce, Bureau of International Commerce (1972), pp. 149–51. Of the

Table 8-1. *Violations of Antimonopoly Law Found by Fair Trade Commission of Japan, by Type of Offense, 1947–73*

Offense	Number of violations in							Total violations, 1947–73
	1967	1968	1969	1970	1971	1972	1973	
Price-fixing agreements	11	27	20	43	32	16	64	...
Other collusive agreements[a]	0	0	3	1	4	9	2	511[b]
Unfair trade practices	7	7	2	0	1	3	0	64
Resale price maintenance	2	4	0	0	0	2	0	...
Tying arrangements	0	0	0	0	1	0	0	...
Refusal to deal	0	3	2	0	0	1	0	...
Other	5	0	0	0	0	0	0	...
Mergers and intercorporate shareholding	0	0	2	0	0	...	...	...
Other	0	0	0	1	0	2[c]	0	33[c]
Total	18	34	27	45	37	30	66	608

Sources: Japan, Fair Trade Commission, *Annual Report, 1969*, pp. 156–57; *1970*, pp. 211–12; *1971*, pp. 222–23; *1974*, p. 28; and Fair Trade Commission, *Dokusen kinshi seisaku 20 nenshi* [History of Twenty Years of Antimonopoly Policy] (1972), pp. 322–33.
a. Distribution-channel agreements and quantity restrictions.
b. Price-fixing agreements and other collusive agreements.
c. Mergers and intercorporate shareholding and other offenses.

Even the offenses subject to active enforcement may not be effectively deterred. This possibility is suggested by the number of repeated offenses among violations taking the form of price-fixing and other collusive agreements (the first two lines of table 8-1). In four recent years the number (and percentage) of repetitions were: 1970, 16 (36.4 percent); 1971, 16 (44.4 percent); 1972, 8 (32.0 percent); and 1973, 32 (48.5 percent).[6]

The first significant case concerning monopolization was decided in 1972 against Toyō Seikan (Toyō Can Manufacturing Company) for controlling competitors in the metal container industry.[7] The FTCJ found that the firm, occupying 56 percent of its market, had controlled the activities of four competing companies (ranking third, fourth, fifth, and eighth in the industry) through shareholding and interlocking directorates. The company had also refused to deal with packers who sought to manufacture their own cans. The commission enjoined the refusals to deal, forbade a pending merger between Toyō and the third-ranking company (Hokkai), prohibited restrictive arrangements limiting Hokkai's freedom of action, and compelled Toyō to reduce its shareholdings in Hokkai to 5 percent of the total shares issued. Because the Toyō Seikan decision is unique, one cannot judge its implications for future enforcement.

The FTCJ's approvals of cartels under the provisions for depression

seven large companies dissolved horizontally by the deconcentration measures of the postwar occupation, four have been reassembled through mergers—Yukijirushi Dairy in 1958, Teikoku Textile in 1959, Mitsubishi Heavy Industries in 1964, and Shin Nihon Steel in 1970.

6. Japan, Fair Trade Commission, *Wagakuni ni okeru kasenka no keikō* [Trend toward Higher Concentration of Economic Power in Japan] (1974).

7. FTCJ decision of Sept. 18, 1972, 1972(R) no. 11.

cartels have been quite generous at times. Although its approvals in the 1972 economic slowdown were less numerous than in earlier periods, they covered relatively large segments of industry. Depression cartels have sometimes been sought by industries having trouble working out clandestine arrangements, and it seems likely that legally authorized cartels have sometimes continued to collude secretly after their expiration dates. Sometimes the FTCJ has approved depression cartels for tactical reasons, preferring formal but temporary cartel arrangements to the alternative of administrative output curtailments managed by MITI.[8] Indeed, the general flavor of antimonopoly enforcement is strongly influenced by the relations between the FTCJ and MITI and other ministries.

The events of 1973 and 1974 brought both an upswing of enforcement and a proposed major revision of the Antimonopoly Law. In 1973 many cases surfaced of price-fixing agreements among large enterprises in large-scale industries, in contrast to previous emphasis on exposures of collusion in smaller scale industries with relatively numerous sellers. In a notable example, the Petroleum Federation was accused of "unabashed collusion of the oil refiners and distributors to restrict supply and raise prices."[9] In early 1974 the cartel was enjoined by the FTCJ but defended by the parties on the ground that they acted under the administrative guidance of MITI, and therefore the alleged violation was not a criminal act. The FTCJ persisted, bringing indictments before the Tokyo High Court, and in an unprecedented move the High Prosecutor's Office decided to proceed with the case.

In September 1974 the Fair Trade Commission proposed extensive revisions of the Antimonopoly Law that would greatly extend the law's scope and increase the commission's enforcement power. Companies with "extremely" high market shares could be divided into smaller units, and cost data on near-monopoly products could be published. Prices charged by cartels could be rolled back and unfair profits surcharged. Fines would be raised, and shareholding by both banks and large nonfinancial companies limited. The proposal became embroiled in heavy controversy, and in 1975 failed to secure passage.

Exemptions from Antimonopoly Law

Since its passage in 1947 the Antimonopoly Law has been under recurrent attack. Opponents have campaigned to repeal important sections outright or create blanket exemptions for anticompetitive practices. But industry

8. Iyori, *Antimonopoly Legislation*, p. 30.
9. "Administrative Guidance Questioned," *Oriental Economist,* vol. 42 (September 1974), pp. 6–10 (quotation p. 6).

groups have also sought escape through specific statutory exemptions, or through administrative intervention by the Ministry of International Trade and Industry or other competent ministries. During the early 1950s certain sections of the law were repealed and some economy-wide loopholes appeared. Despite the incursions, the law survived with only modest excisions and the added provision for depression and rationalization cartels. Circumvention of the law by exemptions through special legislation or administrative action, however, is fairly common.

How important are these officially sanctioned cartels in Japanese industry? In 1963 the Fair Trade Commission, in a survey of manufacturing industries at the six-digit level of disaggregation, found that statutory or administrative cartels governed 336 of 1,748 commodity groups (19.2 percent) in the domestic market, either directly or as an adjunct to an export agreement. Weighted by value of shipments (from the 1960 census), those items accounted for 28 percent of the total value of goods shipped by these groups. But when agreements ancillary to a joint restriction of exports are removed, only 12.0 percent of the commodity groups and 19.7 percent of the value of shipments fall under cartel arrangements. Cartels seem more common in the less concentrated and less differentiated manufacturing sectors: 78.1 percent of the value of shipments in textiles; 64.8 percent in clothing; 50.0 percent in nonferrous metals; 47.0 percent in printing and publishing; 41.2 percent in stone, clay, and glass; 34.5 percent in steel products; and 37.2 percent in food products.[10] Although these cartels surely ran the gamut in degrees of effectiveness (see chapter 3 above), their mere presence in such broad stretches of the manufacturing sector attests to their importance.

The total number of exempted cartels reached its peak level in 1966 (see table 8-2). The total rose from 248 in 1956 to 595 in 1960 and has remained close to 1,000 since 1964. About three-fifths of the cartels are organized in local markets, authorized under legislation designed to help small and medium enterprises. Another tenth have been sheltered under the Act Concerning Proper Operation of Business Requiring Environmental Sanitation (protection for small-scale service industries). About a fifth are in international trade, the export cartels often organized to restrict shipments at the demand of importing countries.[11]

Although the exemption laws are singular by their nature, they follow certain patterns. Iyori classifies the exemptions roughly by purpose, noting that some must be ascribed to political influence pure and simple. His list

10. Figures quoted by Hiroshi Iyori, "Cartel and Concentration Trend in Japan," *Internationales Asienforum*, vol. 4 (1973), p. 423.
11. Iyori, *Antimonopoly Legislation*, pp. 24–25 and 131–34, and "Cartel and Concentration Trend," pp. 420–21.

Table 8-2. *Japanese Cartel Agreements Exempted from Antimonopoly Law by Fair Trade Commission or Competent Ministry, by Exempting Statute, 1964–73*[a]

Statutory basis for exemption	1964	1965	1966	1967	1968	1969	1970	1971	1972	1973
Depression cartels	2	2	16	1	0	0	0	0	9	2
Rationalization cartels	14	14	14	13	13	12	10	13	10	10
Export cartels	201	208	211	206	213	217	214	192	175	180
Import cartels	1	2	3	4	3	4	4	3	2	2
Cartels under Medium and Small Enterprises Organization Act	588	587	652	634	582	522	469	439	604	607
Cartels under Environment Sanitation Act	106	122	123	123	123	123	123	123	123	123
Cartels under Coastal Shipping Association Act	15	14	16	15	22	22	22	21	19	19
Cartels under other statutes	43	50	44	44	47	48	56	53	34	42
Total	970	999	1,079	1,040	1,003	948	898	844	976	985

Source: Japan, Fair Trade Commission, Staff Office, *The Antimonopoly Act of Japan* (1973), p. 27.
a. Number in force in March of each year.

includes exemptions associated with other government regulation, exemptions of trade associations or cooperative arrangements to protect small enterprise, export or import cartels, cartels to combat depression or excessive competition, and rationalization cartels. In many cases the cartel arrangements must be approved by the competent ministry, which is required to give notice to, consult with, or obtain the consent of the FTCJ. The competent ministries may revoke or modify approved cartels if conditions change significantly after approval. Under some laws, especially those bearing on small enterprise, the competent ministers may issue orders restricting the activities of members or nonmembers affecting the cartel's performance.[12] Thus there remains a semblance of public control over producer cartels, but also public complicity in their enforcement.

Industrial Policy and Administrative Control of Competition

Competition policy in Japan has been applied only as a facet—and not a major one—of a broader set of industrial policies. Yet those broader policies have existed not as an integrated whole—logically plotted to achieve coherent long-run objectives—but as a group of ad hoc measures and compromises arising out of political interaction between the business and government sectors.[13]

12. Iyori, *Antimonopoly Legislation*, pp. 104–07.
13. See Kaplan, *Japan—The Government-Business Relationship;* Organisation for Economic Co-operation and Development, *The Industrial Policy of Japan* (Paris: OECD, 1972); Chitoshi Yanaga, *Big Business in Japanese Politics,* Yale Studies in Political Science, no. 22 (Yale University Press, 1968); and William W. Lockwood, "Japan's 'New Capitalism,' " in William W. Lockwood, ed., *The State and Economic Enterprise in Japan: Essays in the Political Economy of Growth* (Princeton University Press, 1965), chap. 10.

Japanese industrial policy represents not the unfolding of a coherent plan but the pushing and hauling of the sometimes dissonant interests of business groups and the government bureaucratic apparatus. Each side has its objectives—the former a straightforward pursuit of self-interest, the latter the achievement of policy objectives that may change over time and wax and wane in importance.

Each sector of the Japanese economy has a cliental relation to a ministry or agency of the government. The ministry, in addition to its various statutory means of dealing with the economic sector, holds a general implied administrative responsibility and authority that goes well beyond what is customary in the United States and other Western countries. While the Ministry of International Trade and Industry (MITI) plays the most prominent role, its operations are not distinctive. "The industrial bureaus of MITI proliferate sectoral targets and plans; they confer, they tinker, they exhort. This is the 'economics by admonition' to a degree inconceivable in Washington or London. Business makes few major decisions without consulting the appropriate governmental authority; the same is true in reverse."[14]

The goals of the Ministry of International Trade and Industry have varied over time in weight and composition, but some have recurred regularly since the ministry's founding in 1949. One has been to promote the movement of resources toward certain favored industries—first to the heavy and chemical industries, then to a group in which Japan seemed to enjoy a comparative advantage in international markets. Another goal has been to promote larger operations in certain industries—larger plants because of an abiding faith in economies of scale, and larger firms in the belief that (as controls on foreign trade and investment were lifted) Japanese firms should be as large as their American competitors in order to compete with them effectively. This goal has led at times to a considerable enthusiasm for mergers and the restriction of new entry into industries of interest to MITI. The ministry has encouraged the importation and dissemination of new technology, promoting industry-wide cooperation in its use. And it has sought to protect Japanese markets from the intrusion of foreign competition through imports or foreign investment.

The means for pursuing these policies have been various. A major sanction until the mid-1960s was MITI's authority over the allocation of foreign exchange for purchasing essential inputs. For example, Sumitomo Steel during the 1965 recession refused to restrict the growth of its capacity in line with guides recommended by MITI, and the ministry retaliated by limit-

14. Lockwood, "Japan's 'New Capitalism,' " p. 503.

ing the firm's access to imported coking coal.[15] Another well-used control is licenses to import foreign technology which can be rationed to restrict entry into various industries and to keep oligopolists from gaining excessive leads over their rivals. This control is now relaxed in all but a few industries. Control over foreign exchange was used to require the purchase of domestically produced computers (a category that did not include IBM's Japanese subsidiary) unless the would-be buyer could convince MITI that only an imported unit would serve his needs.[16]

The ministry offers positive inducements through its influence over access to the generous lending facilities of the public Japan Development Bank. For instance, they were used to promote the computer industry when MITI first developed a high regard for its potential. And its control over access to capital does not stop with special public sources of funds. "The government's support for the project at hand . . . is most helpful in obtaining loans from the commercial banks. Japan's . . . 'city banks' with their numerous branches are closely supervised by the Bank of Japan and the Ministry of Finance."[17] Direct subsidy has not been a major tool of policy, though tax concessions have been heavily relied on to promote the development of new industries. A 1956 enactment, the Extraordinary Measures Law for the Rehabilitation of the Machinery Industry, allowed MITI to channel government lending at favorable terms to target industries for which specific goals of rationalization and modernization had been chosen in advance. This law was used to promote concentration in the auto-parts industry, with some apparent success in standardization and economies of scale during 1956–66. Later efforts to use public funds to encourage mergers among auto producers, however, were unsuccessful.[18] Periodically, MITI has sought legislation to support its efforts to cartelize and rationalize industry, as in the 1962 campaign for a bill to support various forms of promotion and five-year exemptions from the Antimonopoly Law for designated industries. This "Development Bill for Specific Industries," drafted with the automobile industry especially in mind, was successfully opposed in a bitter campaign by the Fair Trade Commission, the socialists, and the automobile companies who saw a clear maximum limit in the amount of government interference that was in their interest.[19]

The Ministry of International Trade and Industry has plied its "administra-

15. Kaplan, *Japan—The Government-Business Relationship*, pp. 146–48; and Lockwood, "Japan's 'New Capitalism,' " pp. 501–03.

16. Kaplan, *Japan—The Government-Business Relationship*, pp. 85–86.

17. Ibid., chap. 4, especially p. 37; see also OECD, *Industrial Policy*, chap. 2.

18. Kaplan, *Japan—The Government-Business Relationship*, pp. 117–21.

19. Ibid., pp. 64–65 and 123.

tive guidance" through trade associations and industry-wide coordinating groups, and now depends mainly on this technique. A prominent concern of these groups is deciding on the rate of expansion of capacity and dividing the increments among competing firms.[20] Harmony does not always come easily. Controls over international transactions have often served as a club when gentle persuasion failed. Dividing up additions to capacity among rival producers is not easy when large-scale plants are involved.[21] The ability of MITI to get its way is limited when its goals clash with the interests of business firms or other government agencies. For example, MITI's desire to consolidate the auto industry around Toyota and Nissan served the interests of those firms and of struggling smaller firms whom they might absorb, but not the stronger medium-sized firms who carried on independently; the alliances made by the latter with U.S. automobile producers hardly served MITI's preferences. Sometimes MITI clashes with other government agencies, as it did in a dispute with Japan Telephone and Telegraph over the use of telephone lines for time-sharing systems.[22]

Conflict with the Fair Trade Commission has, of course, been endemic. But MITI's position as an administrative agency has in general given it the upper hand. The FTCJ has not been able to attack the cartels of large enterprises promoted by MITI, and has found itself periodically battling efforts by the ministry to weaken the Antimonopoly Law or provide new bases for exemption.[23] The FTCJ has suffered chronic weakness in its role as a law-enforcement agency dealing with ministries having general policymaking authority. In contrast to the United Kingdom Monopolies Commission, which has been formally dependent on ministries for enforcement action, the FTCJ has had to operate behind the scene and enjoyed few opportunities to mobilize public opinion in support of its position.

In the 1960s, however, the FTCJ's defensive efforts became somewhat more effective. Indeed, in 1966 in a joint memorandum of understanding MITI agreed to avoid undermining the Antimonopoly Law, securing in return from the FTCJ a pledge of a more permissive attitude toward mergers and forms of joint action. That willingness gained a dubious test three

20. The auto industry association "is the formal link between government and business in such matters as producer rationalization programs, capacity allocations, and export cartels. Its responsibilities are major, particularly in programs such as auto parts, and often offend American standards of antitrust." Ibid., p. 117. Also see William C. Duncan, *U.S.-Japan Automobile Diplomacy: A Study in Economic Confrontation* (Ballinger, 1973), especially chap. 7.

21. Kaplan, *Japan—The Government-Business Relationship*, pp. 144–48.

22. See the case studies in ibid., pp. 77–158.

23. Iyori, *Antimonopoly Legislation*, pp. 25 and 28–32; Yamamura, *Economic Policy*, chap. 5; and Kaplan, *Japan—The Government-Business Relationship*, pp. 64–65.

years later when the FTCJ ultimately faltered in its opposition to the Yawata-Fuji steel merger, strongly supported by MITI.[24]

Only scant evidence is available on the effects of MITI's custodial efforts on economic welfare. There is no doubt that the ministry's policies have engendered some allocative inefficiency by strengthening collusion and some technical inefficiency by distorting incentives for additions to capacity and diverting rivalry into nonprice channels. Furthermore, our statistical evidence from chapter 7 lends support to the doubts expressed by others over the gains flowing from MITI's preoccupation with large-scale plants. On the other hand, there are probable gains that might be substantial. MITI has beaten down substantially the price that Japan pays for technology imports. Some of its efforts at standardization and rationalization have surely lowered real costs. Indeed, in oligopolistic industries with partial collusion it is logically possible that firms become inefficiently diversified, so that an imposed rationalization limiting the items each firm produced could potentially attain scale economies without giving away a significant increase in monopolistic restriction.[25] The favorable and unfavorable possibilities arising from ministerial guidance are strong enough to leave the net evaluation in doubt.

It is important to realize that MITI's policies have not applied across the board to all Japanese industries, or even to all "big business" or "modern sector" industries. Its attention is attracted only by those thought critical to general goals of economic growth or external balance and those raising specific social or economic problems. The scope and intensity of its anticompetitive policies may change—for example, the ministry currently is preoccupied with problems of pollution and the quality of the environment.

Furthermore, not all significant industrial policies lie in MITI's hands. The Ministry of Finance and other ministries of course have regulatory power over economic sectors under their general charge. One area in which MITI has no hand is policy toward small business. It is the responsibility of the Small and Medium Enterprise Agency, formerly lodged in MITI but now cut loose as a separate ministry. Coherent policies toward the small-enterprise sector were introduced around 1953 as the prosperity of the Korean War period faded. The next four years brought legislation authorizing cartel organization and providing certain loans and tax reductions to finance modernization and some forms of export promotion. Over the 1960s new aids were added without the old ones being taken away, so that small businesses now operate under the following principal types of measures:

24. Kaplan, *Japan—The Government-Business Relationship,* pp. 149–51.
25. This possibility is stressed by F. M. Scherer and others, *The Economics of Multi-Plant Operation* (Harvard University Press, 1975), pp. 295–326.

1. Financing assistance is offered through low rates of interest on long-term loans, which are passed through various public financial intermediaries. Modernization loans are provided through prefectural governments. Organizations have been formed to lease equipment and to guarantee loans for small business. Small-business investment companies provide equity capital.

2. Guidance is provided from local public offices on managerial practice and technology. Management training is offered, along with various aids to technical development.

3. Cooperative organizations are authorized, either to reduce "excessive competition" or to handle insurance or other cooperative activities or facilities. The government can order nonmember enterprises to participate in these arrangements.

4. Modernization schemes are promoted via various instruments—advice, loans and tax concessions, and regional planning operations. Also, various inducements to environmental improvement are slanted toward small enterprises.[26]

Depression cartels have been a principal remedy for the problems of small business, although the Agency for Small and Medium Enterprise claims to prefer productivity-raising measures. As of 1964, guidelines on depression cartels were established to make structural rationalization the price of their retention. Possible avenues to rationalization included industry-wide cooperation in modernization to optimize the scales of individual enterprises (while determining capacity for the whole industry), planned approaches to productivity-raising measures at the level of the individual enterprise, and "voluntary structural reform" through mergers (and probably the clandestine continuation of collusive arrangements). After these guidelines were put forth the number of small-enterprise depression cartels was reduced from 116 (in 1967) to 45.

In one test of the value of assistance given to help raise productivity, small industries designated for assistance were followed for several years to compare their progress before and after designation. Their investment rates and capital intensity were stepped up, but there were no detectable effects on the trend of output per worker. Capital availability appeared to be improving somewhat, although perhaps as much due to some shift in the attitudes of large banks as to public efforts. And measures designed to strengthen small-

26. See Japan, Ministry of International Trade and Industry, Small and Medium Enterprise Agency, *Outline of Major Measures for Small and Medium Enterprises in Japan* (1972); Miyohei Shinohara, "A Survey of the Japanese Literature on Small Industry," in Bert F. Hoselitz, ed., *The Role of Small Industry in the Process of Economic Growth* (Humanities Press, 1968), pp. 78–82; and "Overprotection of Small Business," *Oriental Economist*, vol. 42 (July 1974), pp. 6–10.

firm subcontractors in their relations with larger firms have probably helped to raise their independence and stability.[27]

Conclusions

The antimonopoly legislation pressed upon Japan during the occupation following World War II has been enforced by the Fair Trade Commission, an agency created for that purpose. The law restricts monopolizing, horizontal mergers and holding companies, unreasonable restraints on trade, and unfair business practices. Important exemptions are provided, including official cartels to assist depressed industries or promote rationalization and broad exemptions for small business. At times when the law has been under pressure for amendment to legalize broader ranges of cartel arrangements, it has barely been enforced. At other times there has been some enforcement of provisions dealing with price-fixing and unfair trade practices, though not generally against large-scale concentrated industries. Amendments to the Antimonopoly Law proposed to increase the FTCJ's enforcement powers against concentrated industries have not won approval.

In the 1960s legal cartels covered about one-fifth of Japanese manufacturing. Their number has not changed much since then. Competition is also sharply restricted in many important industries by the "administrative guidance" provided by the competent ministries, chiefly the Ministry of International Trade and Industry. Through a clandestine bargaining process, MITI pursues various goals related to market structure and performance: promotion of large scales in Japanese plants and firms, encouragement of the dissemination of new technology and minimization of its cost when purchased abroad, the overall expansion of certain industries, and the protection of Japanese producers from foreign competition and oligopolistic rivalry with one another. These goals are served, directly or obliquely, by MITI's promotion of collusive arrangements among oligopolistic sellers— especially in the installation of new capacity. Clearly, MITI has reduced the cost of new technology and may have speeded its dissemination. Our evidence suggests that its efforts to enlarge plant scales have been overdone, but some gains may have been obtained. Significant costs have been incurred in increased collusion and its consequences—allocative inefficiency, price inflexibility, and diversion of rivalry into nonprice channels.

27. Information supplied by General Coordination Division, Small and Medium Enterprise Agency.

CHAPTER NINE

Reflections and Prospects

DOES INDUSTRIAL market competition work the same way in Japan as in Western industrial countries like the United States? Do Japan's distinctive institutions leave a sharp imprint on the economy's performance? Are there lessons about policymaking or institution-building in Japan to be studied in the United States and other Western nations?

With a few exceptions,[1] empirical research on industrial organization has been concentrated on individual national economies—mostly the United States—and the focus of the research has been on the institutions and policies conspicuous in those economies. Only recently have the statistical methods so useful for examining national data been applied to cross-national data.[2] In this study of Japan's industrial organization we have used research methods devised for the U.S. economy, mindful of the conclusions they have supplied about America's industrial structure and performance. In applying these tools to the Japanese economy we have had to proceed through three stages of analysis and interpretation. First, we have had to decide whether the analytical tools appear to work in a recognizably familiar way when applied to Japan's markets. Second, we have had to determine whether they reveal the influence of Japan's distinctive institutions by showing their net effect on the economic system's operation. Finally, we have considered whether Japan

---

1. For example, Marvin Frankel, *British and American Manufacturing Productivity,* University of Illinois, Bureau of Economic and Business Research Bulletin no. 81 (1957).

2. See, for example, Frederic L. Pryor, *Property and Industrial Organization in Communist and Capitalist Nations* (Indiana University Press, 1973); F. M. Scherer and others, *The Economics of Multi-Plant Operation* (Harvard University Press, 1975); J. Khalilzadeh-Shirazi, "Market Structure and Allocative Efficiency: A Comparative Analysis of U.K. and U.S. Manufacturing," *Economic Inquiry* (forthcoming); and William James Adams, "Corporate Power and Profitability in the North Atlantic Community" (doctoral dissertation, Harvard University, 1973).

offers lessons for other countries to emulate—or avoid—in the institutions she has built or the policies she has chosen.

The framework of analysis that we have used, which serves to explain industrial structures and their effects in other industrial countries, does illuminate the Japanese economy as well. Concentrated industries do earn excess profits. High rates of outlay on advertising do sustain market power. Concentration in Japanese manufacturing industries differs little in average level from that in U.S. industries and varies from market to market in response to similar forces. But our analysis also reveals the effect of Japanese institutions and conditions that diverge from Western norms. In periods of extremely rapid growth the conventional behavior patterns of rival sellers disappear, and the market structures of individual industries have little effect on their performance. Rapid growth appears to be responsible for the relatively strong profit positions of nondiversified large companies, which have evidently kept busy exploiting the opportunities available in their base markets. We also found entry barriers into Japanese industries to differ from those in the United States. Commercial barriers are lowered because collaborative financing is available for new ventures, product differentiation is less solidified, and access to the technology held by firms abroad is open to many firms. But barriers have also been elevated in some industries, where governmental actions have aimed at enlarging the sizes of Japanese firms or insuring the construction of large-size plants.

Economic analysis has proved helpful to an understanding of the role of the bank-centered alliances and successors to the zaibatsu organizations in Japanese industry. The potential mutual benefit to members lies not just in these groups spreading risk or using joint monopoly-monopsony power but also in their pricing internal transactions so as to rationalize the price structures prevailing in imperfectly competitive ambient markets. But from the institutional evidence we doubt that the present-day groups are tightly enough coordinated to annex many of these gains. And our statistical analysis fails to reveal any gains at all. Group firms appear if anything less profitable than large independent companies, after we control for differences in the market opportunities that they face, and we detect only a diversion of profits into the financial institutions that rightly enjoy status as the central organs of today's groups.

In our examination of Japan's distinctive institutions we found a great deal of descriptive evidence suggesting that the nation's cultural traits place their stamp on the management of business enterprises. Yet there is little evidence that the form of business organization and the style of management affect the external behavior of Japanese businesses. Neither the incidence of allegedly cumbersome internal decisionmaking processes nor the effects of heavy burdens of fixed costs can be isolated in the actions of business firms. One area in which we question the distinctiveness of a Japanese institution, if not the importance of its consequences, is the role of small enterprises. Our comparison of Japan with other countries shows that the prominence of small enterprise is not abnormal considering the country's size, its income level, and the speed of its recent growth. Nonetheless, the small-business sector's size and its choice of production techniques clearly reflect the factor-price distortions prevailing in the Japanese economy—and its fate depends on the changes taking place in those distortions. We found that the prominence of these small enterprises in the various manufacturing industries was an important factor in explaining differences in the industries' productivity growth.

Japanese industrial policy appears in some instances to have served the nation's economic interests, in others to have hindered development. Japan's antimonopoly policy has been a hobbled and limited copy of that long used in the United States. Its enforcement has fallen far short of the U.S. model—itself hardly an example of perfect adherence. Its failures have placed significant costs on the Japanese economy in the form of allocative inefficiency and diversion of rivalry into costly nonprice forms. We cannot detect any compensating gains. The obvious industrial success stories rest on new-product ventures not dependent on collusion for either encouragement or protection, or on the penetration of world markets ultimately due to advantages in the real costs of Japanese production. Policy toward small enterprise has been a combination of many measures. Those affecting the manufacturing sector have mostly been sensible in their conception, but we have not tried to evaluate their net effects. Policies toward the distributive sector have been protective and inappropriate until recently. Industrial policy aimed at encouraging the development of large firms has been more opportunistic in practice than its public image would suggest. It may in some instances have speeded the development of large-scale and efficient ventures by reducing the uncertainties surrounding them and helping them to acquire the necessary finance. And it has reduced the rents paid for foreign technology. But we find no evidence that the shift of production toward large-scale units has been a key to industries' success in productivity growth. We conclude that not much of Japan's industrial policy will transplant readily and effectively to other countries.

Our analysis provides some evidence on industrial conditions in a period marked by moderation of Japan's rate of economic growth. As her industrial structure matures, the small-enterprise sectors in many industries will grow smaller and large enterprises will insulate themselves and their oligopolistic rivals with more substantial barriers to new competition. Some consequences of these trends will be adverse for the behavior and performance of Japanese industry. The high cost-fixity of large enterprises makes their profits particularly vulnerable to shrinkage during a period when demand growth is slowing down. That shrinkage will inflate firms' interest in collusive arrangements, and perhaps the assistance supplied by the government in maintaining them. We have argued that Japanese industries are prone to collusive arrangements but also rich in structural incentives for the conspirators to cheat. The net outcome for the gap between actual and ideal industrial output is thus hard to predict, but we do expect increased distortions from sporadic price discrimination, reciprocity, and the diversion of rivalry into uncontrolled nonprice forms. Another effect of these pressures may be to render firms' costs variable with output. Already there is evidence that "permanent employment" gives way when a large enterprise is doing badly.

The maturing of Japan's industrial establishment seems likely to augment barriers to the entry of new firms, which generally have been lower than those in the United States. Product differentiation seems to be solidifying, and the emphasis in Japan on nationwide modes of sales promotion indicates that economies of scale in differentiation will increasingly put small firms at a disadvantage. Changes in the distributive sector, although complex in their overall effects, will assist the larger firms in some industries in differentiating their products. The elimination of labor-cost differentials favoring smaller firms (especially if not accompanied by the removal of capital-market distortions) increases the pecuniary diseconomies of small scale within industries just as it shifts economic activity toward industries whose conditions favor large firm sizes. Fortunately the groups organized around the principal banks and trading companies remain potent bases for generating new entrants into markets where absolute-cost barriers would otherwise be high.

The effect of retarded growth on market conduct and the apparent rise in entry barriers both contribute to and compound the effects of the increasing seller concentration in Japan's manufacturing industries. We have found little evidence to suggest that increased concentration among the largest few firms has significant favorable effects on market performance, and much evidence of unfavorable effects. Hence we expect some deterioration in the average level of market performance as the combined outcome of these forces.

There has been some small trend toward increased enforcement of antimonopoly legislation in the last few years, but the victories have been sporadic at best and not concentrated in the industries whose structures are most involved in the adverse changes. The legislative changes unsuccessfully promoted in 1974 by the Fair Trade Commission would, in their broader outlines, have provided the basis for a more effective policy.

Sources of Statistical Data

THIS APPENDIX sets forth the sources used in the statistical analyses of the preceding chapters and provides further details on the construction of some variables. Four bodies of data were used, two of them for tests reported in more than one chapter.

Seller Concentration (Chapter 2) and Productivity Growth (Chapter 7)

Starting from Japan's census of manufactures, we developed a sample of 99 manufacturing industries by including all that are comparably defined in the Japanese and U.S. standard industrial classification manuals. Fortunately the Japanese classification follows the American one closely except in providing separate classes for indigenous products, and neither country changed its classification system between 1958 and 1967, the outer limits for our data. The sample gives some representation to all two-digit industries and does not have any obvious bias in its industrial coverage. Most of the U.S. industries are from single three-digit categories in the U.S. classification system; some are single four-digit industries or combinations of four-digit industries. All the Japanese industries are three-digit in the Japanese classification or (in a few cases) combinations of three-digit industries.

The data on seller concentration used in chapter 2 are available for both countries in 1963 for industries as defined in the standard industrial classifications. For Japan we used Japan, Ministry of International Trade and Industry, *Seisan shūchūdo chōsa hōkoku, 1963* [Report of Survey of Concentration Ratios of Production, 1963] (1966). The U.S. data are found in U.S., Bureau of the Census, *Census of Manufactures, 1963* (1966), vol. 1, chap. 11, table 2.

Other data were taken directly from the two countries' census reports. To compute the annual average growth of value added per worker in Japan (*JPROD*) we first deducted data for the smallest size-class of establishments employing less than ten workers. Data on productivity in these establishments are quite inaccurate for Japan, and in both countries they often carry out activities quite different from larger firms in the same industry. No attempt was made to adjust figures on the growth of productivity for price changes occurring during the 1958–67 period; the consequences of that omission are discussed in the text. The

Japanese data are taken from Japan, Ministry of International Trade and Industry, *Census of Manufactures, 1958*, pt. 1-3, and the *Census of Manufactures, 1967*, pt. 3-1. The U.S. data come from U.S., Bureau of the Census, *Census of Manufactures, 1958*, vol. 1, chap. 1, table 3, and *Census of Manufactures, 1967*, vol. 1, chap. 1, table 3.

Other variables taken from these same sources were *JKL* and *USKL*, measures of changes in capital per worker in the two countries; *PSZ* and *PLG*, measures of changes in the size of establishments in Japan; and *JP67*, value added per worker in Japanese industry in 1967. They also supplied 1958 values for *JCAP*, *AVSIZE*, and *LGSIZE*, and total value added by the Japanese industry in 1967 (*JVA*), all used in chapter 2.

The variables measuring research and development in Japan and transfers of technology come from sources available only on a more aggregated classification of industries. We can assign each of the 99 industries unambiguously to one of these more aggregated industries, but we had to assume that measures for an aggregated industry pertained equally to each of the 99 included within it. Data on *PAT*, *RDS*, and *RDE* (patents held, research and development expenditures, and research and development staff for fiscal 1968) were taken from Japan, Industrial Science and Technology Agency, *Minkan kenkyū kaihatsu jittai chōsa hōkoku, 1970's* [Survey Report of Research and Development, 1970's] (1970). This survey covers only 582 large companies with more than ¥500 million of paid-in capital. Thus the variable *PAT* indicates the average number of patents held by those firms (including patents of foreign origin), and *RDS* and *RDE* represent their respective rates of research and development expenditure as a percentage of sales and research and development staff as a percentage of total employment. These data are available for only 27 broadly defined industries, so we had to assume that the value for each was appropriate for each of the more finely defined 99 industries included within it. This practice clearly leads to important errors of measurement, although in the 27-industry classification the industries that are grouped together should be similar in their research intensity.

As a substitute for *RDS* we computed an average rate of research and development expenditure as a percentage of sales over the years 1959–67 from Japan, Office of the Prime Minister, Bureau of Statistics, *Kagaku gijutsu kenkyū chōsa hōkokusho* [Report on the Survey of Science, Research and Development in Japan] (1969). The two measures are highly correlated, and it turned out to make no difference for the conclusions which we use.

Data for *TIM*, the number of technology imports, were taken from Patent Agency of Japan, *Tokkyo chō nenpō* [Annual Report of the Patent Agency] (December 1972), pp. 222–25. Being unable to secure data by industry on payments made for technology licenses, we used the annual number of imports classified by twenty-six rather aggregated sectors. Data on these imports are divided into Class A and Class B technology imports, the period of the contract or of the payment being one year or more for the former and less than one year for the latter. The two classes are controlled under different laws. The number of Class B imports by industry is available only on a highly aggregated basis. Because the two classes differ in importance as well as in statistical aggregation, we needed some scheme to weight them. We used average payments made per technology import of each class over 1958–67 as weights, and also assumed that the Class B imports are spread among subindustries in the same way as the (more important) Class A imports. The weighting process converted the data on number of technology imports into an implicit estimate of the value of each industry's technology payments, and that was expressed as a percentage of value added by the industry in order to secure some indication of proportional importance.

Group Affiliation and Profit Rates (Chapter 4); Administrative Costs (Chapter 6)

We selected a sample of 243 large companies (out of about 500 listed in the "first class" stock market) that could be assigned to manufacturing industries encompassing their principal activities and whose financial reports have been published every half-year. Each was in operation continuously over the years 1961–70, made no major change in financial reporting methods, and could be classified as to affiliation with one of the zaibatsu successors or principal bank groups. The asset size distribution of these companies is shown in chapter 2.

The financial reports of these companies provided the source for the firm-specific variables used in the analysis, supplemented by Mitsubishi Sōgō Kenkyūjo, *Kigyō keiei no bunseki* [Survey of Corporate Management] (annual), and Keizai Chōsa Kyōkai, *Keiretsu no kenkyū, 1970s* [Survey of Affiliation, 1970s] (1972). Variables taken directly from or calculated from these sources included *PE, PA, VE, VS, TA, FI, AD, AM, GR, DP*, and the dummies designating group affiliation. Data were also collected on sales-promotion expenses other than advertising for a more comprehensive measure of selling outlays as a percentage of sales, but its performance was inferior and it is not reported in the text. *PE* is negative for 11 firms, so *VE* cannot be calculated; 232 observations are used in equations containing *VE*.

With each firm classified to its principal industry in the standard industrial classification, variables for that industry could also be introduced into the data set. Four-firm concentration ratios in 1963 were taken from the Ministry of International Trade and Industry's *Seisan shūchūdo chōsa hōkoku*, except for four industries taken from Japan, Fair Trade Commission, *Nihon no sangyō shūchū— 1963–1966* [Industrial Concentration in Japan—1963–1966] (1969). *DI*, the specialization ratio of sales in the company's principal industry at the four-digit classification level, was estimated from Nihon Nōritsu Kyōkai, *Kigyō seihin dōkō tōkei, 1970s* [Statistics on Trends of Commodity Production of Enterprises, 1970s] (1972).

Average Profit Rates (Chapter 5)

The data for these 243 firms supplied the basis for the industry-level analysis of allocative efficiency in chapter 5. We selected 35 industries for which the specialization ratio is more than 50 percent. In each industry a weighted average was calculated over values reported by the largest 5 firms in order to secure industry values for profits (*PA* and *PE*), advertising as a percentage of sales, *AD*, and fixed costs as a percentage of total costs, *FC*.

The variable *GD* measures the average annual growth of industry shipments over 1961–70 and is taken from Japan, Ministry of International Trade and Industry, *Kogyō tōkeihyō* [Census of Manufactures] (annual), for the appropriate years. A measure of exports as a percentage of shipments, *XR,* for the same years was developed from Japan, Ministry of Finance, *Bōeki tōkei nenpyō* [Census of International Trade] (annual). Some judgment was necessary in reconciling the industrial classification used for exports with the standard industrial classification used in defining the other variables. We experimented unsuccessfully with a measure of regular employees as a percentage of total employees; it was taken from Japan, Office of the Prime Minister, *Jigyōsho tōkei chōsa hōkoku* [Census of Establishments] (annual), and averaged for 1963 and 1968.

Also unsuccessful (and unreported in detail in the text) were variables designed to measure economies of scale at the plant level. These were constructed identically to variables in U.S. studies cited in the text from data appearing in *Jigyōsho tōkei chōsa hōkoku* for 1963 and 1968 (averaged).

Small-Enterprise Population (Chapter 6)

Data on employers, own-account workers, family workers, and total economically active population for numerous countries are collected by the International Labour Office and appear in its *1972 Year Book of Labour Statistics,* table 2A. The data are based variously on national censuses, sample tabulations of census returns, and labor-force surveys. The year to which the data pertain also varies; an effort was made to concentrate on data for the late 1960s, and the absence of a figure later than 1963 counted as an argument (not always decisive) for excluding a country from the sample. Notes to the tabulated entries for some countries make it clear that their data are noncomparable—for example, when women family workers are excluded. The figures for family workers reported for a few countries are unbelievably low, prompting their exclusion even when notes in the ILO source revealed no specific bias. We wanted to secure a fair representation in the sample of countries less developed than Japan and therefore admitted them under somewhat less strict data requirements. After the winnowing process we were left with the following 34 countries: Egypt, Argentina, Brazil, Canada, Colombia, Chile, Ecuador, Mexico, Peru, United States, Uruguay, Ceylon, Indonesia, Iran, Japan, Korea, Pakistan, Philippines, Thailand, Austria, Belgium, Denmark, Spain, Finland, West Germany, Greece, Italy, Norway, Netherlands, Portugal, Switzerland, Sweden, United Kingdom, Australia.

The two dependent variables defined in the text were constructed as follows: *Y1* by dividing total employers and own-account workers by total economically active population; *Y2* by dividing total employers and own-account workers plus family workers by total economically active population. Both were expressed as percentages. The same ILO table provided data on *size,* the variable defined as total economically active population (in millions).

Data on gross domestic product per capita in purchasers' values, 1969, expressed in thousands of U.S. dollars at going official exchange rates, were taken from United Nations, *Statistical Yearbook, 1972,* table 188. A satisfactory figure was available for every country but Ceylon. The same source (table 183) supplies data on the percentage of gross domestic product originating in agriculture, hunting, fishing, and forestry for 1969 or the nearest available year. No data are available for two countries, Egypt and Switzerland, because the published breakdown of sectors did not conform.

The variable *growth* was computed from a table of index numbers of general industrial production published in United Nations, *Statistical Yearbook, 1972,* table 50. General industrial production is defined to include mining, manufacturing, electricity, gas, and water. For less-developed economies it thus tends to measure the growth rate of the modern sector. For four countries (Chile, Peru, Philippines, and Greece) the index pertains to manufacturing only. The starting year was 1953, the terminal year 1970 whenever possible; later starting years were accepted for four countries, an earlier terminal year for a fifth. The change in the index was expressed as a percentage of its initial value and a corresponding compound annual growth rate calculated and expressed in percent. Satisfactory data were available for 28 of the 34 countries.

Because of missing observations, the degrees of freedom of the equations reported in table 6-1 range between 21 and 24. When the only variables included are *income* and *size,* 31 degrees of freedom are available. In regression equations computed over this enlarged sample the coefficient of *size* is positive and nonsignificant. The negative coefficients (sometimes significant) reported in table 6-1 may therefore reflect the omission of certain less-developed but large countries such as Indonesia and Thailand.

Index

Abegglen, James C., 9n, 13, 14n, 37n, 39n, 40n, 56n, 115, 116n, 117n
Act Concerning Proper Operation of Business Requiring Environmental Sanitation, 147
Adams, Thomas F. M., 54n, 56n
Adams, William James, 96n, 155n
Advertising: effect on administrative costs, 120–21; effect on profits, 76, 77–78, 93–94, 95; firm entry and, 30, 34, 74, 78; product differentiation and, 30–32, 34; by Zaibatsu, 66
Agriculture, 4, 36, 105, 106, 108
Allocative efficiency, 4, 56, 58, 88–89
Antimonopoly Law, 49, 62, 141; enforcement of, 144–46, 158; exemptions from, 143, 146–48, 150, 151; proposed revisions in, 146, 158; provisions of, 142–43
Antitrust policy, 6, 62, 157. See also Antimonopoly Law
Aonuma, Yoshimatsu, 11n
Archer, Stephen H., 108n
Ariga, Michiko, 142n
Automobile industry, 150, 151

Baba, Masao, 18n, 121n
Bain, Joe S., 26n
Ballon, Robert J., 8n, 14n, 44n, 73n
Bank groups, 63, 65, 67, 68–69, 72–73
Banking system, 3, 4, 39, 40, 150
Bank of Japan, 39, 150
Bisson, T. A., 2n, 60n, 83n
Blumenthal, Tuvia, 36n
Broadbridge, Seymour, 102n

Capital: availability of, 37–38; bank loans for, 39, 150; cost of, 4, 34–35, 38, 89; intensity, 23, 25, 111, 138, 139; for new firms, 34–35. See also Equity capital
Cartels: antimonopoly cases involving, 144; depression, 143, 145–146, 147, 153;

development of, 48–49; effect on technical efficiency, 57; legally sanctioned, 52, 143, 145–46, 147; rationalization, 143, 147; regulation of, 49, 142
Caves, Richard E., 7n, 42n, 61n, 75n, 94n
Chung, William K., 124
Cobb-Douglas production function, 132, 139
Comanor, William S., 22n, 30n, 89, 114n
Competition, 49–53, 56, 63, 149–52
Computer industry, 51, 150
Concentration, in industry: capital intensity and, 23, 25; compared with U.S., 18, 19–26; determinants of, 20–21; domestic investment and, 98–99; effect on administrative costs, 120–21; effect on productivity, 138; industry entry barriers and, 90, 91, 158; in largest nonfinancial corporations, 16–18; market size and, 25; plant size and, 21–22; prices and, 97–98; profits and, 74, 76, 88–89, 90, 156; relations between R&D and, 127, 128; technology imports and, 129; trends in, 26–28; wages and, 96, 97. See also Cartels; Mergers
Consumer goods, 33, 116, 125, 177
Corporate business, 10–14, 68–71. See also Concentration, in industry
Costs: administrative, 119–22; capital, 34–35, 38, 89, 95; fixed, 4, 93; wage and salary, 40, 41, 93, 108–09, 113
Culture, effect on economic behavior, 1, 13, 156

Dai-ichi, 63, 67
Dalton, James A., 98n
Denison, Edward F., 124, 125
Development Bill for Specific Industries, 150
Distribution sector, 1, 32–33, 51, 116–19, 157
Downie, Jack, 57n, 119n

165

Dual economy, 4, 107, 108, 111
Duncan, William C., 151n

Economic growth, 1, 5; contribution of knowledge to, 124–25; as incentive for entry of new firms, 37; macro- versus micro-, 35–36, 90; productivity growth and, 118
Economic Planning Agency, 98
Economies of scale: capital intensity and, 23, 111; in distribution sector, 116–17, 158; as industry entry barrier, 94–95; influence on profits, 94–95; in manufacturing sector, 21–22, 23; MITI efforts to insure, 54–55
Education, 9, 10, 13, 14
Efficiency. *See* Allocative efficiency; Technical efficiency
Electrical appliance industry, 50–51
Electrical machinery industry, 8, 127
Employment, permanent, 2, 119; benefits to company from, 14; contribution to fixed costs, 4, 41, 93; effect on management personnel, 12, 13
Entry into industry: capital-cost barrier to, 34–35, 89, 95, 156; effect on concentration in industry, 90, 158; growth rate as determinant of, 37, 91, 157, 158; MITI role in, 55, 91; product differentiation as barrier to, 34, 74, 121; rivalry related to, 52
Equity capital, 78–82
Esposito, Frances F., 92n
Esposito, Louis, 92n
Exports, 36, 42, 92
Extraordinary Measures Law for the Rehabilitation of the Machinery Industry, 150

Faerber, LeRoy G., 108n
Fair Trade Commission of Japan (FTCJ), 20, 26, 29, 33, 70n, 97; approval of cartels by, 145–46, 147, 148; conflict with MITI, 151–52; responsibility for Antimonopoly Law enforcement, 6, 142–44, 158
Family, role in business, 7, 102–03, 106
Foreign exchange, 149, 150
Foreign Investment Law, 91
Frankel, Marvin, 155n
Fringe benefits, 4
FTCJ. *See* Fair Trade Commission of Japan
Fuji bank group, 63, 67, 68n

Gale, Bradley T., 72n, 74, 75
GDP. *See* Gross domestic product
Gilbert, David, 77n

Glazer, Herbert, 8n, 44n
Government: aid to small business, 152–54; guarantee of bank loans by, 39, 150; relations with industry, 1, 6, 8, 53–56; restrictions on competition by, 149–52. *See also* Antimonopoly Law; Fair Trade Commission of Japan (FTCJ); Ministry of International Trade and Industry (MITI)
Gross domestic product (GDP), per capita, 102, 103, 115

Hadley, Eleanor M., 2n, 26n, 39n, 48, 49, 54n, 60n, 62n, 63n, 64n, 65, 67, 68, 70n, 83, 141n
Hall, Marshall, 72n, 75
Hamm, Larry G., 28n, 34n
Hattori, Ichinō, 14n
Henderson, Dan Fenno, 43n, 44n, 52n
Higuchi, Yoshishige, 18n, 20
Hijikata, Bun'ichirō, 128n
Hirose, Yūichi, 11n
Hirschmeier, Johannes, 7n, 9n, 10n, 48n
Horie, Yasuzō, 7n, 9n
Hoselitz, Bert F., 102n, 153n
Huntsman, Blaine, 12n
Hurdle, Gloria J., 78n

Iguchi, Tomio, 17n
Ikeda, Katsuhiko, 77n
Imai, Ken'ichi, 127
Imports: competition with domestic market, 92–93; liberalization of, 42; technology, 34, 44, 124, 125, 137, 150
Income. *See* Gross domestic product, per capita
Industrial organization, 2–3, 6–14
Industry: capital market leverage, 39–40; efficient-scale plants for, 54–55, 57; prevention of excess capacity in, 54–55; product differentiation in, 30–32, 34, 74; tax concessions for, 150; unfair business practices of, 49–52, 54, 142–45, 158. *See also* Concentration, in industry; Corporate business; Entry into industry
Interest rates, 40, 73, 75, 78, 80–81, 82
Investment: domestic, 98–99; foreign, 42–44
Iwasaki, Akira, 98, 99n, 121n
Iwauchi, Ryōichi, 12n, 13n
Iyori, Hiroshi, 49n, 144n, 146n, 147, 148n, 151n

Jacquemin, Alex, 77n
Japan Development Bank, 150
Japan Telephone and Telegraph, 151
Joint selling agencies, 51

Joint-venture enterprises, 43–44
Jones, J. C. H., 92n

Kanazawa, Yoshio, 142n
Kaplan, A. D. H., 18n, 55n
Kaplan, Eugene J., 40n, 144n, 148n, 150n, 151n, 152n
Kawaguchi, Hiroshi, 108n
Keiretsu, 67
Khalilzadeh-Shirazi, Javad, 30n, 92n, 94n, 95n, 155n
Kobayashi, Noritake, 54n, 56n, 98
Kobayashi, Yoshihiro, 97
Kobayashi, Yōtarō, 73n
Komiya, Ryūtarō, 10n, 88n
Kotaka, Yasuo, 12n, 13n, 14n
Krause, Lawrence B., 60n
Kumagai, Hisao, 41n

Labor costs, 40, 41, 93, 113, 115. See also Wages
Labor force: education and training of, 13, 14; family workers in, 102–03, 106; shift from agriculture, 4, 36, 108; small business and, 102–03, 105–06
Labor-management relations, 40
Larner, Robert J., 11n
Laudadio, L., 92n
Legalism, 2
Levenson, Albert M., 108n
Levine, Solomon B., 41n
Lewellen, Wilbur G., 12n
Licensing of technology, 125, 126, 131, 150
Lockwood, William W., 7n, 41n, 55n, 148n, 149n, 150n

Mansfield, Edwin, 130n
Manufacturing sector: cartels in, 147; concentration in, 16–26; dependence on exports, 36; product classification, 19–20; product differentiation, 30–32, 34; productivity growth rate, 130–39; small businesses in, 103, 106, 107; subcontracting in, 3, 107, 112–15; wages in, 109–10; worker productivity in, 110
Market conduct: collusive aspects of, 48–53, 56–58; effect on prices, 47, 96; government role in, 53–56
Masson, Robert T., 10n
Matsushiro, Kazuo, 88n
Matsushita, 50–51
Meiji period, 1, 2, 8, 48, 107
Mergers: effect on seller concentration, 27, 29; permissive policy toward, 28, 30, 151–52; regulation of, 142
Mikitani, Ryōichi, 79n
Ministry of Finance, 151
Ministry of International Trade and Industry (MITI), 6, 147; administrative guidance by, 53, 150–51; conflict with FTCJ, 151–52; efforts to insure efficient-scale plants, 54, 57, 152; promotion of favored industries by, 149–52; role in industry entry, 149–52; role in technology importation, 125–26, 152
Ministry of Small and Medium Business, 115
MITI. See Ministry of International Trade and Industry
Mitsubishi, 60, 63–64, 65, 75, 84
Mitsubishi Economic Research Institute, 37n, 79n
Mitsui, 60, 63, 64, 65, 67, 75, 84
Miyagawa, Kimio, 128n
Miyazaki, Yoshikazu, 52n, 69n, 84, 86
Monopoly. See Antimonopoly Law; Antitrust policy; Cartels; Mergers
Mueller, Gerhard G., 73n
Mueller, Willard F., 28n, 34n
Murakami, Yasusuke, 127n
Musashi, Takehiko, 88n, 89

Nakamura, Tsunejirō, 88n
Nanbu, Tsuruhiko, 41n
Napier, Ron W., 3n, 109n, 110, 111n
Niida, Hiroshi, 89n
Nishikawa, Shunsaku, 27, 28n, 98
Noda, Kazuo, 10n, 11n, 12n
Nylon technology, 55–56

Occupation of Japan, 62, 141
Oil crisis, 50
Ono, Akira, 89n
Ono, Jirō, 28n
Organisation for Economic Co-operation and Development, 126
Orr, Dale, 91n
Ōtsuka, Kazuhiko, 129n

Palmer, John, 10n
Pashigian, Peter, 22n
Patent holdings, 137, 139
Patrick, Hugh, 5n, 42n, 60n, 124n, 125n
Peck, Merton J., 125
Percy, M., 92n
Petrochemical industry, 54–55
Petroleum Federation, 146
Pharmaceutical industry, 50
Porter, Michael E., 94n, 95n, 119n
Prais, S. J., 18n, 134n
Prices: collusive arrangements relating to, 49–52, 54, 143, 144, 146; flexibility of, 97; market conduct and, 47; seller concentration and, 97–98; of Zaibatsu transactions, 61
Product differentiation: advertising and, 31–32, 34; as barrier to firm entry, 34,

74, 121; effect on competition, 30; effect on profits, 77, 78
Productivity: in distribution sector, 116–19; effect of capital intensity on, 111, 132, 138, 139; effect of concentration on, 138; effect of technical change and invention on, 131–32; effect of R&D on, 133, 137, 139; enterprise size and, 3, 4, 110, 137; factors influencing, 7–10; measure of growth of, 130–31, 134–39; plant size and, 133–34, 136
Profits: effect of concentration on, 74, 76, 88–89, 90, 93–94, 156; effect of group affiliation on, 72–73, 75–77, 78, 83; firm's diversification and, 77, 78; growth of sales and, 74, 75–76, 80, 89; influence of advertising on, 76, 77–78, 93–94, 95; market variables affecting, 73–74; maximization of, 7, 12, 37, 48, 53, 61, 66; on owners' equity, 72, 73, 75, 92, 93, 94; on total assets, 72, 73, 75, 77, 78, 92, 93; U.S. and Japan, compared, 96; windfall, 36, 74, 90, 92; of Zaibatsu members, 61, 66
Pryor, Frederic L., 20, 134n

R&D. See Research and development
Rapp, William V., 37n, 40n, 42n
Resale price maintenance, 49–50, 116, 143
Research and development (R&D), 126–28, 133, 137, 139
Retail establishments, 116–18
Retirement, 4
Rhoades, Stephen A., 74n, 77n
Rieke, Luvern V., 142n
Ringisho system, 14
Rosen, George, 35n
Rosovsky, Henry, 5n, 60n, 124n, 125n
Rotwein, Eugene, 26, 57n, 62n
Royalty, on imported technology, 125

Saëz, Wistano, 77n
Samurai, 7–8
Sanwa, 63, 67
Scherer, F. M., 32n, 57n, 130n, 152n, 155n
Schumpeter, Joseph A., 132, 133
Sekiguchi, Sueo, 60n
Sellekaerts, Willy, 61n
Seniority, 4, 12, 13
Sherman, Roger, 40n
Shinjō, Kōji, 97
Shinkai, Yōichi, 97n
Shinohara, Miyohei, 5n, 18n, 102n, 107n, 108n, 109n, 111n, 114n, 115, 153n
Shiseido, 33
Small and Medium Enterprise Agency, 111, 152, 153
Small business, 3–4; acquisition of tech-

nical information by, 129; capital for, 107–08, 153; capital-labor ratio, 111; compared with U.S., 3; competition from imports, 42; family workers in, 102–03; government aid to, 152–54; industries best suited for, 112; labor force size and, 103, 106; managerial talent in, 107; prevalence of, by country, 102; productivity of, 3, 4, 110, 137; relation between GDP and, 103, 106; relation to regional income, 115; role in economic system, 106–07, 157; as subcontractors, 112, 129, 154; wage costs of, 108–10
Sony Corp., 51
Steel industry, 55
Subcontracting, 3, 51, 107, 154; benefits to parent company from, 113–14; among competing firms, 51; contract provisions for, 112; costs of, 41, 113, 115; efficiency of, 114–15; industries engaged in, 113
Sumitomo, 55, 60, 63, 64, 65, 67, 75, 84, 149

Takamiya, Susumu, 14n
Tamura, Shūji, 125, 126
Tanouchi, Kōichi, 118n
Tasugi, Kisou, 32n
Tax concessions, 150, 152
Technical efficiency: administrative costs and, 119–22; in distribution sector, 115–19; effect of collusive practices on, 56–57; of small business, 101–15
Technology: exports of, 126; imports of, 34, 44, 124, 137, 150; licensing of, 125, 126, 131, 150
Teraoka, T. W. M., 73n
Tokugawa period, 9
Tokyo High Court, 143, 146
Tollison, Robert, 40n
Toyō Rayon, 55
Toyō Seikan, 145
Trade associations, 50, 141–42, 144, 148, 151
Tsukui, Jinkichi, 127n

Uekusa, Masu, 41n, 89, 94, 128, 129
Unfair business practices, 49–52, 54, 142–45, 158
United Kingdom, 18, 30, 95
United States: allocative efficiency, 95; barriers to entry into industry, 90; capital structure leverage, 40; concentration in manufacturing sector, 18, 19–26; determinants of profits, 76, 77n; education of business executives, 9; industry management and control, 10, 11; mergers, 28; product differentiation, 30,

31; productivity growth, 130, 131, 132; R&D expenditures, 126; relation between productivity and R&D, 137; small business, 3

von Mehren, Arthur T., 142n

Wadaki, Matsutarō, 8n, 14n
Wages: in concentrated industries, 96, 97; firm size differentials in, 4, 108–10, 115, 158; industry differentials in, 109–10
Wallich, Henry C., 5n
Wallich, Mable I., 5n
Weiss, Leonard, 72n, 75
Wholesale establishments, 116–18
Williamson, John, 7n
Williamson, Oliver E., 114n, 119, 120n
Wilson, Thomas A., 22n, 30n, 89

Yamamura, Kōzō, 27n, 49n, 52n, 54n, 141n, 151n

Yamey, B. S., 75n
Yanaga, Chitoshi, 148n
Yao, Jirō, 79n, 82n
Yasuda, 60, 67, 84
Yoshida, Hiroshi, 73n
Yoshino, M. Y., 7n, 10n, 11n, 13n, 14n, 32n, 33, 34n, 51n, 114, 115n, 116n, 117n, 118n, 119n
Yui, Tsunehiko, 7n, 9n, 10n, 48n
Yukizawa, Kenzō, 36n, 135n

Zaibatsu: collusive versus rivalrous actions by, 83–86; competition among, 67; dissolution of, 10, 62–63; group banks, 63, 65, 67, 68–69; holding companies' control of, 60, 63; linkages among, 60–61, 63–66; pricing arrangements among, 61; profits of members, 72–73, 75–77, 78, 83; purging of executives of, 9–10, 63; reciprocal business transactions among, 65–66, 67–68; reorganization of, 63